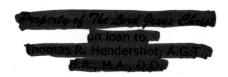
I BELIEVE
IN
MIRACLES

Burton W. Seavey

With Donna J. Seavey

xulon
PRESS

WHAT OTHERS ARE SAYING ABOUT THIS BOOK:

"I Believe In Miracles" is a perfect 29th Chapter for the Book of Acts. The mantle of anointing that was upon the life of Jesus and his disciples was truly passed on to this contemporary prophet who also healed the sick and caused miracles to occur. This book is the story of a spiritual journey, the journey of one of God's anointed prophets that has produced hundreds of contemporary miracles. It is not a discourse about the contemporary possibility of miracles, nor is it simply an exegetical study of the Biblical role of miracles in today's world. Rather, this is a book that shares testimonies of actual miracles that took place in recent times.

"I have known Rev. Burton Seavey for over thirty-five years and have personally observed the phenomenal anointing of the Holy Spirit upon this man. He has experienced the supernatural in a way that few people in contemporary culture have.

"This is a book that you need to read and will not be able to put down! However, you will never be able to read it without developing a hunger for the supernatural. I suggest you read it with a heart open to God. You will discover that God has planned a supernatural ministry for you as well."

Bishop Rev. Thomas F. ("Tommy") Reid
Senior Pastor, The Tabernacle, Orchard Park, NY; Author; TV Host; Founder, Buffalo School of the Bible; Founding Member/ Executive Secretary, Churches United in Global Mission; Board Member: David Yonggi Cho's Church Growth Int'l, Zion Bible College, Elim Bible Institute.

"Burton Seavey has always been a man of the Spirit. He has demonstrated the truths of the Word of God and the reality of the Holy Spirit throughout his ministry. I have known Burton's ministry for many years and have seen the fruit of it.

"The kingdom of God is not only about preaching but in *demonstrating* the Holy Spirit's works. The upcoming generation needs impartation and revelation concerning the kingdom and it's power. Burton Seavey is a pioneer who has opened the way for others to follow. He has taught and trained many to understand and believe the Word of God and to operate in the Spirit.

"This book will inspire you and stir your faith to believe for miracles. God confirms his word with signs following and the world is in desperate need of miracles. Jesus commanded us to do the same works that He did—and even greater *(more)* works. Unfortunately, not everyone today believes in miracles. Burton Seavey does. The faith and power he has experienced can be imparted to you.

"As you read this book, believe for an impartation of faith and trust God for greater things. Receive wisdom from this man of God and allow his life to be a blessing to you. God has sent him for that purpose. Never underestimate the wisdom and understanding you can receive from an anointed book. You will receive a blessing just by reading this book. As you read, prayerfully consider what the author has written; and may the Lord give you understanding in these things."

Dr. John Eckhardt
Founder and Apostolic Overseer, Crusaders Church Chicago
and IMPACT, an International network of Prophetic and
Apostolic Churches; Author of over 150 books

"This book is a must read for everyone who yearns to see the miraculous power of God at work in their life and service for the Lord. It will be particularly helpful to young preachers who desire to flow in the supernatural because Burton explains how to flow in miracle ministry as well as what to expect on a personal level! Once you start reading this book you won't want to put it down!"

Apostle Trevor M. Newport
Author; Founder and President of Life Changing Ministries Global Outreach, Stoke-on-Trent, United Kingdom

"Burton Seavey has had a long and productive relationship with Zion Bible College and currently serves on our Alumni Board. Many attest to his prophetic ministry. Brother Seavey has written a fascinating account of a ministry spanning over fifty years, filled with testimonies of miracles. It is my prayer that the Lord will use his inspiring book to bring men and women to a living Christ and build faith in the supernatural within Christ's true Church."

Dr. Charles T. Crabtree
President, Zion Bible College, Haverhill, Massachusetts; 25 years as pastor of A/G churches in Iowa and California; 14 years as Assistant General Superintendent of the Assemblies of God

CONTENTS

FOREWORD

Because the experiences related herein took place in my own life, personal pronouns have been utilized frequently throughout the book. Every effort has been made to keep these to a minimum and the author hopes his readers will understand that the use of such does not in any way indicate an attempt at personal aggrandizement. Rather, their frequency is a matter of necessity when all anecdotes are excerpted from one's own life.

The accounts in this book are all true and took place at various times and places throughout my fifty years (to this present date) in ministry. Some attempt has been made to group them into similar categories. This has not always been possible however, nor has it been practical, due to instances where particular miracles or areas of giftedness overlapped within the same anecdote. For instance, a *word of knowledge* regarding the past sometimes led into a *prophecy* concerning future events; this in turn encouraged *faith* that resulted in a *healing* miracle, to mention only one possible scenario.

In other cases, several events of differing kinds took place during a single service or at one specific crusade location. These have been grouped together in the re-telling. The reader can thus appreciate the difficulty encountered in attempting to accurately categorize each and every experience.

It is my fervent hope that this retrospective of my own spiritual journey will provide blessing, encouragement and challenge to everyone who reads this book. My prayer for all of my readers echoes the words delivered to the Early Church by the Apostle John: **"Beloved, I pray that in all respects you may prosper and be in good health, just as your soul prospers."** *III John 2 NASBU*

Gratefully,
Burton W. Seavey

IN APPRECIATION

No lifetime is the result of a single person's efforts and no book is the product of its author alone. My own life and ministry have been aided and greatly enriched through the input of many cherished individuals, as has this book. To these precious people I am and will forever be indebted; and wish to express my love and appreciation.

To
The late Ethel Ruth "Gerry" Dennen Seavey,
my devoted mother and powerful woman of God.
Her steadfast love and prayers sustained me
Throughout her lifetime.
The extent of her influence on my life
can never be adequately measured,
nor can my gratitude ever be fully expressed.

To
My wife, Donna.
Your love, patience and unwavering support
have sustained me throughout the many
happy years of our marriage.
You have enriched my life in countless ways
and your accomplished writing and editing skills
have made an invaluable contribution to this book.

To
Brian, Barry, Brent, Eric and Heather,
Our beloved, talented and accomplished children.
You are each a unique gift from God—and we are
overwhelmingly grateful that you have blessed our lives!

To
Megan, Diana, JoAnn and Nathan,
The wonderful mates God
has given to our children—and to us. You have added
to our family and to our lives in so very many ways.

To
Calvin, Cole, Rachel, Kyle, Annika and Elliot,
Our beautiful and amazing grandchildren.
Each one of you is a constant source of delight and pride.
We love you beyond words!

IN DEDICATION

This book is gratefully dedicated
First and Foremost,

To
My God:

Almighty Heavenly Father;
Incomparable Lord and Savior, Jesus Christ;
Abiding Comforter, the Holy Spirit.

**Without the constant presence, love, patience and never-failing
guidance of my loving Lord, this life would have been
a totally barren and unproductive one.**

And to

The Reverend
Thomas "Tommy" Reid

Sr. Pastor, The Tabernacle
Orchard Park, New York

**Over the years, your friendship, concern and
unwavering support have been a mainstay and constant
source of encouragement in my life and ministry.
The effectiveness of your counsel can never be overstated.
Neither can my appreciation ever be adequately expressed.**

**Thank you, Tommy.
It is an honor to call you my friend!**

"Then Gideon said to him, 'O my lord, if the LORD is with us, why then has all this happened to us? And where are all His miracles which our fathers told us about...?' "
Judges 6:13

"Seek His face continually. Remember His wonders which He has done."
Ps 105:4,5

"Thus speaks the LORD God of Israel, saying: 'Write in a book for yourself all the words that I have spoken to you.'"
Jer 30:2

"You are to take His message everywhere, telling the whole world what you have seen and heard."
Acts 22:15 (NLT)

"...I assure you, I am telling you what we know and have seen..."
John 3:11 (NLT)

The Reader's Challenge:

"Let this mind be in you, which was also in
Christ Jesus: Who, being in the form of God,
thought it not robbery to be equal with God…"

Phil 2:5-6

*   *   *

"Man's mind, stretched to a new idea,
never goes back to its original dimension."

Oliver Wendell Holmes, Senior

*   *   *

May these profound truths be indelibly impressed
upon all who read this chronicle.
It has been written to encourage the readers to stretch
their own minds until they come into full agreement
with the miraculous Word of God, the Holy Bible.

*   *   *

I BELIEVE
IN
MIRACLES

"Write this for a memorial in a book."
...Exodus 17:14

...I have herein done as He directed me. (Author)

CHAPTER ONE

GOD'S POSITION
ON THE SUPERNATURAL

Throughout my decades of fruitful, supernatural ministry during which tens of thousands of unbelievers have been ushered into the Kingdom of God, I have weathered many attacks from critics and skeptics who decried and denied anything and everything supernatural. Their contention has always been that, since we now have the written Word of God, signs, wonders and miracles are no longer a necessary component of ministry. However, many years ago I discovered and embraced a simple philosophy—the person with an experience that conforms to the Word of God is never at the mercy of the person with an argument that does not conform to the Word of God! Therefore, let us here briefly examine what the Word of God says about the validity of miracles in the ministry of the church today.

Just a Bit of Doctrine

It has always troubled me deeply when born-again Christians who truly love the Lord criticize miracles such as these I've chronicled in this book. Such people declare that miracles were only for the First Century Church, and today, since we have the Bible, the written Word of God, signs (in the Greek, *se meon*, "attesting miracles") are no longer necessary. Actually, since *attest* means "to testify to the truth (veracity) of something," we must conclude that signs and miracles testify to the validity, veracity and truth of God's Word, both to believers and to unbelievers as well.

Therefore, this renders the previous argument as useless as a blind man in a dark room looking for a black cat that isn't there! Such a contention simply cannot stand when confronted with the Word of God. Let's further analyze that argument by calling the Bible to the witness stand and allowing it to speak for itself.

- Nowhere in Scripture do we find that, since we now have the written Word of God, supernatural signs have been terminated. Try as one might, not one verse can be found to support that theory.
- On the contrary, the New Testament is replete with references pertaining to the supernatural power of God at work in the lives of believers. If that be true, and it is, then as long as there are believers, there should be supernatural signs that attest to their message.
- Jesus Himself believed that signs (attesting miracles) were necessary. This was born out whenever the pure, undiluted Word of His Father poured forth from His own lips. Let's further examine Jesus and His ministry. The Bible says of Him:

"In the beginning was the Word, and the Word was with God, and the Word *was* God."
John 1:1 (Emphasis mine.)
"And *the Word became flesh*, and dwelt among us..."
John 1:14 (Emphasis mine.)

Jesus *was* and *is* the Word—the *Living* Word! There is, never was nor ever will be a greater Word of God than Jesus Christ. He was the Word of the Father spoken directly to mankind. Jesus said of Himself:

"...'Truly, truly, I say to you, the Son can do *nothing* of Himself, unless it is something He sees the Father doing; for whatever the Father does, these things the Son also does in like manner.' " *John 5:19 (Emphasis mine.)*

"But the witness which I have is greater than that of John; for the works which the Father has given Me to accomplish, *the very works that I do, bear witness of Me*, that the Father has sent Me." *John 5:36 (Emphasis mine.)* **"For I did not speak on My own initiative, but the Father Himself who sent Me has given Me**

commandment, what to say, and what to speak." *John 12:49*

"Do you not believe that I am in the Father, and the Father is in Me? The words that I say to you I do not speak on My own initiative, but the Father abiding in Me does His works." *John 14:10*

From these we see that every word that proceeded forth from Jesus' mouth was spoken directly from the Father God *through* Jesus to mankind. Today we have the written Word, while He was and is forever the *Living* Word. He spoke these words and we now can read these words. If Jesus Himself felt that it was imperative for His words (actually, the Father's words) to require the attestation of signs, wonders and miracles, then we must conclude that the *written* word does, also! Why would anyone exalt the written Word over the Father's own Words, spoken through Jesus and subsequently proven true by the signs, wonders and miracles that followed throughout His life and ministry?

Even though the Father's infallible words were channeled directly through Jesus, God recognized that fallen, sinful people needed confirmation of those words. That was accomplished through Jesus' supernatural actions. Contrast the ministry of Jesus with present-day, supposedly well-trained ministers who teach their congregations that since we now have the *written* Word of God, it negates the need for supernatural displays of the Holy Spirit's power. Yet, Jesus the Christ relied heavily upon such works for validating proof every day throughout His ministry. I'm convinced that most of today's anti-miracle protestations are merely smoke screens behind which powerless ministries hide their ineffectiveness.

"And they [Jesus' disciples] **went out and preached everywhere, while the Lord worked with them, and** *confirmed* **the word by the signs** [*attesting miracles*] **that followed."** *Mark 16:20 (Emphasis mine.)*

3

Those who deny that supernatural gifts are a necessary component in today's church embrace the belief that the gifts of the Holy Spirit ended with the passing of the First Century Church. Such a belief would require one to blindly disregard the writings of highly respected church fathers whose writings span the entirety of church history. These writings are readily available to anyone who is willing to take the time to read them. Consider this quote from the writings of Irenaeus, a prominent church father who wrote during the Ante Nicene period from 130 to 200 AD, the Second and Third Centuries after Christ. The quote is taken from his manuscript entitled, *Against Heresies* in which Irenaeus labels as a *heretic* anyone who denied the existence of supernatural gifts in the Church of his day.[1]

> **"Wherefore, also, those who are in truth His disciples, receiving grace from Him, do in His name perform miracles, so as to promote the welfare of other men, according to the gift which each has received from Him. For some do certainly and truly drive out devils, so that those who have thus been cleansed from evil spirits frequently believe in Christ, and join themselves to the church. Others have foreknowledge of things to come: they see visions, and utter prophetic expressions. Others still, heal the sick by laying their hands upon them, and they are made whole. Yea, moreover, as I have said, the dead even have been raised up, and remained among us for many years. And what shall I more say? It is not possible to name the number of the gifts, which the church, scattered throughout the whole world, has received from God, in the name of Jesus Christ... Calling upon the name of our Lord Jesus Christ, she [*the church,* ed.] has been accustomed to**

---

[1] *Heretic:* "…A person who professes a heresy." *Heresy:* "Any opinion…opposed to official or established views or doctrines." *Webster's New World College Dictionary.*

work miracles for the advantage of mankind, and *not to lead them into error* (*emphasis mine*)."

The above quote from Irenaeus' manuscript makes it obvious to even the most casual reader that the Lord continued to work miracles through His followers (even raising the dead!) well into the Third Century! This should be evidentiary proof that signs, wonders and miracles were not discarded after the First Century Apostles had passed from the scene. The writings of later church fathers also firmly establish that miracles did not and should never have ceased to be important elements in the life and ministry of the church. If miracles *have* ceased in some churches, could it be because men have replaced supernatural acts with polished entertainment followed by well-scripted sermons that fail to produce effective results in the lives of the listeners? No wonder many Christians today view the Word of God as being similar to a buffet dinner where one can select what is personally appealing and ignore the rest. Under Holy Spirit inspiration, Saint Augustine wrote:

"If you believe what you like in the Gospels, and reject what you don't like, it is not the Gospel you believe, but yourself."

Ramsay McMullen is an Emeritus Professor of Classics and History at Yale University, where he taught from 1967 to his retirement in 1993 as Dunham Professor of History and Classics. His scholarly interests are in the social history of Rome and the replacement of paganism by Christianity. A *summa cum laude* graduate of Harvard College, he was honored for a lifetime of scholarly achievement at the 2001 annual meeting of the American Historical Association with the Award for Scholarly Distinction. The award citation called him "the greatest historian of the Roman Empire alive today. Considering his impressive resume it is safe to assume that his assessment of the events surrounding the early church bear considerable weight when considering the role of supernatural happenings in the church today. In his impressive book, <u>*Christianizing The Roman Empire, A. D. 100-400*</u>[2] he presents some wonderful details of the supernatural activities of the Holy Spirit in signs, wonders and miracles which continued to occur regularly in the Early Church up to and including the Fifth Century. His educated conclusion was that the Christianizing of the Roman Empire was *largely* due to signs, wonders and miracles that included casting out demons!

---

[2] I highly recommend this book to my readers. Although authored by a learned scholar, it has been written in a casual, eminently readable style. Try it—you'll like it!

CHAPTER TWO

ANSWERING THE CRITICS

"The signs of a true apostle were performed among you with all perseverance, by signs and wonders and miracles."
2 Cor 12:12

S ince the beginning of time, God has revealed His existence through signs, wonders and miracles. The creation of the universe itself attests to His astounding power. The Old Testament is yet another revelation of God as His prophets proved that the God of Israel was the *only* true God—and they accomplished that through performing many miraculous acts.[3]

In the New Testament, we observe Jesus as He ministered in the Holy Spirit and performed signs, wonders and miracles. These supernatural actions attested to His divine credentials as the Son of God. (We will examine this in more detail later in this book.) The Book of Acts records the continuation of Jesus' miraculous deeds in the lives of His faithful disciples, as they were motivated and empowered by the Holy Spirit, resident within them.

Many Christians in today's church disclaim and disdain the existence of miracles, their argument being that such things were only performed during the days of the early apostles. I agree. However, I contend that the days of the apostles have never ceased; they are still here today! When you consider that the Book of Acts is the only New Testament book without a closing, and that

---

[3] Please read *I Kings 18:20-39*.

miracles were still in the church throughout the epistles and existed long after the original apostles had died; one must assume that such supernatural acts were meant to continue until the return of Jesus. With the world of today becoming progressively even more wicked than it was then, should the modern-day church of Jesus Christ exhibit any less of His power than did the Early Church?

Following my Baptism in the Holy Spirit with the evidence of speaking in other tongues, I recall a conversation with my Baptist pastor whom I deeply loved and respected. His position was that speaking in tongues was not for today because the days of miracles had passed away when the last of the original twelve apostles died. My response to him was, "You should have told me that weeks ago, because I've received it already!" (Remember, the man with an experience is never at the mercy of the man with an argument.)

In view of all that God is currently doing through His anointed servants throughout the world, how could anyone logically argue that position? Some theologians attribute such happening to the works of Satan; but that position is as weak as the broth made from the shadow of a chicken that starved to death. I have personally proclaimed the Word of God accompanied by acts of power in many nations around the world and, as a direct result have led thousands of people into the kingdom of God. Convincing people of the Gospel's validity and leading them to salvation has never been the work of Satan—not in days gone by, not now nor will it *ever* be! How could it possibly be to Satan's advantage to weaken his own kingdom and drive souls into the arms of Jesus? I would far rather hold to these words voiced by the Apostle Paul:

"My message and my preaching were not in persuasive words of wisdom, but in demonstration of the Spirit and of power, so that your faith would not rest on the wisdom of men, but on the power of God." *I Cor 2:4-5*

Another argument used to counter the existence of modern-day miracles is that the cures experienced have been psychosomatically induced and are simply products of the mind, rather than having been accomplished through any supernatural means. The several experiences related below should serve to rebut the fore mentioned position that all healings, if they occur at all, are simply manifestations of psychosomatic phenomena.

*   *   *

A Very Bright Dog Indeed!

A few years ago, my son Barry called one day with an urgent prayer request. His beloved dog Bubbles, a beautiful female Boxer, had been suffering for years with recurring cancerous skin tumors. She had been through several surgical procedures to excise them, but now another growth had appeared. I asked Barry to summon Bubbles and place his hand on the tumor while I prayed for the Lord to heal her. He did, I did—and God did! Barry became so emotional over what had happened that he hung up the phone without another word. Several minutes later he called again and tearfully reported that he had felt the tumor disappear completely from under his hand. The moral we can gain from this is: if that particular miracle had been *psychosomatically* induced, we should have featured Bubbles on the nightly news; because that would have made her the most intelligent dog who ever lived!

*   *   *

On a similar note, the following healing miracle illustrates the impossibility of all healings being the result of mental and emotional conditioning and therefore psychosomatically induced within the context of an emotionally charged service.

Hildy's Miracle

I love animals and I'm convinced that my Lord does also. After all, He created so very many of them. My family once owned a beautiful, silver point miniature schnauzer we nicknamed Hildy (an affectionately shortened version of her official AKC registered name, Grand Duchess Hildegarde). For those who are unfamiliar with schnauzers, silver points are black with silver markings on the lower legs, feet, chest and beard and Hildy was a beautiful specimen of the breed. The whole family loved her, but she was partial to me and she remained my beloved companion throughout the entire fifteen years of her life. Even now, several years after her death, I still miss her dearly.

One beautiful summer afternoon, I took Hildy with me for a ride in the car, one of her favorite activities. Because the weather was so perfect, instead of using the air conditioner, I had opened the driver's side window to enjoy the breeze. The car was moving along at twenty-five miles per hour when Hildy suddenly spotted a squirrel and just as suddenly leaped over my lap and straight out the open window. She struck the pavement hard, rolled over twice, and began making a terrible sound of extreme anguish. I had never before heard any animal make those same sounds, nor have I since.

Hildy was unable to walk because the bone of one leg was obviously broken, the jagged ends protruding completely through the flesh at an odd angle. I carried her back to the car and raced toward home where I planned to tell my wife what had happened and then rush Hildy to the vet. I was concerned that she might have sustained other injuries, also; and she continued to make those pitiful sounds of excruciating pain. Desperate to ease her suffering, I laid my hand upon her and prayed that God would comfort her and bring healing. When I did so, she instantly became calm and quiet.

10

My stomach was churning when I reached the house where my wife was working in the front yard. When I opened the car door to relate what had happened, Hildy leaped over my lap, onto the concrete driveway and over a small concrete retainer wall around the perimeter of the lawn. Then she ran across the lawn and began to jump up for Donna's attention, as though she were saying, "Jesus healed me! Jesus healed me!" Indeed He had. There was never any further evidence of her catastrophic leap out of the car. Indeed, our God loves and has compassion for animals—despite the fact that they have absolutely no psychosomatic abilities!

*   *   *

The Psychosomatic Photo

For a period of several months, I conducted Friday night miracle services in a Southern suburb of Chicago. On one of those nights, I was impressed of the Spirit to ask people to bring to the next week's service a photograph of someone who needed prayer, but couldn't attend the meeting. The Holy Spirit's plan was that I would lay hands on the photographs together with a prayer cloth to be taken or sent to the person in need of healing. [4]

The following week, a young man brought a photo of his father who lived in a Western state and was suffering with terminal cancer. As I prayed for the man's healing, I became aware of an exceptionally powerful anointing of the Holy Spirit. The following week, the young man returned with a glowing testimony. He hadn't informed his father in advance of the previous week's service that we would be praying for him, because the man was not

---

[4] "God was performing extraordinary miracles by the hands of Paul, so that handkerchiefs or aprons were even carried from his body to the sick, and the diseases left them and the evil spirits went out." *Acts 19:11-12*

11

a believer. When the young man went home after the meeting, he had received a phone call from his father who wept as he related to his son that at a certain time (allowing for the time differential, it coincided with the exact time we had been praying for him!), his house had been *shaken,* a great warmth had enveloped him and he knew, beyond a shadow of a doubt, that he had been healed of the cancer.

When the son told his father that God had healed him in answer to our prayers, he was then able to lead the man to Christ. Subsequent medical tests performed that week confirmed that the cancer had vanished. The young man joyously told of his plan to join his father for a three-month traveling vacation to renew and enrich their relationship. If anyone can find a psychosomatic explanation for that miracle, please let me know. (FYI: I won't hold my breath waiting!)

CHAPTER THREE

MY INTRODUCTION TO
THE SUPERNATURAL REALM

By the ripe old age of sixteen, the future direction of my life had been fairly well decided upon—to my satisfaction, at least. I had been studying for a future as an electrician and, due to my Aunt Millie's influence as president of the most powerful telephone company union in New York City, I had been guaranteed a position in my field following graduation from high school. At that time, I was unaware of the verse in Jeremiah that indicated God just might have His own plans for my life: **"For I know the plans that I have for you, declares the LORD, plans for welfare and not for calamity to give you a future and a hope."** *Jer. 29:11*

The Holy Spirit is the ultimate Grand Master of this chess game we call life. He knows how to align the pieces on the board to place us at just the right place at the opportune time. When a friend invited me to join him for a conference at Columbia Bible College in Columbia, South Carolina, I gladly agreed and looked forward to the trip. I would never have believed that this casual invitation would signal the beginning of a lifetime marked by the supernatural manifestations of the Holy Spirit.

At mid-morning on the first day of the conference, I stood in the lobby of the main building idly chatting with friends as we waited for the chapel service to begin. I turned aside momentarily and, when I turned back, my friends had all gone. Although I was oblivious to it then, God had separated me from my companions because He was preparing to unfold *His* plan for my life—a plan very different from the one I had chosen.

Call to Ministry

Aimlessly, I wandered into the bookstore and was attracted to one book in the rack, the title of which I can't now recall. I casually opened it to scan a page or two and see if it would be of interest to me. Suddenly, the text on that one page was cast into deep shadow, except for one line. That line was illuminated with a golden glow and read, *"The Lord your God shall speak to you in a still small voice."* Immediately after I read that line, the chapel bell rang, signaling that the service was about to begin. Puzzled by such an unusual event, I shivered, shook my head and hurriedly replaced the book. I was mystified and at a total loss to explain the meaning of that strange manifestation. It is certainly true that "God moves in mysterious ways, His wonders to perform,"[5] and I was soon to move into phase two of God's revelation.

The speaker's topic that day was *"How to Find God's Will for Your Life."* Up until that day, I had never considered any career other than a comfortable one with the telephone company. The possibility that the Lord might not have been in agreement with my career choice had never once occurred to me. However, as the speaker's sermon progressed, inexplicably I began to weep as though a hidden fountain within had suddenly been opened. By the time the service ended, I was awash in tears and shaken to the core of my being, though I had no idea why.

A college student who had observed my strange behavior invited me to join him in the garden, and we sat there for some time while he explained that he knew precisely what I was going through because he had been called into ministry through a similar experience. He told me further that I should not to be ashamed of my tears, because what was happening to me was an outward response to the inner working of the Holy Spirit Who was likewise calling me. As he spoke, every fiber of my being cried out in agreement, *Yes! Yes!* At that very moment I yielded my will and

---

[5] From <u>*The Biblical Illustrator,*</u> Copyright (c) 2002, *AGES* and *Biblesoft, Inc.*

my entire future to the will of God—and I have never looked back. Over the years I have always been grateful to that unknown student whose personal experience and perceptive insight into the ways of the Holy Spirit guided me accurately at that critical juncture in my young life.

Upon graduating from high school at the age of 17, I faced the necessity of choosing a college that would prepare me for the ministry. The thought of applying to a Pentecostal school never entered my mind because I still considered myself a Baptist, in spite of having been drawn to attend a Pentecostal church. I knew there was something compellingly different about those full gospel people; but I still had strong reservations about some of their doctrines that seemed strange to me.

Training for Ministry

Later that summer, my Aunt Millie asked me if I would like to join her and the family for a vacation trip through Canada. Of course I would like to go—Canada was a *foreign country,* and I'd never even been outside of the U.S.A! (In retrospect, I smile now when I consider how many trips I have made around the world since then! My ministry has taken me to over twenty countries, some of them repeatedly.) But there was one small technicality— the final stop on our journey would be at the Spring Conference of Zion Bible Institute, then located in East Providence, Rhode Island. (Over the ensuing years, the Institute became Zion Bible College and relocated to a new campus in Barrington, Rhode Island. It's most recent move has been to another, larger campus in Andover, Massachusetts.) I knew it was a setup, but I was even willing to attend a Pentecostal conference in exchange for the chance to travel in a "foreign" country.

We arrived at Zion a day early and, after settling into our motel, we visited the campus. As I wandered into Zion Gospel Temple, I stood in awe. It was more than the impressive size and beauty of the sanctuary that had overwhelmed me, however. It was the sense of the sweet Presence of the Holy Spirit that hovered over the building. Something (actually *Someone*—the Holy Spirit) spoke quietly in my spirit and assured me that this was where I belonged. I couldn't comprehend why the Lord wanted me to enroll in a school whose doctrine I didn't fully subscribe to; but there was no mistaking the certainty that He was leading me to that place.

In the fall of that same year, this 17-year-old excitedly came on campus to begin my very first year of preparation for a life of ministry. Having been on the National Honor Society throughout high school, I was eager to hit the books. I soon learned that Zion was very different from most other ministry prep schools. It wasn't just about books and learning—it was also a place where young men and women were introduced to the ways of the Holy Spirit—how He moved; how to respond to His voice and how to respond to the gifts He bestowed.[6] In addition to teaching Bible truth, our teachers were engaged in the serious process of preparing their students to combine future ministry with Holy Spirit power.

Revival Begins

Because I was a quiet, serious and "bookish" person at the time, I had difficulty understanding the importance of speaking in tongues; and I was uncomfortable with "emotional outbursts" of spontaneous praise. On more than one occasion, I was known to discreetly poke fun at some of these "antics" of people who were praising God in this unique (to me) fashion. On more than a few occasions, my fellow students would ask, "If you don't like what you see and hear, what are you doing here?" Good question! For want of a better answer, I would always reply, "I don't know why I'm here—except that God told me to come."

---

[6] See: *I Corinthians, Chapters 12 and 14*.

16

The following narrative will describe the beginnings of a truly remarkable and spontaneous, six-week visitation of the Holy Spirit at Zion Bible Institute during which all classes would be suspended. It was literally an around-the-clock move of the Holy Spirit that drew people from around the United States and Canada. They came by the hundreds to witness, participate in and receive from that glorious time of refreshing. During that protracted time of divine outpouring, the unexpected happened to me, as it so often does in God's program! I could never have predicted or even conceived in my wildest dreams what God was preparing to do in my life.

The student body was in the midst of exams and I was deep in study the night the revival began. It had started when a small group of male students in my dorm had gathered to pray for a classmate who was suffering an asthmatic attack. As they prayed, the young man was instantly healed. He then joined the group in praying for another student who was also afflicted with asthma—and he was healed as well.

Needless to say, an abundance of noise soon erupted right outside my door as the group exuberantly praised the Lord for these two miraculous healings! My ground-floor dorm room was situated on the perimeter of a very wide entry hall where students gathered before meals to await entrance into the dining hall on the lower level of the building. It was an ideal place to congregate— and congregate they did, with loud vocal worship accompanied by musical instruments of all sorts! Soon the accordions, guitars, horns and tambourines grew to peak volume along with songs of praise enthusiastic rejoicing. The crowd, like Topsy of old,[7] grew and grew—and so did the noise!

---

[7] From _Uncle Tom's Cabin_, the classic mid-1880's novel on slavery by Harriet Beecher Stowe

The Persistent Roommate

My roommate, Jimmy came to our room and urged me to "come and see" what God was doing. I replied in no uncertain terms that there was no need to go *outside* my room in order to hear what was so blatantly obvious. Had everyone been inside my room, it couldn't have been any louder. I asked him to leave so I could study for tomorrow's test and he did—temporarily. Jimmy soon returned and we went over the same dialogue as before, only this time there was a little more "steam" in my boiler, and I bluntly told my roommate to "get out." He did. But he returned; and I threw him out again, this time with considerably more vehemence.

By this time, the flame of the Holy Spirit had also been ignited in the women's dorms. Since men and women were not allowed in each other's dorms at that time, both groups of worshipers then moved to the lower level of Zion Gospel Temple where the chapel and prayer room were located. I breathed a sigh of relief. They had finally left the immediate premises and peace and quiet had been restored. Finally I would be able to study in peace, or so I thought.

But then Jimmy returned. He invited me once again to "come and see/hear" what God was doing. I glared at him and this time I threatened, "Jimmy, if you come here *one more time*, I will strangle you with my bare hands! Do you understand me?" (A lovely attitude for a fledgling minister, don't' you think?) He withdrew quietly, closed the door and retreated to the chapel. I returned to my books, smugly confident in the fact that I'd had the last word.

You guessed it. Just when peace and quiet had been restored and my studies were progressing so well, Jimmy returned again! I heard the now all-too-familiar sound of the door cautiously opening; only this time he didn't even come into the room—he merely poked his head around the half opened door and said, "Burt, you simply *must* come take just one look at what God is

18

doing." It was clear to me then that either I would have to make good on my threat to strangle my roommate or I would have to go with him and "take a look." Since violence was a repugnant option even by that point, I opted for the latter—on one condition. "Jimmy," I said grimly, "If I go and take one look, will you promise that you will leave me alone for the rest of the night?" He agreed and we made our way to the prayer room.

As we walked to the Temple, I'm sure my body language conveyed my sullen frame of mind. Jimmy and I never spoke a word as we entered the chapel and made our way to the prayer room. Oh, the sounds that emanated from that room—sounds of boisterous praise, such as this Baptist boy had never heard before! Since I had promised Jimmy that I would "take a look," that meant I would have to work my way through the other observers who were standing around and in the two open doorways which led into the prayer room where all the activity was taking place.

The Transformation of a Baptist

When I reached the front of the crowd and surveyed the length of that long room, I observed a strange panorama. Some students were kneeling in prayer, others were dancing before the Lord in joyful abandon and others were weeping or laughing. My Baptist mind didn't know how to process this atmosphere of "emotionalism," and I wanted nothing more than to turn and run. To this day, I don't know who was responsible for what happened next—whether it was Jimmy, some other person or perhaps an angel. Suddenly, I felt a hand between my shoulder blades and it firmly but gently pushed me into that room.

It is impossible to describe how deeply embarrassed I was—to be thrust into the midst of that unfamiliar atmosphere of raw emotion! I looked around desperately for an inconspicuous place where I could wait until I found an open path to leave, but found none. Although I was mortified by my situation, fortunately for me most of the people present never even knew I was there—they were too preoccupied with their own worship.

The prayer room had been set up with chairs around the perimeter and others placed back to back down the entire center length of the room, except for both ends and a three-and-a-half-foot break in the middle that served as a pass-through.

Frantically, I looked for a seat. (My plan was to sit there until an opening in the crowd would allow me to leave as inconspicuously as possible.) When I spied one empty chair against the left wall, I hurriedly sat down. As I bowed my head in an attempt to disguise my presence there, I saw a familiar pair of shoes and knew instinctively it had to be Jimmy. Sure enough, when I looked up I saw him standing there with a big smile on his face and one hand outstretched, as if to shake mine. At the time, my only thought was, "If I don't shake his hand, he will *never* leave!" So I shook his hand.

Suddenly!

No sooner had our hands met than I was immediately stricken with what felt like a bolt of electricity, but I felt no pain. The force of the Spirit's impact catapulted me out of the chair, spun me around twice and left me lying flat on my Baptist back between the chairs in the very center of the prayer room. So much for inconspicuous! As I lay there dazed and wondering what had happened to me, my only thought was, "What in the world am I doing here? I'm a *Baptist!*"

Some minutes later (I have no idea how long it was), I stood up on rubbery legs, staggered gratefully to my still vacant seat and assumed the same pose as before—with embarrassed countenance and bowed head. Suddenly, the same familiar shoes were in front of me again, and that could only mean one thing—Jimmy was standing in those shoes. I glanced up and saw his hand, extended as before. Since I knew what had happened the first time,

I'll never know what impulse compelled me to shake his hand a second time; but when our hands met I was again overcome with that intense power, catapulted out of the chair and spun around. Then, just like the first time, I found myself lying flat on my Baptist back in the very center of the room! However, this time something totally different was happening! A profound sense of God's Presence swept over me in wave after wave—and I found myself exuberantly speaking in another tongue! At that moment, my only thought was, "I don't know what this is, but *whatever* it is—I never want it to stop!" I have absolutely no idea how long I lay there while God's Presence filled me; but of one thing I was certain—my life would never be the same again! Then the Lord spoke clearly within me and said, "I want you to know that *I'm* God—and *you're not!*" (*Good concept—and one I've not forgotten since!*)

What I had just experienced was a divine demonstration of God's sovereignty, a life-changing event when God inserted Himself into my life without asking for or receiving permission to do so. I know that statement may ruffle some doctrinal feathers, but the Word of God bears out its validity. For instance, the Psalmist reflected on the sovereignty of God when he penned the following words: **"But our God is in the heavens;** *He does whatever He pleases."* *Ps 115:3 (Emphasis mine.)*

Sometimes, when God deals with us in a manner that is contrary to our will and diametrically opposed to our doctrinal belief structure, we are inclined to say, "That can't happen; God never imposes Himself upon our free will." Granted, it's rare for God to override a person's unwillingness to yield to His overtures of love and grace—but sometimes He does just that. Read Chapter Nine in the *Book of Acts,* and see how a divine visitation from the risen Christ threw Saul of Tarsus (an avowed enemy of Jesus and His followers) to the ground, blinded him and, within three days commissioned him to preach the Gospel. In a later chapter of this book, I write of several instances from my own ministry that illustrate times when God's sovereignty overrode someone's unwillingness, in order to accomplish His own agenda. Always remember, Almighty God possesses the absolute *right* to do whatever He pleases!

From that moment when the Lord sovereignly filled me with His Holy Spirit accompanied with the evidence of speaking in other tongues, my life was never to be the same. Soon thereafter, I developed a voracious appetite for prayer that resulted in many wonderfully intimate times with the Lord. If someone were ever looking for me, they had only to visit the prayer room first. It seemed as though I couldn't get enough time alone with my Lord. Thus my love for and devotion to Him grew rapidly.

Called Into Prophetic Ministry

My second year at Zion began much the same as the first one had ended—in diligent study, interspersed with an ongoing pursuit for God's Presence and anointing on my life. When my mother called to tell me that William Branham, a great prophet of God was coming to minister at Maranatha Temple in Brooklyn, New York (the church where Claire Hutchins served as pastor), my spirit leaped with excitement and I immediately made plans to attend the services. (In years to come brother Hutchins and I would become good friends.)

The services were everything I had expected, and more. Night after night I witnessed the Holy Spirit in action in a manner I had never seen before. The hidden thoughts of people's minds, as well as their sicknesses and other details were revealed through that humble servant of God and many healing miracles followed.

Before one service, my mother asked me to take a handkerchief to the front of the church and place it with other prayer cloths over which the prophet would later pray on behalf of those who were unable to attend.[8] When the service ended, I went to retrieve Mom's handkerchief that she intended to take to a sick friend. As soon as I touched the pile of handkerchiefs, an actual wind began to swirl around them! It moved over my left hand and up the arm, passed over my head and then engulfed my entire body. So powerful was this anointing that I stood transfixed and shaking even after it had gone. When I delivered the handkerchief to my mother, I related what had happened to me and exclaimed in amazement, "WOW! What a powerful anointing there was in those handkerchiefs!" Little did I know how accurate that assessment was; throughout the years to come I would frequently experience that same anointing power.

Approximately one month after my strange experience during the Branham service in Maranatha Temple, I was assigned to preach before my homiletics[9] class. (As someone once said, "It's a dirty job—but someone has to do it." Smile!) When I finished my sermon, I suddenly saw a vision of a classmate seated in the audience. In the vision, the young woman was seated on the front steps of her family's home. She was debating whether or not to return to Zion after the Christmas holiday. I described the Victorian-style house in detail, including the unusual "gingerbread" trim around the roof. I then revealed the girl's thoughts as they had been given to me in the vision. Discouraged, she had been deliberating whether or not she should leave school and abandon her call to the ministry. The prophecy continued with the encouraging message that God's hand was indeed upon her life and He did have a ministry for her to fulfill. The student wept at the word of the Lord and agreed with the accuracy of the prophecy, including my description of the house.

Immediately afterward, I received another vision that pertained to another female classmate. The content was similar to

---

[8] "God was performing extraordinary miracles by the hands of Paul, so that handkerchiefs or aprons were even carried from his body to the sick, and the diseases left them and the evil spirits went out." *Acts 19:11-12*
[9] Homiletics—the art of preparing and delivering a sermon.

that of the first girl, but I have since forgotten the description I gave of the house, except for the fact that it had a front porch with center steps comprised of large, smooth stones. The prophecy to her also addressed the need for her to continue her Bible education and prepare for the ministry God had ordained for her future. The second student also confirmed that her vision was also accurate in every detail.

Following those two visionary experiences, the Lord reminded me of the unusual happening at Maranatha Temple, when the wind of the Holy Spirit had swept over me so powerfully. At that moment I recognized the fact that my experience had carried more significance than simply a manifestation of God's Presence over the prayer cloths. It had also marked the beginning of my own anointing for service in the prophetic realm. Since that time I have functioned as a seer-prophet[10] and countless numbers of revelations have been shown to me in visionary form. (We'll discuss further aspects of visions in Chapter Seven.)

*   *   *

---

[10] Bible scholars have differentiated two main categories among those whom God anoints for the office of prophet. One category is the *nabe* (pr. <u>nah</u>-bay) prophet; one who mentally receives words or impressions or who hears audible communications from God. The other is that of *seer* (adj. <u>see</u>-er, lit. "one who sees") prophet; one who receives visions of past, present or future events and is directed to describe or "act out" what the visions reveal.

CHAPTER FOUR

AROUND THE UNITED STATES
IN (PLUS OR MINUS) 80 DAYS!

The Grand Scheme

"*O*nce upon a time, three daring young men decided to spend their summer break in ministry." If this sounds like the opening line of a fairy tale, you could say it probably *was* that for us, but God was in it. At the conclusion of my second year at Zion I asked two fellow students, Jim Haupt and Norman Eastman, to join me for an awesome ministry tour across the entire country, an ambitious undertaking for anyone, let alone for the "greenhorns" we were then. We never considered the possibility that such an enthusiastic plan wasn't at all practical. In ministry, sometimes it's true that ignorance (coupled with a big dose of faith) *is* bliss—and we were totally ignorant of the obstacles facing such a venture. As though a preaching tour of this magnitude weren't fairy tale enough in itself, when we initially planned this adventure, we also had no money, no contacts and no scheduled place to preach—except for a single meeting a classmate had arranged with his pastor father's church in Klamath Falls, Oregon! Shortly after securing that one commitment, we received invitations from a church in Hampstead, Maryland and another in Jackson, Tennessee. These were followed by an opening in Jim's home church in Greencastle, Pennsylvania; another at a church in Chambersburg, Pennsylvania and still another in Tulle Lake, California. Needless to say we were overwhelmed with excitement over these opportunities!

The classmate from Oregon also wrote to another pastor (a great prophet in Antioch, California) and requested an invitation for we three budding "evangelists" to minister in his church. His response (which I still have among my memorabilia) was tactful and kind, but it was a refusal nonetheless. The reason given was that his was a large church and only scheduled ministers who possessed renowned international healing ministries and were affiliated with an organization called The Voice of Healing.[11]

Just so you will understand how very "well" we had planned this monumental venture, I will say only that as we approached the start of our great adventure, I was the proud owner of a ten-year-old Cadillac of questionable powers of endurance, but I had no money. Actually, none of us had any money or resources. What we apparently *did* possess were vast reserves of faith!

The plan was that Jim (not the former roommate referred to in Chapter Three) and I would alternate the preaching duties and Norman would lead worship and perform trumpet and vocal solos. (Not *simultaneously*, of course! What a miracle *that* would have been!)

Just prior to our departure, one sympathetic sister in the Lord gave me a twenty-dollar bill toward our trip. With this princely sum we launched our great adventure of faith. Before long, two other people also gave us small amounts of money and we set out for Maryland and our very first evangelistic crusade.

An attempt to relate all the details of our countrywide evangelistic tour here would be impossible, but I will highlight several of the most notable events that occurred during that memorable summer. We begin with the story of my very first public miracle. It took place at the Church of God in Hampstead, Maryland, a small town situated thirty miles southwest of Baltimore. (Little did I know then that I would return to pastor that church the following year.)

---

[11] At that time, a loosely-knit fellowship of anointed healing evangelists. The group also published a magazine named *The Voice of Healing* that published reports of their crusades around the United States and the world.

*   *   *

Spinal Surgery Averted

James Lambert was a quiet man, one who never sought to be in the limelight. He worked for a millionaire attorney and gentleman farmer as the manager of his large ranch that bred prize Black Angus cattle. James suffered from two badly ruptured discs in his lower back and was in constant pain and distress. After x-rays established that surgery was inevitable, he was given a steel reinforced corset to wear during every waking hour and ordered to totally avoid manual labor, including the operation of all types of machinery. The neurosurgeon and James' employer then left for two weeks of grouse hunting in Scotland, following which the necessary surgery would be performed.

The very first night I preached, James was at the front of the prayer line. His wife had previously told me of his serious problem, and I fervently wished that someone with a lesser ailment were standing there in his place! (Remember, I was greener than grass at this business of praying for the sick and this was my very first venture into public healing ministry.)

James stood about eight feet away from me as I began to pray a short, simple prayer. (Throughout my many years in ministry I never again saw anything even remotely similar to what followed.) Suddenly, James uttered a loud shout, ran past me and jumped off the platform. Then, in one bound he leaped from the floor to the back of the front pew. He then ran across the tops of the pews and between the seated people up one entire side of the church. When he reached the back pew, he leaped across the aisle and onto the opposite pew and repeated the procedure down the other side of the church. All this was accomplished with his eyes tightly closed, yet he avoided every person and never missed a step! (I told you it was a totally unique event!)

After the service, James shared his amazing experience with me. He reported that *all* pain had disappeared and he could now sit, stand and turn with no discomfort whatsoever. In his own words, this is what he related concerning the unique events surrounding his healing.

"I looked at you and, as you began to pray, a small ring of brilliant light started right there." He pointed to the solar plexus area just below my ribcage. "Then," he continued, "as the light approached me it grew bigger and bigger until it totally covered my entire body. That's when I knew I was healed and I took off running." He assured me that he had never before done, as he described it, "that running thing." (When I later became his pastor, I found him to be indeed the most modest and reserved person in the church; and I never observed another outburst of emotional fervor on his part throughout my tenure there.)

When he returned home that night, James removed his brace forever. The following day he resumed his full duties on the farm. When his employer and his surgeon returned to the farm and saw him operating the tractor, they took him to task for disobeying the doctor's orders. James then told them of his miraculous healing after which the physician said imperiously, "*I'll* be the judge of that!" He insisted that James submit to more x-rays, after which he was reluctantly obliged to give James a clean bill of health. Needless to say, James never again suffered a recurrence of his back problem.

*   *   *

Our Arrival on the West Coast

After holding more meetings in several other states and driving the breadth of the country with very few stops, we finally arrived in Klamath Falls, Oregon for our next scheduled engagement. Thoroughly exhausted, we arrived at four thirty in the morning and parked in front of the pastor's house, intending to wait for a decent hour to announce our arrival. (It's not advisable to awaken a pastor that early in the morning if you hope to be welcomed with any enthusiasm whatsoever!) We unsuccessfully attempted to sleep in the car but after an hour of frustration, Jim finally gave up. Desperate for sleep, he rang the doorbell.

Our astonished classmate opened the door and, with sleep-filled eyes and a look of surprise asked, "What are you guys doing here? Didn't you get our letter?" Apparently, his father had written to cancel the services, but we hadn't received the letter! This was before the days of e-mail, there were no cell phones and it was difficult for mail to catch up with us considering our hectic schedule. (We never did get most of it that summer—in fact, the postal system is probably still trying to find us!)

Our friend's father was a wonderfully kind person and, when he saw our exhausted and bedraggled condition, he invited us in and cooked us a homemade breakfast. When he realized that we hadn't received his letter of cancellation he said, "I can't allow you to come this far and not minister for me!" He then scheduled a four- night meeting beginning the following Sunday. (Can you spell *relief?*)

Gunshot Wound Disappears

God performed miracles every night during those services. Some of them will be included in later chapters, but this particular one stands out in my memory. Following the service on Monday evening, we were preparing to leave when the pastor mentioned that a man from his church was waiting outside with his young son who was in desperate need of prayer and had been in too much pain to sit through the service. There on the steps of the church he told us the story.

The boy had been playing with his father's twenty-two-caliber pistol when it suddenly discharged. The bullet had penetrated his lower arm and shattered the bone. Following surgery, during which a pin had been implanted to secure the bone, the arm had been placed in a cast. A few days later however, infection had set in accompanied by a high fever and intense pain.

When I laid my hands on the boy and prayed, I felt the fever go down immediately and he said he felt fine. When the father asked what he should then do, I advised him to take his son to the surgeon, explain what had happened and ask for the cast to be removed. The following day, the father did as I had instructed him and, predictably, the doctor said he couldn't remove the cast that soon after surgery because the bone would not have healed. When the father promised him if there were no signs of a miracle, he would pay for the cast to be replaced, the reluctant doctor acquiesced. Imagine his amazement when, not only was there no scar where the bullet had entered or exited, neither was there any sign of a surgical scar. The surgeon then ordered x-rays that revealed the astonishing fact that the bone showed no sign of a break and the implanted surgical pin had also vanished. Now *that's* a miraculous healing!

*   *   *

A Reversal of Fortune

The Klamath Falls pastor was so excited by the miracle above and subsequent ones that he promptly called his friend in Antioch, California. (This was the same pastor-prophet who had previously responded negatively to our request for meetings.) Upon hearing his friend's enthusiastic recommendation, the other pastor replied, "If these fellows are good enough for *you*, send them to me and they can minister here for a week." Because the Lord moved so powerfully in the services, the scheduled week expanded to two. After the final service, the prophet/pastor asked me to come and serve with him as associate pastor. What a total reversal—this time *I* had to refuse *his* generous offer of a pastoral post in order to complete my final year at Bible College.

*   *   *

Judgment At Tulle Lake

The concept of God's judgment isn't one I like to consider, but sometimes it becomes necessary and only God can determine where, when and to whom. One unusual incident involving God's judgment comes to mind. During our ministry time in Tulle Lake, California, God led me to do something extremely unpleasant, at least it was to me, on a personal level.

After several nights of ministering with a heavy anointing, the momentum of the services unexpectedly hit the proverbial brick wall in the spiritual sense. In that particular service, it seemed as though the Holy Spirit had stayed home from church. Since that time, whenever faced with a spiritual void in a service, I have learned to stop whatever I'm doing and seek the Lord for clarification and direction; but that night was to be my initiation into that spiritual situation. Aware of my inexperience, the Holy Spirit told me the reason for the lack of spiritual breakthrough in the service and gave His directions for dealing with it.

Within my spirit I discerned that a man in the congregation that night had been engaged in an extramarital affair for quite some time. He had repeatedly refused to repent, despite the Lord's patient attempts to cleanse and restore him, and God had determined to confront his sinful behavior again that night. When I asked the congregation for bowed heads and closed eyes (so the offending party would not be unduly embarrassed), I observed one man at the rear of the sanctuary who had refused to comply and who was glaring at me defiantly. Resisting the temptation to be intimidated, I stared back at the man and told him what God had revealed to me. Without flinching, he continued to glare his defiance. After I repeated the Spirit's call for repentance without

31

result, I had no choice but to resume the service. I sensed the Holy Spirit was grieved and knew that He had not finished dealing with that man.

The next night was a repeat of the previous one, except the man added to his insolence by folding his arms in an even more blatant display of rebellion. By the third night, God's mercy and patience had been exhausted and I found myself pronouncing His judgment. Quoting Paul's words when dealing with an adulterous member in the Corinthian church, I declared, "Because you have rejected the mercy of God, I now turn you over into the hands of Satan for the destruction of your body, so that your soul may be saved!"[12] The man's answering smirk bore mute testimony of his continued rebellion against the prophetic word; and I knew in my spirit that his time of judgment was imminent.

The following afternoon, the pastor received a phone call from the wife of the man in question. Since the couple did not attend that church and the wife had not been present in any of the services, she knew nothing of her husband's sin and rebellion toward God. She said her husband had been admitted to the hospital and been told that he had at best only three more months to live. (Remember, these unexpected events had taken place in less than twenty-four hours!) The distraught man had asked his wife to relay this cryptic message: "If those young men are still at the church and will pray for me to be healed, I will be in the service tonight. *They'll know what I mean.*"

We *did* pray for him and he *was* healed. True to his word, the man came to the service that night and sat in the very same

---

[12] "You have become arrogant and have not mourned instead, so that the one who had done this deed would be removed from your midst. For I, on my part, though absent in body but present in spirit, have already judged him who has so committed this, as though I were present. In the name of our Lord Jesus, when you are assembled, and I with you in spirit, with the power of our Lord Jesus, I have decided to deliver such a one to Satan for the destruction of his flesh, so that his spirit may be saved in the day of the Lord Jesus." *1 Cor. 5:2-5*

seat. Although it was the same seat and the same row, he wasn't the same defiant man!

Before preaching, I gave an opportunity for people to come forward for salvation. The newly repentant man literally ran down the aisle and threw himself on the altar railing with such force that it broke loose from the floor. If ever I heard someone crying out for God's forgiveness, it was that night. (I guess a little judgment produces very big results!)

There was so very much more that happened on that trip. (Yes, my aged car *did* manage to get us back home. It kept running for another three months before it finally gasped its last and went to the Great Junkyard in the Sky—or wherever tired old autos go!) While some of those experiences do appear in later chapters of this book, to relate all of them would probably fill another book—and those would be only the things I can still remember! That amazing summer of ministry left a deep and profound impression on my life, one that would serve for an example all through my life. The Lord's unfailing Presence in the services, His miracle-working power and His faithfulness in supplying all our needs set high standards for my future ministry. The fact that God would *always* perform His Word was no longer just a mental concept for me, but a proven assurance that has never diminished with the passage of years.

*   *   *

CHAPTER FIVE

MIRACLES OF
PERSONAL PRESERVATION

I've heard it said that one way to determine the value of a person's life and ministry is to take note of how many times Satan has attempted to kill them. There is a certain note of truth in that saying—at least it has proven to be so in my own life.

Childhood Paralysis

At two years of age I contracted a severe case of scarlet fever that resulted in paralysis of both legs. Doctors could do nothing to affect my healing. When told by doctors at the hospital that there was nothing else they could do for me, my mother gathered me up in her arms and ran out into the cold crying inconsolably. Though I was only a young child, that day is indelibly imprinted on my mind.

Refusing to accept the doctors' prognosis, my mother began to massage my little legs with warm oil every day. She had no knowledge of divine healing, yet she prayed as she worked with me and she believed that God would heal my legs and help me to walk again. Although my mother was not born again at that time, she had always felt that I had a special destiny in life. I believe that knowledge had been divinely implanted within her and God honored her faith in that promise. I was never told how long she worked with me, only that strength gradually returned to my atrophied legs and I began to walk. And I haven't stopped since! (In case you're wondering—I've never been troubled with even a slight limp!)

*   *   *

An Attack of *Malaria?*

At the age of sixteen, I was suddenly taken ill with a mysterious malady. Within a very short time, I became severely weakened and ultimately bedridden. Frequent bouts of fever gripped me mercilessly, followed by icy cold chills that caused my entire body to tremble uncontrollably. I had absolutely no appetite (you *know* I was sick!) and I began to lose weight rapidly. As the pounds melted from my six-foot, three-inch frame, I grew increasingly gaunt and extremely weak. Doctors were unable to diagnose the cause of the symptoms and were even at a loss to know what the illness itself was, much less how to prescribe a remedy. (Some years later, I overheard missionary friends describe the symptoms of malaria and recognized them as being identical to those that had so ravaged my body in my youth.)

At my lowest point, the doctor declared that, if I were no better when he came the next day (they still made house calls back then!), that he would have to admit me to the hospital despite my objections. I had vehemently resisted going to a hospital, but not for religious reasons—I was simply afraid of hospitals. When they heard the doctor's intentions, my mother and her sister Millie called several Christian relatives to come that evening and join with them in a time of prayer for my healing. Later that evening, they all gathered around my bed, held hands and prayed. Aside from my mother and aunt, the others present had only recently come to the Lord and the prayer of faith was a new concept for them. Despite their inexperience in such matters, they prayed with fervor and God answered their cry. He healed me instantly! All symptoms ceased immediately, my strength returned and so did my appetite. Suddenly I was ravenously hungry and said so.

Aunt Millie asked what I would like to eat and I replied without hesitation, "I want a steak!" There was a brief debate as to whether or not I should have something that substantial since I had eaten nothing solid for nearly two weeks—but the steak won out.

My mouth watered in anticipation of how wonderful that steak would taste—and it did! (Come to think of it, I feel another "steak attack" coming on as I remember that night!)

When the doctor arrived the next day, he was startled to find me answering the door. After he heard the events of the previous night he went away puzzled, saying he'd never seen anything quite like that before. Instead of being treated by that fine doctor, I had received the far superior services of Doctor Jesus, the only Physician Who has never lost a patient—and never will.

As a footnote, I have a theory regarding the supposed "impossibility" of my having contracted such an unlikely tropical disease in Brooklyn, New York. Since we lived within a few blocks of the waterfront where huge freighters from around the world docked every day, it would have been easy for a malaria-laden mosquito to hop aboard any ship coming from a tropical nation. In fact, someone who worked the waterfront once told me that one of the major dangers dockworkers face when unloading produce from tropical freighters is the presence of venomous spiders. It's my firm belief that if spiders could make the journey from far distant infested areas, then it would also be possible for mosquitoes to do so.

*   *   *

A Near Fatal Mis-Step

During the construction of our first house, I found it a financial necessity to do much of the interior work myself. I arrived to work at the house one day to find that a water pipe in the unheated sub-flooring had burst and flooded the entire floor of the nearly completed basement below. As I quickly descended the ladder from the first floor to check on the damage (the stairs had not been installed at that point), I felt an urgent check in my spirit and suddenly paused on the bottom rung, with one foot extended just inches above the water below. Looking down, I saw that a live electrical wire had fallen into the water and would have electrocuted me had I lowered my foot onto the flooded floor in which it lay! Once again, the Lord had warned me of impending danger and preserved my life.

*　　*　　*

Arranged "Accidents"

Time and space prohibit me from recounting all the various ways Satan has attempted to hinder, injure or even kill me over the course of my lifetime, not the least of which were several auto accidents. One 70-mile-an-hour accident was caused by a tire blowout on a busy highway that propelled our vehicle across multiple lanes of traffic and over a steep embankment where we coasted to a stop without rolling over. (My wife and I walked away from that one unscathed, except for a tiny glass "souvenir" in one eye that soon worked its way out with no negative aftereffects. Another involved a head-on collision, which resulted in a broken neck and other injuries that could have killed or left me paralyzed for life, except that God had further plans for me.

For the remainder of this chapter, I will relate three episodes in which dreams played a crucial role.[13] In two of these instances, I was given three dreams in which the Holy Spirit forewarned and prepared me to walk through potentially fatal conditions with faith. In the third episode, a life-threatening condition was likewise revealed through three dreams. In this instance, the dreams warned me in time to avoid my "inevitable" fate.

*　　*　　*

---

[13] "In a dream, a vision of the night, when sound sleep falls on men, while they slumber in their beds, then He opens the ears of men, and seals their instruction…" *Job 33:15,16*

Healed of Cancer--Twice

While my family and I were living in Beverly, Massachusetts in the mid-nineteen seventies, the following three dreams were repeated on three consecutive nights.

In the first dream, my wife and I were standing inside a church when, somewhere outside the building, there were two explosions of such great magnitude that we thought they might have been caused by atomic bombs. I ran outside to see what had caused the explosions and, as I looked around to see the damage, I heard the voice of God say, *"These are not to destruction!"*

As I was walking alongside a stream in the second dream, I stooped over to run my hand through the cool water. As I extended my hand, a weasel-like creature with two heads lunged forward, sank its teeth into my hand and held on tenaciously. Again I heard the voice of God say, *"This is not to destruction!"* and I seized the creature by the throat and strangled it until it loosened its hold and died.

In the third dream, I was once again walking beside a stream when I stooped down to admire some beautiful item on the ground. Suddenly, a two-headed rattlesnake lunged forward, sank its fangs into my hand and held it painfully. Once again I heard the voice of God saying, *"This is not to destruction!"* I grasped this third creature by the throat as well and strangled it to death.

Needless to say, these three dreams (of *two* explosions, a *two*-headed weasel and a *two*-headed snake) were a cause for concern, because divine warnings concerning future events often come in threes; and these *three* dreams clearly indicated the coming of *two* separate life-threatening attacks. However, it was also comforting to know that the content of the dreams assured me of one very important fact: whatever the two attacks consisted of,

God had already determined that my destruction or death would not be the final result.

Shortly after I received the dreams, my family became engaged in preparations to relocate to the Chicago area and we had begun to pack for the move. During this time, I noticed a recurrence of bloody stools accompanied by acute pain. My first reaction was that I possibly had developed a case of hemorrhoids. I sought medical opinion and the doctor put me through extensive hospital tests.

It is necessary to interject here that I am not against doctors or hospitals. I believe they have been enabled by God to perform a valuable function and to fill a great need in this world, because people often don't possess sufficient faith to believe God for a supernatural intervention in their physical problems. My own purpose in seeking a diagnosis then was so I would know how to pray and could focus my faith toward defeating my enemy.

During the subsequent days while I awaited the test results, we completed our packing and loaded the trucks for the trip to Chicago. The week of our departure, I sat in the doctor's office and waited eagerly to hear the test results. When he entered the office, the physician's somber expression spoke volumes. I will never forget his words, "I'm sorry to inform you that your test results have confirmed *inoperable* colorectal cancer. Although surgery is not an option, radiation and chemo-therapy may be of some help to you."

At this point, I interrupted him, thanked him for his concern and told him I wasn't interested in any further medical treatment. (I had already determined to trust God alone for my healing, whatever the test results.) In addition, in two days we were embarking on our move. We had already sold our home and our family of seven needed to be in New York by the following weekend when I was expected to officiate at my brother Ronald's wedding. Apparently the doctor didn't appreciate the urgency of our moving schedule, because he insisted I enter the hospital immediately and he emphatically stressed the word *immediately.*

The ensuing argument led to a heated debate but changed nothing on my part. When all was said and done and the physician realized I was adamant in my decision, he gave me the name and telephone number of the leading cancer specialist in the Chicago area and insisted that I contact him immediately following our arrival there. I took the information and thanked him for his concern.

A week later we pulled the trucks up to our new home and, for the following three weeks, we spent many hours making repairs, re-painting and doing other necessary chores one encounters when taking possession of a different house. Immediately following that settling-in period, I had to leave for a month to fulfill a ministry commitment in Toronto, Canada.

Over the years I have been scheduled for one or two weeks of services in a church, only to have the meetings extended to a month because the Lord was moving so marvelously. This time, however, Pastor Hope Smith of Evangel Temple in Toronto had actually scheduled an entire month in advance. The services were accompanied by outstanding manifestations of the Holy Spirit's power and every night there were signs and wonders, healings and miracles. It was literally a taste of heaven in the midst of that great city!

At the very beginning of that rigorous schedule, the Lord prompted me to enter a time of concentrated prayer and fasting for the services and for my personal healing. Accordingly, I engaged in hours of earnest prayer every day. In addition, I alternately fasted for two full days and ate only one hearty meal every third day. This pattern was repeated throughout the duration of that month of services.

At the conclusion of the final service, over two hundred people gathered at the front of the church to extend their thanks and wish me well. For thirty days I had totally spent myself in ministry to the people and suddenly I found myself the object of their ministry in return as they expressed gratitude and assured me of their continued prayers. Because I had told no one (including my wife) of my physical condition, their pledge to uphold me in prayer touched me more deeply than they realized.

At one point during this greeting time, an elderly lady (who doesn't seem as elderly to me now!) stood on tip-toe from behind two rows of people in the crowd, pointed a bony forefinger at me and prophesied forcefully, "You're *not* going to *die*! You're going to *live! Thus says the Lord!*" Having delivered the message, she quickly turned and slipped away. I tried to follow, but she had completely disappeared into the crowd. I have often wondered since that time, if she might possibly have been an angel. I'd like to think so, but only God knows for sure.

Shortly thereafter, another woman approached me bearing a gift. "I was shopping today when the Lord impressed me to buy this for you," she said almost apologetically, as she handed me a large, gift-wrapped box. She added, "*He* said *you'd* know what this meant."

I thanked her for her thoughtfulness and, when I got back to my hotel room, I opened the box to find a large painting. Rendered in deep blues and blacks, the nighttime seascape depicted a solitary shaft of silvery moonlight shining through ominous clouds. In the midst of the light, two seagulls flew upward together. Darkness surrounded the pair and the only light that guided them came from above. To me, the symbolism was an obvious portrayal of my wife and me flying through this serious situation together while focusing on the Light from above. Though I hadn't yet told Donna of my condition, we were in this together nevertheless, because we had always functioned as "one flesh" in every circumstance throughout our marriage. To this very day that painting still hangs

42

in a prominent place in our home, as it has for many years. It has moved with us to several homes and serves as a constant reminder of the enduring mercy and faithfulness of the Lord.

Shortly after my return to Chicago, we held a previously scheduled miracle service in a local church. The auditorium was filled and, following the prayer for healing, I asked those who had been healed to come forward and testify. A large number of people responded and lined up across the front of the church. I started at one end where I asked a Chinese brother what illness he had been healed from. In broken English he replied that he had come to receive the Baptism in the Holy Spirit. Since I had asked for testimonies, I summoned one of my ushers to explain the purpose of this particular altar call and then pray with him while I moved on down the line.

When I had gone only a few feet away, the Lord said, "You go back and pray for him, and I'll fill him with the Holy Spirit." (Since He's my Boss, when He gives me a course correction, I have no choice but to obey.) I went back and explained to the brother what the Lord had said. When I laid my hands on him, he was immediately filled with the Holy Spirit and began to speak loudly in another language, neither Chinese nor English. When he had finished speaking in tongues, a lady at the rear of the auditorium stood and interpreted his (the Holy Spirit's) words,[14] directed personally to *me*. The words prophetically stated, "You are *not* going to die—you are going to *live* because I've called you to minister many times around the world." Further, the prophecy went on to speak of future healings and miracles that would accompany my ministry.

Needless to say, the message greatly encouraged me and, in the days following that service, I scheduled an appointment with the oncologist recommended by my initial physician in the Boston

---

[14] "…to another various kinds of tongues, and to another the interpretation of tongues." *1 Cor 12:10*

area. I presented the records from the prior examination and asked for his truthful assessment of my condition based on those records. His conclusion was identical to the first—inoperable colorectal cancer. I asked to be put through the tests again and he agreed to do so.

After the test results were in, they told a far different story from the previous one. The oncologist said, "Everything in the prior report indicates the presence of inoperable colorectal cancer, but I can't find any trace of it on any of these test results. You are definitely cancer free!"

When I returned home that day, I told my wife and we praised the Lord together. We two "seagulls" had indeed flown into the light of God's healing power! Since that day I have never stopped praising Him for that wondrous miracle in my body—and I never will!

*   *   *

Satan's Encore Performance

Seventeen years later the colon cancer symptoms returned, only this time their intensity had increased. The pain was greater and the passage of blood was much heavier. As I had done during the previous attack, I kept the news from my wife pending manifestation of the miracle I fully expected to receive. The reader might legitimately question my motive for doing this; however, in both dreams that foretold these two attacks I had been alone. In addition, I possessed His promise that death would not be the result of these attacks. That promise gave me a deep peace and the assurance that I would ultimately emerge from this trial with my health totally restored. I felt that to have told Donna would have caused needless anxiety and concern on her part.

Often, I would awaken in the night and retreat to the bathroom where I would pass blood and grit my teeth so as not to cry out in pain. My frequent question was, "How long, Lord, how long? I know you're going to heal me—but *how long* will it be?" Despite His silence in the matter, I knew the outcome would be positive and inevitable.

In anticipation of my healing, I determined that, when I had been symptom free for thirty days, I would tell Donna about this latest trial of faith. The day came when I realized I had been symptom free for quite some time and I counted backward to the day I had last exhibited physical signs of the disease. I then added thirty days and looked forward to soon being able to tell my wife of this second victory in my body.

The end of the thirty days fell in the middle of a prophetic conference in Florida. (Could that possibly have been orchestrated by a higher Power? I wonder...) Donna and I attended a prophetic presbytery on the day I planned to reveal my healing. We had gone to the presbytery hoping to hear a word from the Lord, but we received far more than we had anticipated. That morning, as so often happens with me, the presiding prophetess singled me out of the crowd and spoke to my exact situation. In addition to many other things, she rebuked the spirit of death and forcefully declared that God had answered my prayer and I had been delivered from the fear of death. She assured me that not only would I not die, but that I would live to see an increase in future ministry.

As we walked away from the presbytery afterward, Donna pointedly asked, "Is there something you'd like to tell me?" I confessed that I had indeed intended to tell her on the patio immediately after the prophetic presbytery—but the Lord had beaten me to it. We both enjoyed a good laugh at that!

*   *   *

"Watch Your Wrist!"

As a result of impact during an automobile accident, I developed *ganglion*[15] cysts on both wrists that required surgery to remove. One wrist was particularly bad and had to be redone and nerves were extensively damaged. Because of this damage, I was warned at the time that I would suffer ongoing pain in the wrist. The surgeon predicted that the pain should decrease in intensity, though never be completely gone. Over the years, the pain did decrease somewhat, but was always there and made the wrist very sensitive to pressure of any kind. I thought I had learned to tolerate it quite well, but it was always annoying to me and over time it became more acute. Since I had been warned of pain in advance, I assumed I would just have to continue living with it. Then one night, I had a strange dream.

In the dream, the tide had just gone out and I was digging in wet sand, searching for treasure. Since treasure hunting is an avid hobby of mine, there was nothing unusual in the dream up to this point, except for one peculiarity—I always use a metal detector in my searches. In this dream however, I was just digging with my hands; taking special care to avoid injuring my perennially sensitive wrist. Shortly, my labors uncovered a chest shallowly buried in the sand. It was very ornate, obviously very old and resembled illustrations of the old pirate's treasure chests. (This was every treasure hunter's dream—no pun intended!)

When I opened the chest, I discovered that it was filled with beautiful wristwatches. All of them were men's watches and appeared to be extremely valuable. I began to inspect each one and, as I did so, I kept putting them over my right wrist until my arm was covered with wristwatches. As I was thinking that I must tell my wife of my find, I woke up.

---

[15] A mass of scar tissue caused by traumatic injury or the stress of frequent, repetitive actions.

While my wife and I prepared for our day, I told her about the dream. We both laughed and said perhaps I was going to find some nice watches on my next metal detecting foray on the beach. I didn't think there was any real spiritual significance to the dream; that is, until it was repeated the next night and again on the following one. By that point, knowing that the Lord frequently speaks through dreams; I began to seriously ponder a possible hidden meaning contained in my dream.[16] Over lunch on the day following the third recurrence, my wife and I again discussed the significance of this experience. Suddenly, Donna looked at me and said, "You've been covering your *wrist* with *watches* for three nights now. Perhaps the Lord is saying, *Watch your wrist!* I think you should see your wrist specialist again." Since her theory seemed to make sense, I made an appointment that very day.

When the x-rays were evaluated, the surgeon's opinion was that it would be necessary to open the wrist again and correct whatever was causing the presence of a dark, oval-shaped object that could be clearly seen on the films. His opinion was that it was probably a *neuroma*[17] that would need to be removed; though we were soon to learn that the Holy Spirit knew far more than these initial x-rays had revealed.

After the surgical procedure, when the doctor met with me in the recovery room, he revealed the astonishing facts that had been discovered during the course of the surgery. The dark growth had indeed been a *neuroma;* however, that had been only part of the discovery. Contained within the mass were another *ganglion* cyst *and* a large *aneurism.*[18] The latter could have caused my death

---

[16] "In a dream, a vision of the night, when sound sleep falls on men, while they slumber in their beds, then He opens the ears of men, and seals their instruction…" *Job 33:15,16*

[17] A mass of scar tissue that fuses together on the ends of severed nerves—the result of traumatic injury and/or surgery.

[18] A weakness in an arterial wall that causes blood to gather in one area. The resultant bulge then continues to grow, until the size of the mass causes the artery to burst and hemorrhage—a potentially fatal condition.

47

had it gone undetected for much longer! As the surgeon put it, "Had that *aneurism* burst, you would have been conscious of intense pain, but may not have realized that you were hemorrhaging internally—until it was too late. You could very well have died from this!" (Since I am generally stoical when confronted with pain (and tend to wait until it becomes unbearable), that outcome had been a distinct possibility.

The surgeon went on to state that, throughout his many years of experience with surgeries of the hand and wrist (his specialty), he had never encountered the presence of these three conditions within a single area. In addition, the presence of an *aneurism* within the wrist was extremely rare. Once again, my faithful and loving Heavenly Father had warned me of impending danger—and my life had been spared as a result.[19]

* * *

The remainder of this book will be devoted to ministry vignettes I have attempted to cull from the countless wonders I have witnessed over the years. The reader can vicariously take part in miracle services that took place in many different locales. Through these pages, you will witness firsthand some of the things I have been privileged to see. I invite you to join me in this journey down memory lane and perhaps you will rejoice along with me!

* * *

---

[19] "The Lord's lovingkindnesses indeed never cease, for His compassions never fail. They are new every morning; great is Your faithfulness." *Lam 3:22,23*

CHAPTER SIX

I BELIEVE IN ANGELS

At some point during my first summer of ministry (related in Chapter Four), Satan made an all-out attempt to thwart God's plans for further Divine manifestation. We had reached California when I found myself becoming increasingly overwhelmed with the constant pressure of ministry. Though I prayed earnestly about it, my situation intensified until one day I prayed in desperation, "O, God! I need special help to minister tonight! Please send an angel to assist me."

Prior to service time that evening, as I sat on the platform quietly praying, suddenly I felt the distinct presence of someone standing to my right side and actually leaning against that side of my body. My immediate thought was, "Who would have the audacity to disturb me like that while I'm obviously praying?" When I opened my eyes and looked, I saw no one there, though the pressure against my side continued. Then a familiar voice said with amusement, "You asked Me for an angel—didn't you?"

Immediately upon hearing the Lord's assurance, I leaped to my feet and began to prophesy to an elderly couple seated in the second row. I told them that in the current process of selling their home, they had felt uneasy about their realtor and didn't know the reason. I told them their uneasiness was a warning from the Lord because the property was worth far more than they had been told. Their realtor was untrustworthy and had been trying to influence them to sell at a reduced price for his own personal gain. The Holy Spirit further revealed that God would protect them by exposing the realtor and the details of the deceptive transaction. The couple wept profusely and spoke with me further following the service. They confirmed their prior hesitation regarding the realtor and the entire situation. They said the prophecy had validated their feelings and they now intended to dismiss the current realtor and engage another, and they felt confident the Lord would lead them to His choice.

*   *   *

This incident signaled the beginning of a life-long angelic presence in my ministry. To this day I will not minister in the supernatural realm without first sensing the presence of my angel to minister with me. For many years I made no public mention of the angel, although occasionally others reported having seen him.

For example, during services at the Full Gospel Tabernacle (now simply *The Tabernacle*) in Orchard Park, New York, pastored by Rev. Thomas "Tommy" Reid, the Holy Spirit blessed us with many outstanding healing miracles. A woman approached me after one service and, glancing about furtively as though we were spies engaged in a covert meeting, she timidly asked if I would think her strange if she told me she had seen an angel ministering alongside me during the healing service. I replied that I would not think it strange at all and asked her to describe what she had seen.

Among many others that night, I had prayed for a man who had been wearing a very distinctive green plaid lumberjack shirt and he had received his healing. The woman said she had seen the angel while I was praying for that man. The following is her statement of the details as she related them to me. She said, "When you stretched forth your left hand and laid it on his cheek, the angel stretched forth his right arm and placed his hand on the man's right cheek. The man then fell to the floor under the Holy Spirit's power and he was healed."[20] I thanked her warmly and continued to greet other people.

---

[20]"Do not neglect to show hospitality to strangers, for by this some have entertained angels without knowing it." *Heb 13:2*

Not more than ten minutes later, another woman approached and spoke briefly about the service and how wonderful the Presence of the Lord had been. I can nearly always tell when an individual's opening statements aren't *really* what they want to discuss, and this was definitely one of those times. She finally broached the core issue behind her comments and, listening to her story was like a déjà vu experience[21] for me. Nearly word for word, she repeated the entire scenario related by the first woman, even to her description of the man's green plaid lumberjack shirt. She likewise stated that when I had extended my left hand and laid it on the man's cheek, the angel had placed his right hand on the man's other cheek and he had fallen to the floor and received healing for his ailment. I thanked her also and assured her that, since another woman had told me the very same thing, she needn't feel at all peculiar!

*   *   *

More Angelic Experiences

For a long time I made no public mention of the angel's presence, but in later years I have made occasional references to him as a means of explaining why I wait for the manifestation of angelic presence before beginning to pray for the afflicted. My reason is that doing so signifies to me that the Holy Spirit is ready then to perform miracles. Perhaps this is also an indication of my own attempt to be completely subservient to His exact timing. (See *John 5:3,4*.)[22] Whatever the reason, I know He has always worked that way with me.) I never publicly reveal the angel's position in relation to where I stand in order to avoid any attempt by people to

---

[21] The sensing that one has "been there, done that" at some prior point in time.

[22] "...a multitude of those who were sick, blind, lame, and withered, waiting for the moving of the waters; for an angel of the Lord went down at certain seasons into the pool and stirred up the water; whoever then first, after the stirring up of the water, stepped in was made well from whatever disease with which he was afflicted." *Jn.5:3b,4*

look for the angelic messenger and be distracted from the awesome Presence of the Holy Spirit Himself.

It has always been my practice to make use of "catchers" when I pray for people. These are men who, when the Presence of the Holy Spirit overwhelms someone who is receiving prayer, will gently lower that person to the floor in order to avoid injury to them. I consider it a matter of courtesy, even though I am of the opinion that the Holy Spirit will never cause anyone to be injured. (Incidentally, I am also aware that some people unfortunately will fall down as a gesture of emotionalism or in order to appear "spiritual" in some way. It is these people who are more likely to incur injury in the absence of catchers to cushion their fall!)

Since my healing angel always stands in the same position in relation to me, I always ask the workers to avoid walking there out of respect for his presence as messengers of God. I don't publicly explain this reasoning, just that I would prefer they not walk there.

By way of indulging my somewhat warped sense of humor, I must relate two amusing events that involved my heavenly messenger. The first happened some years ago during a healing service in an Assemblies of God church in Skokie, Illinois. My eyes were closed as I faced the person for whom I would be praying. Suddenly my keen sense of the angel's presence was briefly interrupted. At the same moment, I heard the sound of a body striking the floor. I opened my eyes and looked in the direction of the sound. There, exhibiting a rapturous grin, I saw one of my workers lying prostrate on the floor, where he remained until the conclusion of that lengthy healing service.

When the man was finally helped to his feet, he stood upright on rubbery legs. Smiling broadly, he asked, "Did I walk through your angel?" Scarcely containing my amusement, I smiled and said, "You certainly did!" Still looking dazed and confused, he replied emphatically, "I'll never do *that* again!" That brief moment in time confirmed what I already knew—God does indeed possess a sense of humor!

*　　*　　*

An Ill-Conceived Attempt at Levity

The second incident is tickling my funny bone still, as it probably will for the reader also. At the time I was a much younger, less seasoned evangelist and I present that as a weak excuse for my behavior. (I like to think I have become more mature in the ensuing years—at least experienced enough not to repeat another such silly incident as took place one night at the Full Gospel Tabernacle in Orchard Park, New York.)

After I had already prayed for several people, I looked up to greet the next person in line. She happened to be an *extremely* large woman whose eyes were tightly closed in prayer. I looked past her and smiled knowingly at my two catchers. With the eye farthest from the congregation, I winked mischievously at them. Though no one else saw it, my catchers knew I was indicating sympathy and saying, "You've certainly got your work cut out for you with this one!" (Did I mention that I sometimes have a slightly perverted sense of humor?)

Departing from my usual method, I didn't lay my hand on the side of the woman's face during the prayer. Instead, I stood about two feet in front of her, closed my eyes and raised my hands in praise for the healing she had already received. At that very moment, she sensed the Lord's powerful Presence and she fell—not backward toward the catchers, but directly *forward* at me! Her body hit me with full force and propelled me backward the length of the platform before I could regain my balance. (My just punishment probably should have been to fall spread-eagled in full view of the congregation, but God was merciful to me!) I believe that was the Lord's way of using my angel to teach me a lesson in

53

respect for *all* of His people, regardless of size or shape. Needless to say, God has not found it necessary to repeat that lesson, since I have never repeated that particular attempt at humor!

*   *   *

About Angels...

Although my healing angel has ministered with me for many years, I have never held a conversation with him. He had not spoken with me either, until one time some years ago when I experienced an awesome angelic visitation while meditating in my office chair. My head was bowed at the time when I suddenly became aware of another presence in the room. Head still bowed, I opened my eyes to see who had come into the office. Looking downward I saw two pairs of sandaled feet and the hems of two white robes that extended nearly to the tops of their feet. Though I had never seen one, I knew that my visitors were angels. To say that it was an experience of overwhelming power would be a gross understatement. I was literally overcome with awe, so much so that I didn't dare even to look up, but kept my head bowed in reverence while one of them spoke God's personal word to me. The content of his message will remain private; but to satisfy the reader's curiosity, I will say only that it was a good and encouraging message.

That evening, following the lesson I had taught from my course on personal prophecy, a seasoned prophet whose proven ministry I trusted asked if he could deliver a personal prophecy to me. Of course, I welcomed any word from the Lord and told him so. The prophet said, "Since I am familiar with your ministry, I already know that there is an angel who ministers with you. But the Lord says, 'From *this* day forward, *two* angels will minister with you!'" Until that moment I had mentioned that afternoon's angelic visitation to no one, including my wife.

In the years since that time, I still have never engaged in conversation with either angel, though I am often aware of their powerful presence—especially during healing services. While I cherish that indication of Holy Spirit anointing, I also feel that any communication I initiate should be with my Heavenly Father alone. At the same time, I'm also aware that the Lord frequently used angels as messengers to speak to various individuals in the Bible; and I don't discount the future possibility of again receiving a word of comfort, strength or direction through that same means. Needless to say I would welcome such a gift at *any* time.

*   *   *

Is Angelic Visitation Always Genuine?

A brief word of caution is in order here. Over the years I've heard many people brag about having seen an angel or even the Lord Jesus Christ. With few exceptions, this statement has usually been delivered in an offhand manner accompanied by an obviously prideful attitude. Hearing such a conspicuous tone of voice, I've been absolutely positive of only one thing—that person has never seen nor heard an angel—much less the Savior Himself! I am certain of this because Scripture tells us that, when he received his visitation from the Lord, Isaiah cried out, "Woe is me..."[23]

While it is true that our Heavenly Father desires a close, personal relationship with His children and we should never be hesitant to come into His Presence, this privilege should never be taken lightly or treated casually. The awesome power of God is not a plaything. Heavenly manifestations cannot be summoned by our will or at our convenience; neither can holy things be expected for our pleasure. Christians should be cautioned against becoming

---

[23] Then I said, "Woe is me, for I am ruined! Because I am a man of unclean lips, and I live among a people of unclean lips; for my eyes have seen the King, the LORD of hosts." *Isa 6:5*

overly familiar with supernatural events to the point of considering them commonplace. They are *far* from that!

CHAPTER SEVEN

OUTSTANDING VISIONS

"Then the LORD answered me and said, 'Record the vision and inscribe it on tablets, that the one who reads it may run.' "
Hab 2:2

In our early years, when Donna and I traveled together in evangelism, I made it a practice every day to pray many hours in preparation for the evening service. The time was spent pleading with God for the unsaved and interceding for the sick and afflicted that would be present in the service that night. During those intense seasons of prayer, I often found myself entering into detailed visions.

By way of explanation, I should interject here that in biblical terms a vision is typified as a mental picture that impresses itself upon the mind of the visionary much more clearly than would a mental image generated by one's own thought processes. It's also important to note that God sometimes displays the sequence of *future* events through visions. In these cases therefore, in order for the vision to be fulfilled, everything in the vision must then actually happen in precisely the same order and manner as portrayed, unless the Lord specifically explains any purely symbolic aspects. This has been borne out through the experiences of visionary prophets in the Bible, as well as in the lives of prophets throughout church history. I know it has been consistently so in my own ministry.

At that time, my visions usually pertained to one or more miracles that would take place in the service that night. At other times, visions were given to me at some point in the service itself. However and whenever received, my visions always accurately portrayed the exact details and sequence of events that were subsequently witnessed in the service. When they were described to the congregation, faith for miracles was produced and the events portrayed always happened precisely as revealed in the vision.

Since that time, visions have formed an integral part of my ministry. Through the years, I have ministered to multiplied thousands of people and have received more visions than I can count. Yet I can testify to the fact that the Holy Spirit has never failed to perform any action or event conveyed to me in vision form. God has proven over and over that He will *always* be faithful to fulfill His Word, whether expressed in scripture or through means of an inspired vision.

I'm often asked what emotions I've experienced when describing details of a vision. The answer is that my own emotions are rarely involved one way or the other when I'm operating in the Spirit, because my own senses and thought processes are suspended. (Afterward, however, I'm sometimes shocked at the magnitude of the Holy Spirit's words and I'm always grateful that they were *His* words and not my own!)

Another scenario proposed to me is what I would say or do if events didn't happen exactly as I had described? Since that has never happened, I've never really considered any action I might take if it did. After all, the Holy Spirit is the Source of visions and He alone is responsible for performing them. His reputation is the only one on the line. If I were not totally convinced of that fact, I would probably be terrified of such supernatural events and be driven to pursue some other line of work!

"Blessed be the LORD, who has given rest to His people Israel, according to all that He promised; not one word has failed of all His good promise, which He promised..." *1 Kings 8:56*

* * *

"I'm *Already* Healed!"

The following is an example of a vision that led to a remarkable restorative miracle. During a crusade in Dennisport, Massachusetts, a town on Cape Cod, I received a vision just before the evening service while I sat on the platform, praying. Since my eyes were closed, I was not aware of specific people in the congregation. The crystal-clear vision was of a large African American woman seated in the fourth row on the right-hand side of the church. She was wearing a dark blue dress with a pattern of white polka dots. The Lord spoke to me and said, "When you begin to minister, tell that woman I'm going to heal her of whatever is wrong with her." When the vision faded, I opened my eyes and saw everything exactly as I had seen it in the vision. A large black woman wearing the same dress was indeed seated exactly where I had seen her in the vision.

When I came to the pulpit, I prophesied to the woman that the Lord intended to heal her completely that night. Bear in mind that I had not seen the woman enter the church and was totally unaware of her physical condition. When I called her to the platform after the sermon, her husband and adult son rose to assist her. They were both large men and, without their help, she would have been incapable of walking to the front of the sanctuary, let alone climb the few steps up to the platform. As they came, I saw what the woman's seated position had hidden from my view. Her spine was severely angled to one side and she told me she was unable either to bend or straighten her body from its current configuration. In addition, both of her legs were grotesquely twisted and deformed.

Before praying, I was directed by the Holy Spirit to have her read *I Peter 2:24*, **"... by whose stripes you *were* healed."** I placed particular emphasis on the past tense and explained that her infirmities had already been dealt with on the cross. All that was further required was for her to accept Christ's finished work. We dealt with the back problem first by entering into a dialogue that went something like this:

"On the basis of that scripture," I asked, "do you believe that God has *already* healed you?"

"Well, I think so," she replied.

"Read it again," I said and repeated the same question.

The response was, "I hope it will be tonight."

Patiently we repeated the same process again with no results. After the *third* reading, an expression of comprehension suddenly appeared on her face as her mind finally grasped the simple truth[24] contained in the past tense of the phrase, "you *were* healed." Overjoyed, she cried out, "Why, that means I'm *already* healed!" Instantly, her back was loosed, she straightened up to her full height (which still wasn't all that tall) and began to bend freely in every direction. We all rejoiced with her as she continued to twist and bend.

A brief bit of instruction is called for here. It's one thing to intellectually grasp the meaning of a particular Scripture; but it's an altogether different thing to experience the *rhema*[25] of that word. The meaning of *rhema* is explained by what happens when the Holy Spirit ignites the truth of the Word and it becomes absolute truth to *you* personally. When the *rhema* of the Word of

---

[24] *Rhema*, (Greek): *revelation*. Usually refers to a specific passage or concept and differs from another use of "word*,*" *logos* (Gr.), commonly used in reference to the entire written Bible.

[25] **WORD:** The significance of *rhema* (as distinct from *logos*) is exemplified in the injunction to take "the sword of the Spirit, which is the word of God," *Eph 6:17*; here the reference is not to the whole Bible as such, but to the individual scripture which the Spirit brings to our remembrance for use in time of need, a prerequisite being the regular storing of the mind with Scripture. (From *Vine's Expository Dictionary of Biblical Words*, Copyright © 1985, Thomas Nelson Publishers.)

God comes alive within you, there is no demon, not even Satan himself, who can steal your faith in nor divert your focus from that truth!

Since the woman had already received her first miracle, I thought it would be a simple matter for her to believe for her arthritically twisted legs as well. However, when I asked if she believed that God would straighten them also, she replied much the same as she had before. "It surely would be nice," she commented. So we repeated the same ritual of reading and re-reading *I Peter 2:24*. Then, as happened before, in a moment of time the light dawned and she realized the truth—that she was *already* healed! In that moment she believed that, though her physical appearance and symptoms said otherwise, her healing was an accomplished fact in God's eyes.

At that point I moved to the far side of the platform and instructed the two men to release the woman's arms and allow her to stand by herself. Reluctantly they complied, though they remained poised to catch her if she started to fall. She stood there, wobbling to be sure, but nonetheless without assistance. Her legs were still as twisted as before, but I told her to fix her gaze on me as I beckoned her toward me and encouraged, "Begin to *act* on your faith and walk toward me."

As she struggled to obey, she faltered and the men reached out to support her. I understood the extent of their concern; nevertheless, I instructed them to stand back and allow God to honor her faith as she walked in obedience. Every childlike step brought her closer to me but, since my eyes were riveted on hers in an effort to help her focus, I didn't have the privilege of seeing the actual process take place. I do know that by the time she reached me, her legs were strengthened and as straight as my own. Her exuberant shouts of rejoicing were among the loudest I've ever heard. (I think some of us even mirrored her enthusiastic praise that night!)

Since it was a November evening on Cape Cod and light snow had fallen, her gentlemanly escorts extended their arms to assist her down the church steps following the service. When they did so, she gently pushed their hands aside and said with a chuckle, "You carried me on in here, but you ain't gonna carry me on out!" We all had a good laugh as she straightened her new back and walked proudly down the steps all by herself on her brand new legs.

* * *

Miracle in Maine

It was nearly time to minister the Word at the Assemblies of God church in Caribou, Maine, and we were all standing as the pastor led us in prayer. Suddenly, my surroundings faded away and I was captivated with a powerful vision. In the Spirit, I saw myself standing on a hillside overlooking a dark valley with a river running through it. Midway between my position and the river, I observed a man kneeling over a tree stump in obvious pain and heard his anguished sobs as he cried out to God for relief from his pain. He was a balding, slightly built man and he was wearing an olive-green suit. As I watched, I saw an angel descend from heaven, lift the man in his arms and take him to the river where he baptized him. As the man emerged from the water, the sun illuminated the dark valley and he was immediately healed. With hands raised, he began to shout and praise the Lord.

When I asked the Lord the meaning of the vision, He replied, "The man in the vision is one of My little ones, and the valley is a place of sickness and despair. The river is a river of My healing power and when the angel baptized him into the river of healing he was made whole."

Immediately after the Lord spoke these words, I felt a tap on my shoulder. An usher stood there with an urgent expression on his face. He said, "Please come with me! Brother Clairmond is in great pain and needs prayer." I heard the voice of the Holy Spirit say, "Go, doubting nothing—*this is it!*"

As we descended the stairs to the basement ("valley"), before we ever reached our destination, I could hear the cries of a man in the throes of intense agony. When we entered the room, I saw a balding, slightly built man clad in an olive-green suit. He was kneeling over a chair ("tree stump") at the precise angle I had seen in the vision and he was sobbing while he coughed up blood and pleaded with God to end the pain and heal him. I sat on a chair facing him and tapped him on the shoulder. When he raised his head, I looked into the bloodshot eyes of a face distorted with excruciating physical pain and agony of soul.

I asked what the specific need was and, between gasps and sobs, he told me that his stomach was riddled with bleeding ulcers and he was in great pain. (This event took place on a Saturday night and I would later learn that urgent surgery had been scheduled for the following Monday when a large portion of his stomach would be removed.)

The usher had told me the man's name so I sat down and addressed him by name. I described the vision I'd just been given and assured him that God was going to heal him imminently. I had seen Clairmond standing upright and rejoicing after the angel had baptized him in the river that symbolized his healing. Accordingly, I instructed him to stand and raise his hands over his head. I knew this would be extremely difficult because the natural reaction is to bend over in order to relieve distress when one's stomach is in great pain. In a determined act of faith, Clairmond painfully struggled to his feet, straightened up and, with immense effort, raised his hands high and began to utter feeble words of praise. As he did so, the healing power of the Holy Spirit was immediately released and he began to dance vigorously before the Lord! Needless to say, everyone present joined in with his loud shouts of praise for the remarkable deliverance we had just witnessed!

[In case any reader asks why I didn't lay hands on and pray for this man, the simple answer is that I was only an observer in the vision. I had played no part in the man's healing; to have inserted myself into what I had clearly seen would have been to distort the vision and prevent the sequence of healing as God had shown me.]

The next night, Clairmond talked with me after the service and asked me for counsel regarding the way he should deal with the surgery appointment scheduled to take place the following day. Because he was absolutely free of pain and the hospital was good distance away, he wanted to know if he should cancel his appointment. To illustrate the extent of his freedom from all symptoms, he told me that when he had gone home after church the night before, he had consumed huge portions of a typical Northern Maine Saturday-night meal which consisted of frankfurters, Boston-baked beans, potato salad and homemade bread! My amused reply to his meal description was, "If that meal didn't kill you—nothing will!

I advised my new friend that keeping the hospital appointment wouldn't indicate a lack of faith on his part, but that he shouldn't submit to surgery without first insisting that another set of x-rays be taken. We knew the results would serve as irrefutable proof of his total healing to the medical profession and other skeptics. He agreed that this would be advisable, so he followed through the following day.

When Clairmond requested another set of x-rays, the surgeon argued that such a course of action was unnecessary. By way of proof, he displayed the original films and reiterated that the stomach was overrun with ulcerous lesions and the only viable option was surgery. Clairmond, however, remained adamant until the physician relented and ordered a new set of x-rays. When the results were in, the dumbfounded surgeon was unable to comprehend what they showed; so he ordered a second set. Imagine his amazement when both sets failed to reveal any presence of ulcers. Clairmond was given copies and, when he left the hospital that day he left with a clean bill of health and incontrovertible proof that a miraculous healing had taken place in his body.

*   *   *

Update #1

Many years later, my wife went to visit relatives and friends in Presque Isle, Maine, the hometown of her youth. The city where the aforementioned miracle had taken place was only a few miles away. On the bus trip to yet another city to connect with her flight home, she overheard a conversation between two women who had boarded at a prior stop and were seated behind her. Realizing that they were conversing about the Lord, she joined their discussion. She soon discovered that one of the women was Clairmond Belanger's sister. Hearing this, Donna mentioned his miracle from years earlier and inquired about the current condition of his health. In reply the sister said, "After that night he never suffered another bout with ulcers. In fact, he is still alive and well and serving the Lord."

*   *   *

Update #2

While writing this account of Clairmond's amazing miracle, I was prompted by the Holy Spirit to research his name and phone number on the Internet. When I called the number given, his wife answered and was excited to hear my voice after these many intervening years. She told me, her husband was now eighty-six years of age and had never again experienced a recurrence of stomach ulcers. He had remained in excellent physical condition and, at that very moment he was high on a ladder painting the barn! She called him to the phone and we shared a wonderful time reminiscing about the events of the past and the goodness of our (Lord. If any of my readers should entertain any doubts that miracles are permanent, I assure you that my friend Clairmond has no such reservations!)

* * *

To Sell a House

God had blessed us with a lovely house in a very desirable neighborhood in Lynn, Massachusetts where many respected and influential people had also made their homes. When my family decided to relocate to another nearby community, we listed the house with a local realtor, confident of a quick sale. In such a neighborhood, houses did not remain long on the market and ours should have sold rapidly—but it didn't. It was a well appointed home in excellent condition, the price was reasonable and the spacious back yard was enclosed with a stockade fence—a real plus for families with children. When time passed and the property still hadn't sold, we allowed the realtor's contract to expire. We sought the Lord to give us some reason why we couldn't sell, but He remained silent. Don't you just *love* those times of thunderous silence in your life (*smile*)?

After a brief period of time, we again offered the house "for sale, by owner" this time. We had lots of the usual lookers, those who entertain themselves on a Sunday afternoon by walking through nice homes they have absolutely no thought of buying.

One Sunday afternoon, while we waited for yet another prospective buyer to view the house, I went to my bedroom to seek the Lord. That room was located on the back of the house, so it was impossible for me to view anyone approaching from the front. I had been in prayer only a short time when I received a vision of a family walking up to the front door. I took particular note of the husband who stood out clearly because of his bright red hair. The Holy Spirit then said to me, "There's your buyer!" No sooner had I heard those words, than my wife called me to come down and meet our guests. Before I went, I shared the vision with my mother-in-law and stated emphatically that this was definitely the family who would buy the house. Her only response to me (delivered with a knowing smile) was, "Burt, you're *spooky*." Spooky or not, before they left that day, they had given us a down payment and the house was finally sold!

The vision and its fulfillment further reinforced my long held conviction that the Lord really is concerned with every detail of our lives, even the so-called "secular" ones. He will always be faithful to guide His people at every juncture in their lives, when they listen patiently for and obey His voice.

*   *   *

A Long-Forgotten Injury From the Past

During a crusade in Canada at the Connaught Heights Pentecostal Church near Vancouver, British Columbia I received an unusual vision while praying for the sick. In the vision I saw a little girl I knew in the Spirit to be five years of age. She was playing with her dolls in the attic of her home when she took a step backwards, tripped over a doll's rocking chair and fell, striking her tailbone on the hard wooden floor. The Holy Spirit showed me that her right leg had failed to grow normally after that incident and had remained two inches shorter than the other throughout her lifetime.

Immediately after I received the vision, I turned to that large congregation, related the vision and invited the woman to come forward and receive her healing. My request met with silence, but I was certain the woman was present in the service. A very few moments of waiting elapsed, but it seemed like forever before an elderly woman stood and slowly came forward. She walked with a cane and wore a prosthetic shoe with a two-inch-thick sole. She explained her hesitation to respond by saying that, since the incident I described had occurred sixty years ago, she had

67

been forced to go back in memory through a considerable length of time. However, as she mentally scanned back over the years she was able to remember the incident clearly. She confirmed that everything had happened exactly as I had described it and she was able to recall every detail as though it had occurred the previous day.

Because I've never been accused of being what is commonly known in evangelistic circles as a "leg lengthener," I didn't attempt to pull her leg out. And I'm not "pulling your leg" now when I say that I simply prayed a brief prayer and then declared that the length of the leg had been restored. I was certain of that fact because the Holy Spirit had assured me that the work had already been done. The elated woman marched back and forth across the front of that large auditorium as she loudly proclaimed her healing. She then returned to her seat and, though she continued to limp, she and I were both certain that she'd received a miracle.

As soon as I came to the podium the following night, the same elderly woman rose to her feet and loudly requested permission to address the congregation, all the while waving her cane in the air high above her head. I gave my permission because, among other things, I've learned never to argue with an elderly lady armed with a cane—it could be used as a lethal weapon! (Smile!)

As she walked resolutely to the front of the auditorium, no limp was evident; though she did appear to be somewhat agitated. Apparently she had overheard disparaging remarks regarding the fact that she had been limping when she returned to her seat after her "healing" the previous evening. When she took the microphone, she began to scold the members of the congregation for their unbelief. She ended her remarks by saying, "I'm aware of the fact that I was still limping after my miracle last night. However, had you been observant, you would have seen that my legs were the same length—but my built-up shoe made me limp in the *other* direction!" While she spoke, she paced back and forth without even the slightest limp, all the while triumphantly waving the useless prosthetic shoe and cane over her head and modeling the brand new shoes she had bought that day!

The congregation erupted in praise. Through the means of that vision, God had brought about a restorative miracle and caused a permanently stunted leg to grow two inches within a single moment of time! How encouraging it is to know that our compassionate Savior has a very long memory and He is still as concerned with our individual circumstances today as He was of that woman's needs then.

*   *   *

Another Incident From the Distant Past

During one service at The Tabernacle in Orchard Park, New York, I saw an unusual vision involving a young woman who, in her youth had been out joyriding with friends on a beautiful, sunny summer day. In the vision, I saw an old-fashioned automobile packed full of young people. I saw the young woman in question standing up (as foolish young people were often prone to do) in the rumble seat[26] of an old coupe. As the vision progressed, I saw the driver attempt to negotiate a turn at a considerable rate of speed. As the car swerved in a patch of sand at the shoulder of the road, the driver lost control and it collided with a tree. At the point of impact, the young woman in the rumble seat was ejected from the car and into the tree. She was badly injured and I was made to know in the Spirit that, throughout the many intervening years, she had suffered constant back pain as a result of the accident.

---

[26] In the 1930's and into the early '40's, small, two-door automobiles were popular. In place of our present-day trunk above the rear bumper, many of these vehicles had instead a fold-down exterior seat known as a "rumble seat."

As I made the vision known and called on the person involved to come forward for healing, a middle-aged woman responded and confirmed that the details of the vision were totally accurate. She was subsequently healed from her long-standing condition and the pain she had endured for so many years. Her brother later confided to me that he had never even known the origin of his sister's physical problem, nor had he been aware of the existence of the coupe or its rumble seat!

*   *   *

"Deliver Us From Evil"

The church and its location in this account will remain anonymous, as will the pastor involved who died some time ago. While ministering in this particular mega-church in Canada, I witnessed a startling vision that powerfully illustrates God's intervention and protection in an unthinkable situation.

It was in the days before office-sized and home computers had impacted our world and typewriters still reigned supreme in the business world. (Doesn't that sound like the opening line of an historical documentary, perhaps one entitled *When Dinosaurs Roamed the Earth?*) The basic fact of the matter is that typewriters were essential for letters and I didn't have one with me. I was haunted by the need to write three important letters and I had no way to prepare them. One night during casual conversation over after-church snacks, I mentioned my need to write those letters. The pastor and his wife offered to let me use one of the office typewriters and I agreed to come to the church office the following afternoon.

The next day I became involved with other things and wasn't able to keep my appointment. That evening the pastor's wife reiterated her suggestion and again I made plans to tend to my letter-writing chore the following day. That day however, followed the pattern of the previous one and I became too busy to make good on my intention. Frustrated, I again bemoaned the situation that evening after church. When the offer was repeated again, I declared emphatically, "Nothing will keep me away tomorrow—I will be there no matter what else happens." The Holy Spirit knew my determination, as He always does, so He began to set in motion an encounter that would protect me from a situation of which I was totally unaware.

When I awoke the following morning, I was as determined as I had been the night before and, as I showered in preparation for the day, it was satisfying to know that I was finally going to accomplish my task without any further delay. When I stepped out of the bathroom door, I was startled by an open-eyed vision[27] that suddenly appeared in the center of my room. In mid-air before me I saw a three-foot-high form of a woman's head and I recognized it to be the face of the pastor's wife. As it appeared, I also heard the audible voice of the Lord express an emphatic warning: *"Beware of this woman sexually!"* The vision vanished and I stood there trembling and barely able to move. To say I was in a state of shock would be a gross understatement. I had no intention of disobeying the Father's command. Nevertheless, the meaning behind His words puzzled me because the woman in question was not even *remotely* attractive to me sexually or in any other way. There was absolutely nothing about her plain face and matronly manner of dress that would have suggested a woman of sexual seduction.

Shortly after I'd received the perplexing vision, one of the church's associate pastors called and invited me to join him and his wife for brunch. We shared an enjoyable time, but at one point during the meal he suddenly became serious, stared at me intently and stated emphatically, "God spoke to you this morning, didn't He?" At first, his statement startled me because at that time in my life I was comfortable prophesying to others, but was

---

[27] This is the most powerful type of vision, because the natural senses are suspended and one is able to view what the Holy Spirit is revealing with eyes wide open. "The oracle of him who hears the words of God, who sees the vision of the Almighty, falling down, yet having his eyes uncovered..." *Num 24:4*

unaccustomed to hearing someone deliver a prophecy to me. Nevertheless, I replied in the affirmative and my friend then asked what God had told me. I found it uncomfortable to reveal such a sensitive matter to anyone else and I replied that I preferred to not share that with anyone else. He replied that not only had God told him that He had spoken to me, but the Lord had also revealed precisely what had been said. He had shared it with his wife and had brought her along to confirm his words once I had told them what God had revealed to me.

An inner sense of peace released me to share the entire experience. When I had finished, the couple confirmed the fact that mine were indeed the same words the Holy Spirit had spoken to them. (Then, as on many occasions before and since that time, I was impressed by the many ways in which God chooses to deal with His children. His ways have never become commonplace to me—I am always amazed by their diversity.)

For the next hour these dedicated pastors revealed the details of the sordid life in which the pastor's wife had become entangled. Her demonic involvement with sexual promiscuity over the years had led to recurring extramarital affairs within the several churches her husband had served as pastor. When public exposure of the incidents would appear to be imminent, the pastor would be forced to resign his pastorate and move on to another church; where the same pattern of events would be repeated.

Many unsuccessful attempts at exorcism had been made over the years; including several in which my friend and his wife had participated. The efforts had always failed to produce lasting results because the woman's lack of commitment to the Lord had always led to every increasing infestation. The Bible teaches that attempting an exorcism without the subject's willing cooperation is a disservice, because Satan knows when he is welcomed back and will always take full advantage of the opportunity.[28]

Consider this possible scenario. Had I gone to the church and the woman had arranged for staff to be out of the office while I was there, I would have been vulnerable to the enemy's plans. Had I refused her advances (and I *would* have), she could have retaliated by accusing me of the act anyway in the same way Potiphar's wife had done to Joseph.[29] Since the pastor was well aware of his wife's many infidelities, he would have had no reason to disbelieve her claim that I had followed the pattern of other men in the past.

To this day I continue to be overwhelmed with gratitude for God's watchful protection over my reputation, my marriage and my future ministry. Through this one vision, He had preserved every aspect of my life from the potential repercussions of a devastating situation orchestrated by Hell itself.[30]

"...The Lord knows how to deliver the godly out of temptations and to reserve the unjust under punishment for the day of judgment, and especially those who walk according to the flesh in the lust of uncleanness..." *2 Peter 2:9-10* **NKJV**

*   *   *

---

[28] "When the unclean spirit goes out of a man, it passes through waterless places seeking rest, and not finding any, it says, 'I will return to my house from which I came.' And when it comes, it finds it swept and put in order. Then it goes and takes along seven other spirits more evil than itself, and they go in and live there; and the last state of that man becomes worse than the first." *Luke 11:24-26*

[29] Please read *Gen 39:6b-21.*

[30] You shall not be afraid of the terror by night, nor of the arrow that flies by day, nor of the pestilence that walks in darkness, nor of the destruction that lays waste at *noonday. Ps 91:5-6 (NKJV) (Emphasis mine.)*

You Can't Hide From God!³¹

Whenever I travel in ministry, I prefer to stay in a hotel rather than be entertained in the home of a church member. The anonymity and privacy of a hotel setting provide ample time for study and prayer. However, when a pastor friend invited me to minister for a week at his church, he offered the hospitality of a close friend and loyal church member whose spacious home and private guest suite would allow sufficient private time and yet provide fellowship whenever I wished. His suggestion sounded like an ideal arrangement and I did indeed enjoy my time in that lovely home. My hosts were extremely gracious and spoke glowingly of their pastor who was also the couple's best friend. I admired that attitude because it indicates the loyalty and respect due to one's pastor. My long-held opinion is that church members should *always* speak well of their pastors or otherwise volunteer no comment at all.

The services were blessed and well attended. My hosts had entertained me admirably and, before leaving for the last service, the gentleman and I sat at a small breakfast table and chatted over coffee. He was the engineer of a huge freight train and it was exciting to talk about his experiences. It's probably every boy's dream of someday riding in a locomotive; so I was elated when he promised to let me accompany him for a short, 50 mile run the next time I returned to the church. (His offer certainly exposed the little boy inside of me and my wife recently satisfied that childhood desire by treating me to a Birthday ride in an actual locomotive!)

At some point during the course of our casual conversation, I suddenly found myself involved in another open-eyed vision, the like of which I've encountered only twice in my life. With eyes wide open, I could still see the man's face, but in front of it a semi-transparent drop-down list appeared, similar to one on a computer screen only much larger. The list contained ten grievous sins

---

³¹ "...behold, you have sinned against the LORD, and be sure your sin will find you out." *Num 32:23b*

committed against his pastor and "best friend." While I read off each item on the list aloud, the man's gaze never wavered but remained fixed on mine.

When I had finished reading, the list disappeared and the man said indignantly, "That is *not* the truth!" Immediately the anointing of the Holy Spirit came powerfully upon me and I replied sternly, "You, sir, are not simply talking to a *man*, but to a prophet of the Most High God!" With that, his face crumbled and he lunged forward until his head struck the table. In tears he cried, "It's the truth! It's *all* the truth! What should I do now?"

I told him it was imperative at the very first opportunity for him to go to his pastor, confess his sins and obtain forgiveness. I further advised him that it would be impossible for him to hide his transgressions because I was honor bound to prepare the pastor by revealing what had just happened. Through his tears the man promised to go to his pastor, confess and repent and become reconciled. In my spirit I knew that if he did what the Lord required, the relationship would be restored.

In keeping with my promise, after the evening service I told the pastor everything God had revealed through the vision. Predictably, the pastor had difficulty accepting the ugliness and extent of the sins committed by the man who had professed to be his friend.[32] He kept shaking his head and repeating, "But he's my best friend." To this anguished protestation, I replied, "No, he's not—*he's your worst enemy!* With a "friend" like that, you don't need an enemy!" Knowing him to be a man who loathed any kind of conflict, I attempted to impress upon him the absolute necessity for confronting the offending brother and beginning the reconciliation process. Finally he acknowledged the wisdom of that advice and promised to comply as soon as possible. As I flew home the next morning, I hoped that those two alienated brethren

---

[32] "For it is not an enemy who reproaches me; then I could bear it...But it was you, a man my equal, my companion and my acquaintance." *Ps 55:12a,13* (*NKJV*)

would be able to reconcile and forge a renewed and strengthened relationship from the ashes of that betrayal.

Approximately six months later I received a phone call during which the caller sobbed so hysterically that it was impossible to recognize the voice or discern what was being said. I attempted to calm the caller and, when the crying had subsided sufficiently, I was able to discern the voice of my pastor friend. At that point it was totally unnecessary for a revelation from the Lord to reveal the reason for his call. The sinking feeling in my stomach clearly told me what had happened. I called him by name and implored, "Please tell me you confronted your detractor; *please* tell me that!"

His unbelievable reply was, "I just couldn't go to him. He was my best friend." I reiterated what I had told him before, that the man's own actions had shown him to be the pastor's worst enemy and not his best friend. Then the full extent of the sorry tale unfolded. Because he had not been confronted, the disloyal "friend" had not repented but had continued in his sin, spreading further discontent and division among the people. The predictable finale was that the man's divisive conduct had finally caused the membership to split into two factions and he eventually led away half of them and started another church. Since the church had built a much larger facility in the interim, this development had left my pastor friend and his remaining congregation in a precarious financial position from which the church has never totally recovered. Despite the passage of many years, I can still recall the sorrow I felt that day.

During a recent visit, my pastor friend updated me on the present state of his betrayer. Ultimately, he had been unsuccessful in his attempt to shepherd those people who had joined him in rebellion. It is an accurate observation that a church founded upon deception and treachery has doomed itself to a similar fate and this church had followed the inevitable pattern. Finally, the rebellious "pastor" had abandoned his followers along with the failing enterprise and had retreated into retirement somewhere in Florida.

Only God knows where those badly wounded and scattered sheep are today. In similar situations, many people often become embittered against God, abandon allegiance to any other church and soon find themselves backslidden and lost to the Kingdom of God. How unnecessary and how different the outcome might have been had my friend obeyed the vision and confronted the man at the outset! None of these devastating events would have been possible, had the counsel of the Lord been quickly and decisively implemented.

This true story illustrates the damage that often follows in the wake of a failure to believe and carry out the prophetic mandate revealed through a God-given vision.

*   *   *

CHAPTER EIGHT

THE BENNETTSVILLE SAGA

**"God also testifying with them, both by signs and
wonders and by various miracles and by gifts
of the Holy Spirit according to His own will."**
Heb 2:4

Throughout the early years, God wonderfully blessed our services with signs, wonders and miracles and, as a result, this ministry was steadily in demand. Because evangelists weren't paid very well in those days, it was necessary that our schedule be solidly booked because if we didn't have meetings, we literally didn't eat! Aside from the fact that I thoroughly enjoyed my work in evangelism, I was traveling with a wife and two small children at the time and working steadily was vitally important to me in a purely practical sense. To those of us called to the ministry of evangelism in that era, it appeared that the average church's slogan was: "Lord, please send us a poor, humble man. *You* keep him humble—and *we'll* keep him poor." (Wryly humorous but all too frequently true!)

Though my schedule was usually well filled except for the occasional holiday or rare break taken to rest, at one point I found myself with a two- week vacancy during the spring season, usually a prime time for churches to hold evangelistic services. I've always been a believer in the scriptural admonition that states: **"...just as the body without the spirit is dead, so also faith without works is dead"** (*James 2:26*). In keeping with that precept, when springtime was still a good way off, I contacted ministers who had previously asked me for open dates. Because I was well known at the time and of good reputation in my denomination, I was confident I would be able to fill that slot. No matter which pastor I contacted however, the answer was always a negative one. For a variety of reasons, they indicated their desire to book me, but no one was able to schedule meetings for those dates; so my calendar remained open. Despite the growing concern, I had a distinct sense within my spirit that somehow the Lord Himself would fill the vacancy, and not through the customary channels.[33]

*   *   *

An Unexpected Development

On the closing Sunday night of a week-long meeting in Fayetteville, North Carolina, we had finally reached the end of the last scheduled crusade before the vacancy—and still the dates remained open. Since we had no home base at the time, my family had literally no place to go.

When people came forward for prayer that final night, I was drawn to one particular man and I began speaking to him prophetically about his stomach condition and told him that God was going to heal him. He was visibly moved and after prayer he testified that he had indeed been healed. When the service was dismissed, the man introduced himself to me as the pastor of a church in Bennettsville, South Carolina, a small city a short distance across the state line.

He told me that his sister in another city had called to tell him about the miracles they had witnessed at their church through my ministry. She had enthusiastically urged him to book a meeting with me in his church. When she told him their evangelist's name, he had recognized it because he had often seen it in our

---

[33] "Do not call to mind the former things, or ponder things of the past. Behold, I will do something new, now it will spring forth; will you not be aware of it? I will even make a roadway in the wilderness, rivers in the desert." *Isa 43:18-19*

denomination's national magazine and had previously felt impressed to schedule a crusade with me.

Sometime after that conversation with his sister, a friend in the Fayetteville church had called to tell him about the move of the Holy Spirit they were experiencing there, and again he was urged to invite me to minister in his church. Following the friend's call, he was convinced the Lord wanted him to contact me; but in that day before the advent of cell phones, he couldn't imagine any possible means by which he could reach me during my travels. He was convinced that even if he managed to locate me, arranging a meeting would be impossible because my schedule would most likely be booked up for quite some time.

The previous Friday this pastor had received a physician's diagnosis of a serious stomach disorder, the name of which eludes me now. Troubled by this depressing health report, he had presented the Lord with a *fleece*[34] that would provide an answer to his dilemma. Since he had told no one about his stomach disorder, he determined to come to the Fayetteville service on Sunday evening. The fleece was that, if the Holy Spirit revealed his health problem to me and healed him, he would be certain it was God's will to invite me to his church. Since the Lord had amply fulfilled his fleece that night, he then invited me to come to Bennettsville whenever I had an opening.

Having heard this chain of events, I then told him of the vacancy in my schedule and said we could begin services the very next night. Somewhat taken aback, he said there would be no possible way to advertise the services and he was concerned that we would be unable to attract the church people let alone the townspeople on such short notice. Furthermore, even with advance notice, the church couldn't afford to pay much and the offerings would probably be meager. Because I was convinced in my spirit that the services had been ordained by God, I assured him that I

---

[34] Read *Judges 6:37-40* regarding Gideon's fleece—the test he put before the Lord.

would come no matter what the obstacles and the Lord would take care of the details. Despite his concerns, he gave me travel instructions and agreed to inform the members by phone the next day of that evening's opening service of a two-week crusade. Rarely have I faced such an unlikely opening to a crusade; but then, our God delights in doing miracles in the face of improbable situations!

An Inauspicious Beginning

Because I knew the Holy Spirit had choreographed every aspect of that evangelistic endeavor, I was eager to begin that first service. Despite the pastor's best efforts, however, the attendance on the first night was only eight people including me—the pastor, his wife and five others! Facing those empty pews would have been enough to discourage even the most optimistic evangelist's expectations; strangely enough, it didn't dampen my spirit in the least.[35] (I'm not so sure about the pastor's thoughts on the matter!) The old adage has always been true however, that "little is much if God is in it." I was convinced that God had ordained those meetings and I knew Him to be incapable of failure. Therefore, something wonderful was bound to happen.

When I stood in the pulpit that night, I received a word within my spirit and shared it with the people. "The Holy Spirit has just told me that He intends to perform a miracle tomorrow night. How many of you will agree to fast tomorrow and believe for that miracle?" Every hand went up. I remember thinking we were off to a good start because we had done our part. It was in His hands now and the results would be up to Him!

*　　*　　*

---

[35] "For who has despised the day of small things?" *Zech 4:10*

82

Paralyzed Legs Restored

The next night, while I sat on the platform with my eyes closed in prayer, I suddenly heard a loud noise at the back of the church where the two spring-hinged doors were swinging freely. The disturbance was intrusive and I looked up to see who had been so rude as to allow that to happen during a time of prayer. When I looked toward the doors, I saw that a man on crutches had been unable to restrain the doors and was laboriously making his way down the aisle where he subsequently stopped at the front pew and heavily dropped into the seat.

Satan immediately took advantage of the situation and challenged my emotions by making this jeering remark: "You promised a miracle tonight, didn't you? Do you see that man? Guess what will happen when you pray for him? *Nothing.* That's *exactly* what will happen—nothing! If you thought there was a small crowd last night, just wait until nothing happens tonight; then you'll see how many people show up tomorrow night!"

Let me interject something amusing here. So much of my life has been lived in tune with the Holy Spirit that I sometimes don't consider how my actions appear to others when I engage the enemy in ways others may not understand. Sometimes I'm sure my behavior must appear to be just a wee bit strange, to say the least! That night the congregation probably thought the same, but I wasn't really concerned with anyone's opinion of my actions when I voiced my rebuttal aloud, "Let's just see what the Father has to say about that!" Immediately the voice of the Lord declared, *"There's your miracle!"* That was all I needed to hear. Again I spoke aloud: "Devil, did you hear that?" As expected, there was no reply. The enemy had been exposed and had promptly retreated.

In the opening remarks that preceded my sermon, I explained what had happened earlier and how the Lord had responded to Satan. I assured the congregation that since God had said, "There's your miracle," then He alone would be responsible

83

for performing it. I then addressed the crippled man directly and said, "The Lord *is* going to heal you tonight, Sir. Whenever you're ready, just let me know and I'll pray for you."

I had assumed he would allow me time to preach and build faith for healing, not only in him, but also in the congregation which had now grown to *double* that of the previous night—a *huge* crowd of sixteen people! To my surprise, the man immediately stood up on his crutches, proclaimed his readiness and came forward to the platform.

In an effort to collect my thoughts, I addressed the man with a few words regarding faith and healing. The prayer for healing was brief and to the point and I didn't even lay hands on the man. When I had finished praying, I asked him to hand me one crutch. He looked slightly alarmed but, with a shaking hand, he passed the crutch to me. His look of utter surprise was amusing to see. There he was, standing on his own with the aid of only one crutch. When I asked the man for the second crutch, he hesitated only slightly despite the fact that if he hadn't been totally healed he'd have surely fallen. Cautiously, he removed the crutch from his armpit and passed it to me. For several seconds he stood there motionless. Then, in the next moment the realization struck him— *I'm healed! I'm healed!*

What happened next was amazing. The man didn't walk and he didn't run; he began to *jump* rapidly up and down as though bouncing on a pogo stick. Then he ran several times around the church declaring his healing and shouting praises as he went! Not a typical reaction for a Baptist man who had never been in a Full Gospel church and had never even *seen* a miracle before, much less been the *recipient* of one. (Chalk up another score for the good guys and another no-hitter for Satan!)

As I discovered later, nearly everyone in that community knew this man and were aware of his paralyzed condition. When he was healed, the word quickly spread around the entire area. The news was absolutely contagious, just as it was when Peter and John healed the beggar whom everyone knew at the Beautiful Gate of the Temple![36] People later reported that the telephone party lines had been buzzing as the various people on each line discussed what had happened in the church the previous night. Needless to say, when I arrived early for the service the next night, the church was filled to capacity with an overflow of people who remained standing in the foyer; and it remained that way for the two-week duration of the services. On the last Sunday morning it was estimated that as many as two hundred people stood outside the church and listened to the service through the open windows. (I guess one could say that at that time, more churches were "prayer conditioned" than air conditioned.)

Since that time, the miraculous events that happened during that crusade in Bennettsville, South Carolina have held a special place in my heart. The healing miracles the Holy Spirit performed there were of such immense power and profusion that only a brief overview can be attempted in this book. I will relate the more notable ones here.

---

[36] And a man who had been lame from his mother's womb was being carried along, whom they used to set down every day at the gate of the temple, which is called Beautiful, in order to beg alms of those who were entering the temple. When he saw Peter and John about to go into the temple, he began asking to receive alms. But Peter, along with John, fixed his gaze on him and said, "Look at us!" And he began to give them his attention, expecting to receive something from them. But Peter said, "I do not possess silver and gold, but what I do have I give to you: In the name of Jesus Christ the Nazarene—walk!" And seizing him by the right hand, he raised him up; and immediately his feet and his ankles were strengthened. With a leap he stood upright and began to walk; and he entered the temple with them, walking and leaping and praising God. And all the people saw him walking and praising God; and they were taking note of him as being the one who used to sit at the Beautiful Gate of the temple to beg alms, and they were filled with wonder and amazement at what had happened to him. While he was clinging to Peter and John, all the people ran together to them at the so-called portico of Solomon, full of amazement. *Acts 3:2-11*

"You've Really Cost Me Money!"

I well remember one woman who came before me for prayer. She appeared to be in good health but from a side view her back looked somewhat like that portrayed by the hunchback of Notre Dame in the movie of the same name. A large tumor on her upper back resembled half of a regulation-size football. From the base of her skull it sloped on an angle and crossed over the right shoulder blade. Laying my hand lightly atop the ugly growth, I prayed a simple prayer. Instantly the tumor vanished and her custom-made dress fell against her body and down to the floor in the back. I don't think I've ever seen anyone more surprised than she was. Amused, I said something like, "Well, that *is* what you came up here for, isn't it?" (I'm convinced our God has a great sense of humor also.)

The next night the woman returned and testified to what the Lord had done for her the night before. Then she turned to me and said with a big smile, "You've really cost me a lot of money!" When I asked how that could be, she replied, "Because all my dresses were custom made to accommodate the size of the tumor. Since it's not there anymore, my dresses hang to the floor in the back. Now I'll have to pay a seamstress to remake all of them. But it's well worth the money!" (To which I'm sure the reader will say *Amen.*)

* * *

Locked Ankles Loosed

One twenty-one-year-old woman came for prayer walking stiff-legged and flat-footed. She explained that she had been born with both ankle joints fused and unable to bend which made walking very difficult and awkward and running impossible. When I laid my hands on her head and prayed, she was immediately healed and sat on the altar rail while she effortlessly rotated both ankles and bent them in all directions. I will never forget her elated expression when she was able to accomplish those movements. When a miracle healing has been experienced, many people burst out in jubilant praise, while others tremble or dance before the Lord; but this young woman just sat there and cried copious tears of joy. Jesus had come into her life and twenty-one years of bondage were broken in a moment of time. As the old gospel song puts it: *"When Jesus comes, the tempter's power is broken; when Jesus comes, all tears are wiped away."* How wondrously true!

*   *   *

The Sheriff's Problem

Healings and miracles of many sorts were in profusion on a nightly basis during that crusade. The fact that three services had been scheduled for that last Sunday was a daunting prospect. Much personal ministry would be expected to follow the preaching of the Word in every service, as had been the case throughout the meetings and I knew my physical resources would be strained to their maximum limits. After the morning service ended, there was only a brief interval during which a luncheon was hastily consumed. (I *think* I ate some lunch, anyway!) Immediately following lunch, we went directly into the afternoon service.

The service had just begun and, as had been the case since the third night of meetings, the church was again filled to capacity that Sunday afternoon. In addition there was no other vacant place for people to stand; every aisle had been filled with extra chairs and a crowd had gathered outside to look through the open windows. When a sheriff came in and began conversing with a deacon at the rear of the church, I assumed his solemn demeanor meant he had come to enforce the town's fire codes that were most likely being violated under those overcrowded conditions.

When they had finished their conversation, the deacon came forward and told me of the sheriff's problem. (I immediately thought it had to be about the crowded conditions inside the building, but I was wrong.) The sheriff's dilemma was that traffic had backed up for a quarter of a mile outside the church. Carloads of sick people had been brought for prayer and traffic was at a standstill throughout that main thoroughfare. No one would move until I agreed to come out and pray for the sick. The sheriff had said if I would come and pray in the cars, he and his deputy would direct traffic until I had finished.

Emerging outside, I found that the Sheriff had accurately portrayed the situation and I began to lean into individual cars in order to pray for the desperate people inside. As soon as I had finished in one car, the Sheriff would move it along and signal the deputy stationed up the road to release another one. So it continued until everyone had been ministered to and traffic could resume its normal flow. Following that unique episode, I returned inside to minister again.

*   *   *

"Stretch Forth Your Hand"

In the midst of that anointed sermon, the Holy Spirit abruptly interrupted and directed my attention to one section of the congregation. By revelation I knew that a young woman approximately nineteen years of age was seated in that particular area of the church. I knew also that she had a withered right arm, though I hadn't been aware of any such details among individuals in the congregation before that time. I called the young woman in question to come forward for prayer. As she made her way to the platform, the short-sleeved dress she wore clearly revealed a misshapen right arm.

The young woman explained that she had contracted polio as a young girl and it had left her with an arm that was not only paralyzed, but which had lost all strength and become totally atrophied. It was immediately apparent that absolutely no muscle tone remained and the arm was shrunken and permanently frozen into an upwardly bent position across her chest. The discolored skin that covered the limb bore the brown leathery texture similar to that which is usually seen on a mummified body.

As I prepared to lay my hand upon the affected arm to pray, the Spirit of the Lord forbade me to do so. I withdrew my hand and told her what the Lord had directed me to say. "When Jesus ministered healing to a man with a withered hand, He didn't pray for him. He simply said, 'Stretch out your hand.'[37] So I say the same thing to you. Stretch out your hand!"

Although the arm was permanently bent and there was no physical way she could have moved the hand, the woman didn't ask *how* or hesitate even for a moment. As she obeyed, by faith she was enabled to extend her arm toward me. As she did so, the Holy Spirit performed an amazing recreative miracle by instantaneously reconstructing muscles, sinews, tendons and skin and restoring blood flow and natural color to the limb!

In total awe, I witnessed this miracle from in front of the woman. From her vantage point in the audience however, my wife saw the entire process unfold from a sideways view. Afterward, Donna's comment was that she had witnessed the very formation of muscles beneath the skin of the arm even as it was in motion toward me. She described it as being similar to the way one observes a long, narrow balloon in the process of being inflated. Needless to say, the entire congregation erupted in a deafening roar of praise.

When the praise had diminished somewhat, I said to the young woman, "Thank you for allowing me to minister to you. You may return to your seat while I finish my sermon." To the reader this may appear to have been an offhanded remark on my part; but during and after the entire procedure I was fully aware of

---

[37] "Then He said to the man, 'Stretch out your hand!' He stretched it out, and it was restored to normal, like the other." *Matt 12:13*

the fact that I had not been personally responsible for the outcome of this wondrous event. The Lord Jesus Himself had been in absolute control of my actions and of the situation. I knew that I had simply obeyed His voice and been allowed to speak His command. He then had taken over and done what He does best— Jesus had entered into a humanly impossible situation and totally reversed it!

*　*　*

"I'll Have Faith *For* You!"

On that last Sunday afternoon in Bennettsville, we had conducted an extended time of ministry following the sermon. When the service had finally been dismissed, there had been only enough time for a brief rest and a few refreshments before convening the evening service. Since we had already held two lengthy services that day (plus the time spent in "traffic jam ministry"), this last service would be the culmination of two physically grueling weeks of meetings. It would be a total understatement to say that I was emotionally drained and physically exhausted even before the service began.

On my way down the aisle to the platform that night, I had noticed that a young woman seated in the front row was holding a pair of crutches across her lap. I had stopped and asked her what had happened to her. She told me she had accidentally shot herself through the arch of the foot with a powerful rifle. Physicians had determined that the bones in her foot had been shattered beyond repair and she would never again be able to walk properly.

When I asked if she believed God would heal her that night, her reply was hesitant. She said, "I'm a really new Christian, and I don't think I have that much faith." Our God appreciates honesty and he prompted me to speak before I could even think the words. I heard myself say, "Then *I'll* have the faith *for* you—you *will* be healed tonight!"

After ministering the Word of God I gave an invitation for those who wanted prayer for healing to come forward. I thought it strange that out of that capacity crowd (including many others who were standing outside the building), no one had responded to the invitation. "Since no one else is responding," I said, "I know of at least one person who needs a healing." Having said that, I left the platform and went to the woman who had shattered her foot in a gunshot accident. She stood up on her crutches and I prayed a brief prayer. The power of God was instantly visible on her face as her entire countenance changed from an expression of obvious pain to one of total disbelief and joy.

At my request she handed me her crutches and, as she did so she looked down and saw that her weight was being supported on the injured foot. Without being asked to do so, she began to firmly stomp the floor with the affected foot and then started leaping and dancing with joyous abandon. Her emotions spent, she further demonstrated her miracle by walking normally back and forth across the front of the church.

I had been so intrigued by the unfolding of this miracle that I was unaware of the growing sounds of movement in the room. When I turned toward the audience again, I saw that the entire center aisle was filled with people who had come forward for healing. When I asked why they hadn't responded earlier, many heads nodded in assent when one person replied that I had looked so weary they were hesitant to come forward. I will never forget that selfless expression of love and compassion. They had been willing to spare me at the expense of their own physical need! (Such self-sacrificing servants sound amazingly like Jesus, don't they?)

*   *   *

Of Primary Importance

The first person in line that night was a mother who held her very sick infant in her arms. As I extended my hand toward the child, the mother said tearfully, "Before you pray for my baby's healing, I need to be saved." I prayed with her and led her to Christ. Though we all rejoiced when her baby *was* subsequently healed, I hope everyone present was aware that when a life is surrendered to Christ, that experience of salvation represents the greatest miracle of all.

*   *   *

Disappearing Tumors

A few moments later, a man stood before me who was suffering from an affliction that required no further elaboration from him. I didn't have to ask what his need was, nor did I need a revelation from God, because it was painfully obvious that his face, neck and hands were covered with a multitude of tumors the size of a silver quarter. He told me that his entire body was likewise strewn with the loathsome growths. Before I could begin my prayer he requested, as had the mother with the sick baby, that he wanted to be saved before he could receive prayer for his body. After we had prayed together for his salvation, we discovered that all the tumors had disappeared from his face, neck and hands! The man then excused himself and went to the restroom in order to examine the rest of his body. When he returned, he reported that his entire body was free from all other growths as well.

*   *   *

Unfortunately, the passage of time has erased the details of most of the other miracles that took place that day and throughout that entire series of services. However, in addition to the two people mentioned above the greatest miracles we witnessed in those two memorable weeks were the number of people who had accepted the Lord Jesus Christ as the Savior and Lord of their lives. Many, if not most of the decisions for Christ, had come as the result of having personally witnessed the love and compassion of our Savior exhibited by the many instances of restored health to the afflicted. Add those who were saved in that one crusade to all the others who have been won to Christ over the years and one can see why I am excitedly awaiting the day when heaven's exacting Keeper of the Book of Life will inform me of the final tally!

*   *   *

The "Right" Way to Conduct a Revival

At some point during those two weeks, a member of the church informed me that a young evangelist was simultaneously conducting revival services at another Full Gospel church nearby. This person had visited the church to see how the meetings were going and felt sorry for the evangelist because there had been only six people in attendance. He also said that the evangelist had made public mention of me and of the services in progress. Among other disparaging remarks, he had declared that praying for the sick was not God's method for conducting revival meetings.[38] (I remember thinking how sad it was that both the evangelist and the sponsoring pastor claimed to be believers in the *Full* Gospel but were unable to show the fruit of the Holy Spirit's miracle-working Presence in their own services.)

One night after our service had been concluded, the Holy Spirit spoke clearly to me, "Go outside now—the wolves are waiting for you!" That isn't a particularly encouraging word to hear after a physically tiring meeting; nevertheless I obeyed. When I emerged from the church, I saw that the other pastor and his

---

[38] But the Pharisees went out and conspired against Him, as to how they might destroy Him. But Jesus, aware of this, withdrew from there. Many followed Him, and He healed them all. *Matt 12:14, 15*

evangelist were standing outside. They told me they had been waiting for me to come out and I replied, "I came because the Holy Spirit told me you were here. What can I do for you?"

Being the more vocal of the two, the young evangelist spoke first. Assuming the condescending attitude of one who possesses superior knowledge, he informed me that I had done everything wrong; that praying for the sick wasn't scriptural today and served little or no purpose in conducting a revival crusade. His obvious assertion was that he, on the other hand, knew the proper way to do so.

With no outward sign of anger or disrespect, I inquired how many people had been in attendance at their services and he did not reply. I contrasted that with the fact that we who did everything "wrong," didn't have enough room to accommodate an overflow crowd every night. When I asked how many people had given their hearts to the Lord during their services, again there was no reply. Yet our "improperly conducted" services had produced many converts to Christ.

I then asked the young evangelist if he had ever prayed for a blind person who had received his sight; a deaf person who could now hear; or for a crippled person who had regained the use of his limbs. To all of these, he replied in the negative. Having heard this, my only comment was, "When you have accomplished even some of these things, only then have you earned the right to tell me that I am using the wrong method to expand God's kingdom. Since these were the methods Jesus used, I choose to follow His example and not the 'wisdom" of men.'" (Even after all these years I still feel the same way!)

*   *   *

CHAPTER NINE

MIRACLES IN ARGENTINA

In January of 1973, my wife and I attended a Conference in San Diego conducted by Evangelist Morris Cerullo. During that conference I reconnected with Dr. Alex Ness, with whom I had previously ministered in Toronto. At that time he was serving as Vice President for Morris and Teresa Cerullo's international ministry of evangelism. Between services Dr. Ness introduced me to the Rev. Dr. Omar Cabrera, then known as "the Billy Graham of South America" because of his groundbreaking evangelistic ministry in the predominantly Roman Catholic nation of Argentina. Dr. Cabrera and I were instantly aware of a connection in the Spirit that would over the years develop into a relationship of mutual love and respect. During that initial meeting, Dr. Cabrera invited me to come to Argentina and conduct a miracle crusade. Instantly, I was convinced that the Holy Spirit had orchestrated our meeting and I eagerly accepted the opportunity to minister with Brother Omar in his home country.

A few weeks prior to the date set for the Argentina Crusade, I received a disturbing letter from Brother Cabrera. At that time, conditions in the country were not favorable for foreigners, especially evangelicals, and he was concerned for my safety. Argentina was in the throes of political upheaval, so much so that the very real possibility of a military coup was imminent.

As my new friend poured his heart out in the letter, I could sense his deep distress concerning current religious persecution that was being directed against his own ministry. He detailed many instances of open opposition directed against him personally and against the members of his church. A high-ranking religious leader over the entire province had consistently resisted any attempt by "the evangelicals" to establish a foothold in the city of Rafael or anywhere else throughout the province of Entre Rios. This religious official and the local Communist mayor had formed a mutually advantageous partnership. Through his churches, the religious leader would influence election votes for the mayor. In return, the mayor would use the police force to persecute and harass Brother Cabrera and his church. Speaking of strange bedfellows! It doesn't get much more bizarre than for one part of the Church of Jesus Christ to align themselves with atheistic Communism in order to establish their own part of the Kingdom at the expense of their brethren in any another branch of Christ's body! No wonder on that final agonizing night of His earthly life Jesus felt constrained to pray on behalf of His followers "that they may all be *one*."[39]

As a result of this aforementioned unholy union, the police had broken up Brother Cabrera's outdoor meetings and created pandemonium by turning attack dogs loose on the congregation. In the midst of one service, the police had attacked the people by discharging guns loaded with tear gas canisters into the crowd. In addition, on one Sunday morning the police entered the church during the sermon and arrested Dr. Cabrera, forced the congregation from the building and padlocked the doors. A notice had then been posted on the doors that forbade anyone to enter. As a result of his arrest, Dr. Cabrera was now facing four separate false charges that, if convicted, could potentially cause his imprisonment for a total of sixteen years.

I fully understood my friend's concerns. His lovely wife, Marfa (who was also a powerful evangelist in her own right) and their four young children needed him at home to provide leadership and financial support and it appeared on the surface that risking further public exposure would be foolhardy. Despite the circumstances, I knew in my heart that the Holy Spirit had witnessed with my spirit that I should minister in Argentina at that time. In my letter of reply I explained that, while I fully understood

[39] *John 17:21*

his situation, I still felt strongly that God would somehow remove all the obstacles in order to accomplish His own purposes.

Following my reply, I received another letter in which Dr. Cabrera stated that, though nothing had changed, he would move ahead with arrangements anyway if I still wanted to come. Needless to say, I accepted joyfully.[40]

*   *   *

The First Miracle

Upon my arrival in the country, I preached a service in Dr. Cabrera's headquarters church in Buenos Aires. During the meeting, a man came before me for prayer and his need was obvious to all. His lower jaw protruded grotesquely ahead of the upper one, so much so that the teeth were completely unable to meet. Chewing and other facial functions were difficult and painful for the man. As prayer was offered, the man's jaws became perfectly aligned and the contours of his face were totally transformed! This was a wonderful introduction to our main crusade scheduled to be held further inland in the province of Entre Rios.

*   *   *

An Inauspicious Beginning

Following that brief time in Buenos Aires, I was taken by car to the city of Rafael where we had planned to hold a crusade. Throughout the long trip, we were regularly stopped at armed military checkpoints because of the intense political unrest in the

---

[40] "The steps of a good man are ordered by the LORD, and He delights in his way." *Ps 37:23* (NKJV)

country that had necessitated military intervention and threatened to erupt in civil war. It was quite unnerving to have a grim-faced soldier train a fully loaded machine gun at one's head while checking documents! (I'm certainly glad that none of the guards took a sudden attack of hiccups during the process!)

When we finally reached our destination, I was informed that we would only be able to hold a small meeting in the courtyard of a church member's house that first night. Brother Cabrera warned the congregation that we would have to conduct the entire service quietly because the house was located within two blocks of a police station and we couldn't risk exposure. When we met that night, I ministered as quietly as possible to the forty people assembled there; but God had planned a miraculous conclusion to the service.

*   *   *

The Demonized Woman

Following the sermon an amazing thing happened. A demonized woman went berserk, her arms outstretched at shoulder level as she began to spin around violently, all the while screaming loudly. (As I think back on it now, I'm convinced that her screaming was Satan's attempt to alert the authorities to our activities and cause the services to be shut down.) With great effort, three men were finally able to subdue the woman and stop the spinning, but her struggling and screaming increased all the more. She was yelling at me in Spanish and threatening to kill me. (I don't understand much Spanish, but I do know that *morte* means *death!*) Here I was at the start of my first ministry in Argentina and the devil wanted to kill me—imagine that! Could it possibly have been because I was doing something the devil didn't like?

As the woman continued her demonic rant, I instructed the men to let her go, but they kept telling me that, because of the demon, she was extremely strong and was determined to kill me. I told them that, since I was a servant of God, she wouldn't be able to harm me. Since the woman didn't understand English, she hadn't been informed of this limitation and, when they let her go she dashed forward and skidded to an abrupt halt directly in front of me. Without touching her, I commanded the unclean spirits to come out and they were forced to obey. The woman crumpled to the ground under the power of God. Through an interpreter I led her to Christ and then into the Baptism in the Holy Spirit. What a time of victorious rejoicing!

Despite the events of the evening however, we still faced what appeared to be insurmountable opposition to our ministry, and the possibility of obtaining the necessary permits to advertise and hold a mass crusade still seemed remote.

*   *   *

The Lord Intervenes

Following that first service and its dramatic display of Holy Spirit power and total control over demonic powers, a lady approached and addressed me in English. She said she had heard that Dr. Cabrera and I were encountering difficulties in securing permission to minister publicly. She said the governor of the province was her good friend and asked if I would like to meet with him. *(Would I?* That's about as ridiculous as seriously asking if the Pope is *Roman Catholic!)* I eagerly agreed and the woman declared, "Be ready early in the morning because the governor will see you tomorrow."

The next day, Dr. Cabrera and I received a call at eight o'clock in the morning instructing us to be at the governor's office promptly at ten o'clock. We arrived on time, only to wait for hours while a parade of high-ranking officials passed us by and entered the governor's office ahead of us. Around noontime, the governor's secretary finally summoned us. We entered a huge

99

room, whose ceilings were at least fifteen feet high. The room was remarkable not only because of its great size, but for the grandeur with which it had been decorated. In addition to the marble floors and fine, gilded woodwork, the walls were adorned with many gold-framed oil portraits of past governors. To my mind, it resembled a scene from *"Mission Impossible,"* but we were soon to discover that the Holy Spirit was in the process of changing the situation into His "Mission *Possible*." When the governor, an impressive but diminutive man entered, he extended his apologies for having kept us waiting for such a long time. He explained that he had wanted to get all other state business taken care of so he could give us his undivided and uninterrupted attention. For the next two hours, we were indeed afforded his total attention.

The governor opened the conversation by stating that his friend had apprised him of our difficulties in obtaining permission to hold a crusade in the city. After Dr. Cabrera told of the persecution he and his ministry had endured, I explained that I had come to simply preach Christ and not to attack any existing religious structure within their country. Because of our lengthy conversation with the governor, time and memory preclude me from recalling the entire conversation. However, at the close of the meeting, with tears coursing down his cheeks the governor asked us to pray for his wife who was ill and for himself that he would be healed of cancer. Together, we laid hands on him and prayed earnestly.

Before we left, the governor directed his personal photographer to take a picture of the three of us that I treasure to this day. He then gave us gifts of state and offered the use of his private plane and pilot for the duration of our time there. He pledged his solemn word that henceforth no one would be allowed to hinder the crusade or to attack Dr. Cabrera's ministry in the future. The governor assured us that we had full access to the media and to the use of public property. We had his permission to preach whenever and wherever we pleased with no interference.

We subsequently learned that after our meeting, the governor had publicly humiliated and discredited the mayor of the city, which effectively forced the mayor's resignation. Later, we were also informed that the very day I arrived in the city, the religious leader who had been supporting the mayor had suffered a massive heart attack and died suddenly. Was that mere coincidence? I think not! The God of the universe will not be mocked nor withstood, either from within the religious establishment or as the result of outside forces, political or otherwise.

*   *   *

Opening Day

On the first day of our public crusade in Argentina, we were eagerly anticipating what God had in store for us. However, when I met Dr. Cabrera that morning for brunch, thick, low clouds filled the sky and a steady, drizzling rain had begun to fall over the entire area. My host lamented that this rain signaled an early beginning of the rainy season and, since we had announced that the services would be held at an outdoor soccer field, we might not be able to open that afternoon as planned. Hearing this, the Holy Spirit prompted me to prophesy that before the scheduled time of the meeting, the rain would stop and the wind would blow sufficiently to dry the ground in time for the service.

Not realizing that my statement had been prophetic, Brother Cabrera replied that once the rainy season had begun, it was highly unlikely that the rain would stop throughout this entire day or for that matter, the coming months. Confident that I had heard from God, I smiled and added to the prophecy, "To prove that I'm a prophet, not only will the rain stop and the wind blow; but before I preach, the sun will shine."

101

Incredulously Brother Cabrera replied, "O, my brother, if only the rain would stop, *that* would be enough—but *sunshine?*" Then, with a big smile he added, "Don't push your luck!"

Following our meal, we drove by the soccer field to check on the arrangements there. Despite the rain, many people had begun to gather and were standing under the trees around the perimeter of the field for whatever shelter they could find from the steady drizzle. Already several busses filled with eager people lined the field. Moved, Brother Cabrera and I addressed the people and told them that if they could come out in the rain, we would also come at the appointed time and preach in the rain, if necessary.

Shortly thereafter the rain abruptly stopped, a brisk wind began to blow and the ground dried sufficiently to accommodate the people for the afternoon service. (Of course, there was still the little matter of sunshine to be fulfilled.)

As I stood on the ground level at the side the platform waiting to be introduced, I looked up at the clouds that still covered the sky like an ominous gray blanket as far as the eye could see in every direction. Brother Cabrera had a wonderful sense of humor and, during his introduction in Spanish, every time my name was mentioned he would glance up at the clouds and then down at me with a teasing smile and a twinkle in his eyes. When he invited me to come up the steps, as I placed my first foot onto the platform an opening appeared in the clouds and the sun broke through over the entire field; thus it remained throughout the entire service! At the conclusion of the ministry time, as we dismissed the people the rain began to fall again.

To the glory of God, I can honestly say that the same sequence of events occurred every day throughout the remainder of the crusade. The rain would fall steadily during the first part of the day and stop in the afternoon; a brisk wind would arise and dry the field before service time. Then the rain would begin again at the conclusion of the service and continue a steady drizzle throughout the night. The sun didn't break through again, however; and with good reason—because the subsequent meetings were held at night!

*   *   *

Satan's Challenge

That first meeting posed an obvious threat to the domain of Satan and true to form, he showed up to try to thwart our efforts for the Kingdom of God. When I finished ministering the Word, Satan threw out his first challenge. We had erected a three-foot-high semi-circle of fencing in front of the platform to provide an open area where people could come forward for salvation or to testify to a healing miracle. As soon as we prepared to give the call for salvation, a teen-aged girl standing directly behind the barrier fell to the ground, her whole body rigid as a bar of steel. I immediately recognized this as a challenge from Satan to confront our authority in what he considered to be his exclusive domain.

Later that night, I was told that this sixteen-year-old girl was well known throughout that area because of these demonic attacks. Past seizures had been known to last for periods of anywhere from three days to three weeks. Treatment had been sought from physicians and even the local priest had been asked to perform an exorcism. Neither source had been able to offer a solution and both were equally frustrated by their inability to either prevent or end her frequent bouts with these mysterious seizures.

*   *   *

The Holy Spirit's Response

Insulted by this affront to His authority, the Holy Spirit rose up mightily within me and I instructed my assistants to bring the girl to the platform. Her body was so rigid that it did not bend whatsoever when one man picked her up by her head and the second by her heels and laid her on the front of the platform.

As I prepared to minister deliverance, the Lord commanded me to make a statement to the crowd that Dr. Cabrera later told me he nearly refused to interpret until the Spirit of the Lord intervened and said, "He's My prophet! You say what he tells you to say!" Reluctantly, he obeyed and I made an outrageously bold statement, the like of which I have never had occasion to repeat throughout all my many years in ministry.

I began, "Today you have heard us *sing* about the power of God. Today you have heard us *testify* about the power of God. Today you have heard me *preach* about the power of God. And today you are about to *see* the power of God!" That proclamation would not have caused the least bit of concern to my host. However, the words that followed alarmed him considerably and I'll admit, if our roles had been reversed, I might have felt precisely the same way.

Having the assurance in my spirit that God would be true to His Word, I said boldly, "If at my command, God does not raise this young girl up, then leave here immediately; because if God does not raise her up at my command, then you will know the Word of God that we've preached here isn't true. If you have a Bible with you, throw it away in the trashcan when you leave here. If you don't have your Bible with you tonight, then throw it away when you get home. But, *when* God *does* raise her up, you will know that the Word of God is absolutely true and you *must* believe *every word* of it!"

When I walked over to where the girl was lying, I spoke so softly that, had I not been wearing a microphone, no one would have heard me (no one, that is, except for the demons who were about to release their hold over her). Speaking with the absolute authority given me by the One Who sits upon the throne and Who had commissioned me, I said simply, *"Come out in Jesus name!"*

104

Immediately, the young girl opened her eyes and turned her head in my direction. When I offered my hand to assist her to her feet, she declined and rose under her own power. A great shout of praise erupted from the audience.

Turning to the thousands gathered there, I yelled triumphantly, "Now believe *everything* I've told you about our God!" Then I extended a brief call for people to come forward for salvation and within moments over five thousand people had responded (including the newly delivered young girl) and committed their lives to the Christ who had performed that miraculous deliverance before their very eyes!

[Twenty years later, Marfa Cabrera ministered in a Brazilian city and was approached after one service by a young woman who identified herself as the young girl who had been delivered that fateful night in Rafael, Argentina! She stated that she had married a Christian man, moved to Brazil, and together they had raised their children in the faith. As of that time, the entire family had been saved, filled with the Holy Spirit and were active in their local church. The woman testified that she had never again been troubled with the evil spirit that had caused the seizures in her youth.]

*   *   *

Following that first glorious service, the roadside was crowded night after night with charter busses filled to capacity with people who were coming to attend the crusade. The Holy Spirit, He Who is forever faithful continued to visit us nightly and perform numerous other signs, wonders and miracles. By the end of the crusade, thousands more people from the surrounding areas had committed their lives to Christ. Today in the city of Rafael there is a church of over a thousand members that was birthed out of that crusade. May our God be forever praised!

105

As I flew home from Argentina, I did so on the same plane that carried the United States ambassadorial attaché on the last civilian flight out of the country before a military coup seized control of the government. Because I had been seated beside her, we had opportunity to converse extensively about the precarious state of Argentine politics and the future outlook for the country. Had these events occurred before our crusade, the upheaval in the political atmosphere would have made it impossible for me to enter the country and minister. But by then it was too late—the Holy Spirit had already done His work!

*　　*　　*

CHAPTER TEN

SIGNS AND WONDERS IN NIGERIA

A Series of "Insurmountable" Obstacles

Some years ago, I was invited to conduct a citywide Miracle Crusade in the city of Lagos, at that time the capitol of Nigeria in West Africa. When making advance arrangements for the flight, my business manager had been erroneously informed that a visa would not be needed for Nigeria; all that would be required was a valid passport. As a result, when departure time came I was denied access to my overseas flight, which had been scheduled to arrive in Nigeria two days prior to the opening service. Needless to say, much effort and expense had been expended for this massive undertaking and saturation advertising had ensured that multiplied thousands of people would be gathered in expectation at the soccer field where the services would be held.

Unsure how to handle the urgent situation, I sensed the Holy Spirit prompting me and I said confidently to the boarding agent, "It's alright—everything has been arranged at the other end by those who will be meeting me." (I had no idea what I was saying and was unaware that I was speaking prophetically of the way in which the Holy Spirit would work a series of miracles to make those very "arrangements" I had just predicted!)

*   *   *

The First Miracle

The first miracle in the Nigeria saga occurred immediately. Those who have traveled abroad will understand just how great a miracle it was (even in those pre-9/11 days) for what happened next to have been even remotely possible. Without any further protest, the agent said, "All right, Sir, you may board now." Unbelievable—but true! With no idea what awaited me at my destination but nevertheless possessed of a supernatural sense of God's peace, I embarked on my journey. (After all, I was God's Ambassador and I was on assignment!)

*   *   *

The Second Obstacle

Many hours later, when I deplaned in Lagos and proceeded to Customs and Immigration, imagine my shock and dismay when I was told I would not be allowed to enter the country nor proceed further into the terminal. When I requested permission to at least be allowed to inform my party in the waiting area, I was forbidden to do so. In fact, armed soldiers were promptly dispatched to load me into a military jeep, which summarily escorted me and my luggage *(at gunpoint!)* to a waiting plane bound for Kenya—all the way to the opposite coast of Africa! I had no way to alert my Nigerian hosts of the situation and soon I was in the air and bound for Nairobi, Kenya where I had no contacts at all.

During the long flight I searched my mind for a plausible course of action; and I remembered that a well-known Canadian missionary, Paul Bruton, had been serving in Nairobi for many years and was a man of good reputation and influence in that city. My thought was that if I contacted him, he could arrange an appointment at the Nigerian Consulate in Nairobi where I could obtain an emergency visa and return to Nigeria in time to begin the crusade. As soon as I reached the hotel, I searched the directory for Brother Bruton's phone number, only to find that he was not listed there.

*   *   *

Miracle Number Two

At that point I desperately cried out to the Holy Spirit to help me in my frantic search to locate the man who represented my only hope of returning to Nigeria. As soon as I had prayed, the phone book fell open to the P's (where I would have never looked) and I found that the name had been erroneously listed and appeared in reverse order as "Paul, Bruton" instead of in the customary sequence of surname first, followed by the given name. Much relieved, I breathed a grateful prayer and dialed the number; only to be informed that the missionary had gone to the States and was not expected to return anytime in the near future. Close to despair, I held my frustrated head in my hands and cried, "Lord, why did You miraculously lead me to Brother Bruton's name when You *knew* he couldn't help me?"

The Holy Spirit promptly replied, "I wanted you to realize that *I* am your source, not Paul Bruton!" Thus properly rebuked for relying on my own intellect and reasoning process, I was impressed to go to the Nigerian Consulate the following day. With that plan in mind, I retired for the night.

*   *   *

Miracle Number Three: The Reluctant Diplomat

Early the next day, I started my search for the Nigerian consulate, but the hours passed by without locating it. Finally, I arrived at the building late in the day, only to be informed by the Nigerian Consular General that the office would be closing shortly and the official responsible for issuing visas was out and was not expected to return to the consulate before closing time. As we were talking in the reception area, the visa official returned unexpectedly and passed by on the way to his office, whereupon the Consular General stopped him.

When he was informed of my request, he stated abruptly and unequivocally that he had stopped by only to retrieve something from his office and would have absolutely no time to issue a visa. It was obvious that he cared little for me or for my urgent need; but the Consular General interrupted and ordered him to issue my visa immediately. Unwilling to disobey his superior, the man turned abruptly and literally stalked into his office, gesturing impatiently for me to follow. He made no effort to hide his disdainful annoyance and, when the visa had been issued, he stamped it angrily and threw it at my chest without another word. At that point, his attitude was of no importance to me—I had my visa in hand and could leave for the airport and my imminent departure for Nigeria!

*   *   *

Miracle Number Four

Safely aboard my flight, I realized that I would not be able to inform the crusade sponsor of my arrival time in Lagos. When I asked the pilot to call ahead and alert the pastor of my flight number, he said the trans-African phone service was so poor that I would have already landed before a call could be completed. Imagine my surprise when, upon clearing Customs and Immigration, I was met by a contingent of fifty jubilant Nigerians who were holding up a huge welcome banner, smiling and singing their greetings. When I asked how they had known I would be arriving at that time, the sponsoring pastor smiled knowingly and replied, "The same Holy Spirit Who speaks to you speaks to me also!"

We rejoiced together at Satan's unsuccessful attempts to thwart God's plans. And so began one of the most outstanding weeks of miracles in my entire ministerial career!

*   *   *

110

The Transportation Situation

As we began the crusade, I was confronted by the fact that the entire nation was in the throes of an acute nationwide shortage of gasoline in a city critically dependent upon public transportation. Buses were filled far beyond their capacity and it was not uncommon to observe large numbers of people clinging precariously to the outsides of those buses. These overloaded conveyances were forced to pass by many bus stops crowded with yet more throngs of people waiting to travel to and from work and school or to shopping areas. It was difficult for the natural mind to conceive how we could possibly conduct a successful mass crusade under such adverse circumstances. I still don't know *how* God accomplished it but He did, and people poured into the opening services. So many physical needs were represented there and the Holy Spirit did not disappoint many of those who had come to receive a miracle.

When word of miraculous events spread throughout that large city, by the third night the crowds had grown to more than 30,000 people. With our own eyes we beheld the truth contained in this scripture: **"He does great things past finding out, yes, wonders without number."** *Job 9:10* (NKJV)

Love Finds a Way

One of the people who heard of the miracles was a nine-year-old girl who had never walked in her entire life. As the result of some unknown malady, she had been born with legs that were paralyzed and totally useless. As soon as she was old enough to sit up, her parents had propped her legs into a lotus configuration (seated, with legs bent and crossed over each other) in order to keep her upright during waking hours; and so she had remained

111

throughout every subsequent day of her short life. Over the years, the legs had become fixed in that position until they could no longer be straightened. She had asked her parents to take her to the crusade so she could be healed, but they adamantly refused because they followed the pagan rituals of the local witch doctors. Every day, the little girl asked to be taken to the crusade, but her parents adamantly refused to be swayed.

Having overheard her sister's repeated requests and knowing how badly she wanted to be taken for prayer, her twelve-year-old sister finally told her that, since she was so determined to go, she herself would take her. One would wonder how she could possibly have made good on her promise. Even if the parents had relented and given them money for public transportation, it was highly unlikely they would have been able to board the overcrowded buses. Despite overwhelming obstacles, love alone can sometimes work its own miracles.

One night, the older sister somehow managed to get the younger one onto her back and then she carried her for some miles to the crusade location. She told me later that she would carry her sister as far as she could, put her down briefly in order to rest and get water from some kind stranger. Then she would pick her up again and resume the journey. She did this repeatedly until they reached the huge outdoor soccer field where the meetings were being held.

Such selfless love reminds me of the Boys Town motto, taken from the true story of an older brother who had carried his younger brother a great distance in order to reach that place of refuge. When asked how he could possibly have done it since he had been obliged to carry his heavy sibling for such a long distance, he replied, "He ain't heavy, Father—he's my brother!"

Considering the obstacles the sisters had overcome to be there, they arrived when the service was well under way; and had seated themselves on the ground at the perimeter of that vast sea of people. No one noticed their presence and this evangelist certainly was unaware of their presence in the service. It's comforting to know however, even when you're lost in a crowd or buried under difficult circumstances or suffering from an incurable ailment, the Holy Spirit knows all about you and your situation; and He sees precisely where you are at all times. You are never invisible in His sight!

Following the prayer for miracles to be released, I observed a great stirring in one section at the rear of the crowd. Seeing this, I knew something notable had occurred and I asked the people in that area to allow whoever had been healed to come through to the altar area at the front. Soon those two young sisters emerged from the crowd and were escorted to the platform. Since they were both walking, I had no idea that only moments before one of them had never even stood upright, much less walked. Not only had both crippled legs been straightened, but consider what had also been accomplished in a moment of time. Atrophied muscles had been re-created; sinews, nerves and blood vessels had been formed within; the limbs had been infused with strength and energy; and walking skills had been taught and mastered! What we were seeing was only the final result of the Holy Spirit's work that evening—for the first time in the nine years of her life, the young girl was walking perfectly! (If readers close their eyes and employ their imagination, perhaps they can visualize the radiant smiles that lit up the sisters' faces that night! I know they were matched by my own.)

*   *   *

I Once Was Blind, But Now I See

During the same crusade in Nigeria, I listened to the account of an astounding and heartwarming miracle. Following the healing prayer one night, my workers escorted a very tall man and his little son to the platform to give testimony. The father and son were Masai, members of an African tribe known for its great height, outstanding courage and stoicism; but this man was openly crying unashamedly as he cradled his little child in his arms. Through his tears, the father said, "My son is four years old. He has been blind his entire life. I brought him tonight because I had been told that your God could cure blindness and now I know that's true. My son was born totally blind, but now he can see!" Do I need to tell you that this evangelist, along with the entire congregation, broke into shouts of grateful praise?

*   *   *

The Book of Acts Revisited

During one service, three men came to the platform and requested permission to speak to the people. The three were leading witch doctors and very well known in the area. Through my interpreter I interviewed them and after hearing their stories, allowed them to address the congregation. What follows is a paraphrase of what each of them said to that sea of people.

"I've been a powerful witch doctor and many of you know of me and have marveled at my powers in the spirit world. All of my gods combined can never match the power of this man's God! These past few days I have seen many healing miracles with my own eyes and I have come to believe in this God. I have made a decision to accept His Son, Jesus as my Savior and I urge all of you to do likewise. I now renounce my gods and all the powers of witchcraft."

The other two testimonies were similar. When all three had indicated a decision to accept Christ and renounce the practice of witchcraft, they removed the *juju* bags[41] from their belts and dropped them to the ground in front of the platform. The altar

---

[41] A leather bag filled with magic powders, charms and amulets, etc., used in the casting of spells.

114

workers sprayed them with lighter fluid and burned them. As they did so, a mighty roar of praise rose from the crowd! What we had witnessed that night was a modern-day reenactment of an account in the Book of Acts:

> **"This became known to all, both Jews and Greeks, who lived in Ephesus; and fear fell upon them all and the name of the Lord Jesus was being magnified. Many also of those who had believed kept coming, confessing and disclosing their practices. And many of those who practiced magic brought their books together and began burning them in the sight of everyone; and they counted up the price of them and found it fifty thousand pieces of silver. So the word of the Lord was growing mightily and prevailing."** *Acts 19:17-20*

✳   ✳   ✳

The crusade in Lagos, Nigeria was outstanding in every respect and stands out in my memory as one of the most astounding displays of the miracle-working Presence of the Holy Spirit I have ever seen. His mighty power was in evidence every night and the sheer magnitude and awesome variety of the healing miracles He performed were amazing to behold. Every night we saw blinded eyes that were made to see and deaf ears that could now hear. Useless limbs were restored and began to function once again and many exotic diseases were healed.

When severely maimed and crippled people were healed, they discarded their canes, crutches, braces and wheelchairs, and we added them nightly to the ever-increasing number displayed in an area at the front of the platform. In addition to the restorative and healing miracles that occurred, a great many demons were cast out and their victims were subsequently freed from Satan's bondage.

The miracles we saw were of such magnitude and took place so rapidly, we could allow only a small fraction of those who had been healed to testify from the platform. In addition to the specific miracles recorded here, there were so many more whose testimonies we didn't have time to hear, the particular details of which I will never know this side of heaven. When the crusade came to a close, a conservative estimate put the numbers at fifteen thousand decisions for Christ and at least that many healings. I will remain forever humbled and filled with gratitude to my wonderful Lord for having allowed me to be a part of that move of God. To Him belongs *all* of the glory!

* * *

One Final Word

The retelling of these wondrous events in Africa should be enough to convince many liberal theologians of the error of their commonly held conviction that acts of miraculous healings, signs and wonders are unnecessary in this present church age. The reader is aware that I have expounded my position on this subject at length in earlier chapters of this book. However, I thought it appropriate here to re-state what I consider to be the present-day church's responsibility to this lost and suffering world. To that end, I offer this brief quote from one of my previous books, *The SHOCKWAVE*:[42]

We Christians have faith in Jesus and His Word, but that's our personal decision. We've lived our lives in a culture where (at least with lip service) the Bible is respected as the Word of God and Jesus is regarded as Lord. Why should the heathen (whether here or abroad) toss out their gods and their sacred writings (in which they've believed for centuries) in

---

[42] From *The SHOCKWAVE*,© 1997 by Burton Seavey, Treasure House, an Imprint of Destiny Image.® Available from the author (see product page in the back of this book).

favor of ours? What will convince them that our God is bigger, stronger and better than theirs? Our preaching must be accompanied by a demonstration of Kingdom power sufficient to convince the heathen beyond any shadow of a doubt that what we have is superior in *every* respect. Then they will not only want what we have, but will yearn to embrace it. John G. Lake who, in the early 1900's, had a powerful healing ministry said, "A God without power to heal a sick heathen's body is a poor recommendation of His ability to save his soul."[43]

---

[43] "But so that you may know that the Son of Man has authority on earth to forgive sins"— He said to the paralytic, "I say to you, get up, pick up your pallet and go home." And he got up and immediately picked up the pallet and went out in the sight of everyone, so that they were all amazed and were glorifying God, saying, "We have never seen anything like this." *Mark 2:10-12*

CHAPTER ELEVEN

RECREATIVE MIRACLES

Throughout my ministry career, I have been privileged to witness many instances of miraculous restoration involving various human body parts. A complete accounting is impossible because of the similarity in nature and the quantity and frequency with which they occurred, sometimes within the same service or crusade. For that reason alone they do not stand out specifically in memory, despite their having all been of miraculous origin and inestimable value to the individual recipients. Some specific recreative miracles involving blindness, deafness, crippling diseases and infirmities are detailed elsewhere in this book and some have been specially selected for this chapter.

*   *   *

Severed Spinal Cord

Sometime during my tenure at Zion Bible Institute, I received a telephone call from my mother in New York City. Mom related that she had recently met a young twenty-one-year-old woman whom she had led to the Lord, but who was in desperate need of a miracle. Doctors had previously discovered a tumor on the young woman's spinal cord. The family had been advised that the result of ignoring the tumor would eventually lead to her death; but to remove it posed a substantial risk that the spinal cord could be severed and result in permanent paralysis from the waist down. When faced with those dismal alternatives, the girl and her parents had consented to the surgery.

The surgery itself had successfully removed the tumor, but the spinal cord had indeed been severed. That beautiful young woman's legs had been rendered useless and the obvious prognosis was that she would never walk again. My mother had won her to the Lord and told her about God's power to heal. The purpose for Mom's call was a request for the faculty and students to pray for a miraculous restoration of the severed spinal cord. As she spoke, the Spirit of the Lord came upon me and I prophesied that the Lord was sending me to pray for the young woman and she would be miraculously healed.

When I arrived in Brooklyn, a group of Christians accompanied me to the parents' apartment to pray. Included in the number were my mother, her sister, Millie and Buster, my friend and fellow student who had driven me to the city. But the most important Person by far was the unseen member of our little group—the infinitely compassionate and powerful Holy Spirit. All of us were eagerly anticipating what the Lord would do that night.

As is often the case in Brooklyn, the apartment layout required us to pass through the kitchen in order to reach the young woman's bedroom. Seated around the table were four people, friends and relatives of the family, all of whom were smoking, drinking beer and laughing at our presence there. They mocked us, calling us fanatics, "holy rollers," and other derogatory terms. Conversely, the girl's parents were respectful and gracious hosts who appeared to be embarrassed by their guests' verbal abuse. Strangely enough, the insults left us unmoved; instead it was somehow encouraging to know that Satan was fighting our presence there. It seemed to be an indication that God was with us and hell was resisting the inevitable outcome of our visit.

We shut the door on the sounds of amused mockery and entered the room where the young woman lay in bed awaiting her miracle. Since I was at the forefront of the group, the father (an Italian man and devout adherent to the Roman Catholic faith) asked me in heavily accented English, "Are *you* the healer?" I replied truthfully, "No, Sir, I'm not." Somewhat puzzled, he questioned, "Then which one *is* the healer?" As I pointed toward

Heaven I replied, "Jesus Christ is the Healer and He's here right now, even though you can't see Him."

In the girl's bedroom I observed a pyramid-shaped structure in one corner on which many tiny figurines had been carefully arranged. Placed before each one was a lighted candle. When I asked the significance of the display, the gentleman reverently replied that the altar contained ninety-six statuettes of saints placed in ascending order, at the apex of which was a larger one which represented the Virgin Mary. He explained that the candles were kept continuously burning before each saint as a perpetual plea for their intercession on his daughter's behalf.

I respectfully asked the parents to extinguish the candles and refrain from praying to any of the saints represented there throughout our time of prayer for his daughter. Curious, the father asked the reason and I replied, "Because all of them have had their opportunity to perform a miracle; now it's God's turn. Jesus *is* going to heal your daughter and I don't want there to be any lingering doubt whether the saints could somehow have been involved in the miracle." I told him it was of utmost importance that Jesus alone receive the praise and no one else. The father smiled, agreed that the request was a reasonable one and gave his word that no one in the room would pray to anyone other than Jesus.

We took our places around the bedside where I spoke a few words to encourage the family's faith and quoted several scripture verses pertaining to God's willingness to heal the sick. Following that brief exhortation, we knelt in a circle around the bed and joined hands. I held the afflicted woman's right hand in my left one and offered a brief prayer for healing. A moment later the entire bed began to shake violently! I opened one eye (my own rendition of the biblical injunction to *watch and pray*) and was awestricken to see the girl's legs moving energetically up and down under the covers. That incredible act was taking place before our very eyes despite the fact that a surgeon's scalpel had totally

121

severed the spinal cord and it was a physical *impossibility* for those legs to move! We could scarcely contain our joy as we beheld a true miracle!

Overcome with awe, I rose to my feet and offered my hand to assist the young lady out of bed. She moved my hand aside and politely said, "Thank you, but I don't need your hand." She then threw aside the covers, swung both legs over the side of the bed and stood to her feet. No one had told her what to do next, but she had obviously overheard the mockery of those in the kitchen earlier. So, perfectly erect and without assistance she triumphantly pushed her wheelchair into the kitchen. In shocked disbelief the laughter ceased immediately and in the ensuing silence, some at the table nervously lit cigarettes, while others extinguished theirs. Drinks were either forgotten or hastily consumed. The only unanimous gesture was that every head was bowed in reverence or embarrassment as we left the apartment. Instinctively, they seemed to recognize that the Lord Jesus Christ Himself had come by that night and they had witnessed the awesome result of a genuine miracle.

When an individual receives a doctor's opinion that appears to be inevitable, they should seek another opinion; and that's precisely what we had done that night. In the face of a final and humanly irreversible prognosis, we had sought the advice of the Great Physician. His decision was the determining one. Although an earthly physician had severed the spinal cord, the Great Physician had reattached it with perfect results!

I must tell the reader an interesting observation I made while this drama was unfolding; something akin to the biblical narrative which relates the healing of a blind beggar.[44] When Jesus entered Jericho amid the shouts of an enthusiastic throng, a blind man named Bartimaeus was seated beside the roadway begging for handouts. When he realized it was Jesus Who was passing by, he

---

[44] Please read *Mark 10:46-52* for the full account of this miracle.

cried out for restoration of his sight. When Jesus heard the cry and called for the blind man to be brought to Him, Bartimaeus threw aside the cloak he was wearing and came to the Master.

The significance of his act was that in those times, blind beggars wore a special robe that informed passersby of their infirmity. A modern day counterpart would be the white cane used by blind people today. When Bartimaeus threw aside his blind beggar's cloak, it constituted his confession of faith. By so doing he declared, "I'm going to be *healed* today! I'm going to receive my sight; and when I do, I'll never need this robe again!"

The young woman's actions in this narrative bore a marked similarity to those of Bartimaeus. When she rose from her bed, I noted that she was wearing a robe beneath the covers. Prior to our arrival, she had obviously asked her parents to bring a robe to wear over her nightclothes. Bartimaeus had *removed* his robe and she had *put on* her robe. Both had performed some tangible action in anticipation of receiving their miracle. By those simple acts, they had indicated their faith and that faith was seen by Jesus and amply rewarded.

*   *   *

Recreated Ear Drums

During a healing service in Princeton, Illinois, I personally ministered to afflicted individuals and then prayed a group prayer for those in the congregation who had not come forward for prayer. That night everyone present had been made acutely aware of an extraordinarily powerful anointing of the Holy Spirit in the service. It was one of those times when one was utterly convinced that just about anything good could happen—and very special things certainly *did*.

Because there was no major airport near that small city, I had traveled there by train. After the service I needed to hurry in order to catch the last train back to Chicago that night. As I hurried to leave the church, a woman stopped me in the aisle, eager to share what the Lord had done for her during the healing service. I always make it a point to listen to all such good reports, but that night I was afraid to miss my train connection for home and had not made arrangements to stay overnight locally. As graciously as I could, I attempted to explain why I was in such a hurry to leave, but the woman would not be deterred. "But I can *hear* now!" she insisted emphatically.

I've been blessed with large numbers of deaf people around the world who have had their hearing restored and I never tire of hearing their testimonies. But that night, even while I acknowledged that dear sister's exuberance over her healing, I kept inching toward the door. Seeing my distraction, she spoke up kindly, but firmly, "You don't understand, Brother Seavey. The eardrum in one of my ears was surgically *removed*, but now I can hear perfectly in that ear!" That certainly gained my undivided attention. My waiting train was forgotten while I listened intently to the woman's testimony. Within moments another woman excitedly related to both of us that one of her own eardrums had been ruptured and she had been deaf in that ear for years. Following the healing prayer she likewise had experienced the miracle of restored hearing.

Together we celebrated the fact that the Master Designer Himself had installed those two replacement parts for defective ones. (I'm sure the reader will agree that it would be impossible to do better than that!) The fact that He did so in a moment of time without pain or the use of invasive surgery was a compelling illustration of the way in which the Great Physician operates (dual meaning intended!). The same God who had done this wonderful thing was also mindful of my dilemma and delayed my train just a tad. I was soon on my way home with a grateful heart, rejoicing over the evening's miraculous events.

Every time I reminisce about that night, I sense again the wonder of our God and marvel at His power and compassion. His heavenly "body shop" never runs short of parts or of miraculous ways to install them. If any reader is currently in need of a restorative miracle, be assured that the Great Physician is always in His office; and He has absolutely no need for malpractice insurance![45]

*   *   *

Dejavu in Korea

Before I relate the following incident that happened in Korea, allow me a brief aside here to tell the reader something that has greatly impacted me personally in my ministry. Some years ago, my good friend Pastor Tommy Reid (see Dedication page) sponsored my attendance at a gathering of world leaders for the *John 14:21 Conference* in Singapore. It was a great honor to be invited and I was sent there as a representative from the field of evangelism. During a planned stop in Seoul, South Korea, we attended services at the great Full Gospel Church founded by Doctor Paul Yonggi Cho (now *David* Yonggi Cho). Our United States delegation also met with Dr. Cho for a special session titled "The Fourth Dimension." I was intrigued by the title because it is also the title of one of my own hallmark messages by the same name that is concerned with the Holy Spirit-filled life. At the time I was amazed by the similarity between our two teachings.

Because of our apparently mutual love and respect for this important subject, I briefly stopped by Doctor Cho's seat during our flight to Singapore to comment on how much I had enjoyed his teaching. I was astonished when this great man invited me to be

---

[45] "...Ascribe greatness to our God! The Rock! His work is *perfect*..." *Deut.32:3b,4a (Emphasis mine.)*

seated with him and consequently shared a two-hour conversation regarding our passion for the Presence and work of the Holy Spirit in the church today. I found him to be an extremely personable and humble servant of God and I greatly enjoyed our exhilarating conversation and unusually deep spiritual connection.

Sometime later that year, I attended a conference at which Dr. Cho was the featured speaker and was honored to be invited backstage. Following a brief time of fellowship, he presented me with a copy of one of his books inscribed with his name and the Korean phrase for "I love you," which he promptly wrote out in English as well (see the picture section in this book). Since that time I have had an affinity and spiritual burden for the nation of South Korea, and am grateful for Dr. Cho's impartation of love and concern for his nation. It was my long held hope to minister in Korea and my first series of meetings there took place in the very early part of this twenty first century.

Within the past few years, the Lord has further blessed me on four other occasions with opportunities to minister in several cities throughout South Korea. During my most recent visit in 2006, Prophet Leyff Wenderson and I were privileged to witness over a thousand miracles of healing and restoration during our month-long ministry there. In one very large church alone, we experienced more than four hundred miracles representative of all kinds of infirmity and disease. Out of all those, one particular incident stands out because of its remarkable similarity to that of one Illinois woman's experience.

As I was preparing to pray over the entire congregation for healing during our last service in that church, the Holy Spirit prompted me to first relate one incident from the above account— that of the woman whose eardrum had been restored after surgical removal. I had no idea why I had been directed to postpone praying for the countless needs represented in that congregation of thousands in order to share that one testimony in particular. However, I've learned not to question God. He always has His reasons, whether or not He chooses to reveal them to us. He never asks for our opinion; His singular requirement of us is our absolute obedience whenever He speaks. Accordingly, I related the incident in question and then went on to pray a general prayer for the needs of all those present.

When I prayed that prayer, a powerful wave of anointing swept over the congregation and we knew the Holy Spirit had accomplished many miracles. Throngs of people who had just received a healing and/or miracle poured down the aisles in order to offer their personal testimonies of God's visitation.

Among the varied reports of healing we heard that night, the testimonies of two women bore a marked resemblance to the one I had just related. Separately, they testified to having been totally deaf for years in one ear because the eardrum had been surgically removed; as had also happened to the Illinois woman. As I had prayed the prayer of faith, the Holy Spirit had created brand-new eardrums and their hearing had been totally restored within a moment of time! Although our Lord uses myriads of methods to accomplish His works, sometimes He does repeat Himself!

*   *   *

"A New Back"

Some years ago the Holy Spirit inspired me to write a book entitled, *Why Doesn't God Heal Me?* It deals with many scriptural reasons why some Christians have not received spiritual healing despite repeated prayer. The premise of the book is that one primary reason healing does not occur is that the afflicted person may be out of harmony with principles contained in the Word of God. Each chapter in the book examined a particular scriptural concept that had been unknown, ignored or violated by the reader

127

and this had resulted in their continued state of impaired health.[46] Each chapter also instructed readers in their responsibility to conform to the Word and thereby clear the way for their healing. The book, published by Creation House (now *CharismaLife*) proved to be a best seller in both the Christian and secular markets.[47]

Testimonies were received from people around the world who told of their deliverance through reading the book and applying one of the scriptural remedies to their own situation. One such woman wrote from Australia. After coming in contact with my book, she wrote me an excited letter telling of the miracle the Holy Spirit had brought about in her life.

The woman explained in the letter that all the discs in her spine had deteriorated to the point where medical science could offer no further viable options. She had been in a constant state of extreme pain that even the most powerful medications had been unable to alleviate. Finally, in desperation she had asked her doctor if there was even a slight hope of restoring her to health. His facetious response was, "Your only hope now is *a new back*." Neither he nor his patient had any way of knowing that his statement, spoken in abject frustration, would prove to be prophetic.

The letter continued by saying that she had "happened" to come across my book in a drugstore bookrack while on a trip to Singapore. She had read it, applied the scriptural truth contained in one chapter and had subsequently received a complete and total restoration of her spinal column. (May I state emphatically here that it wasn't happenstance that led her to the book. The Holy Spirit Himself had directed her to it as a means by which He could speak to her and thereby release her healing.)

---

[46] Please read *I Corinthians 17-31* for an example of this concept.

[47] "*Why Doesn't God Heal ME?*" is now being prepared for an updated and revised second printing. See the back pages of this book for ordering information.

Since that time I've often wished the woman had told me which chapter and scriptural principle had spoken to her situation. The letter simply stated that she had responded to the truth contained in one of the chapters and rectified something in her life that was contrary to the Word of God. When she returned to her doctor to be examined, he had reported, in absolute amazement, that she had somehow been given what he termed *"a new back!"*

*   *   *

Mangled Finger Restored

I will conclude this chapter with the account of a lesser miracle albeit a very important one to me personally. When I was a very young man, I accepted the pastorate of a small church in Northern Maine that was unable to pay a living wage for our family of four. As a result, I had secured employment selling home appliances at a large department store. In the course of my duties, I sometimes found it necessary to visit the warehouse to oversee delivery arrangements for my product sales.

On one such occasion, I was standing at the opening to a large freight elevator equipped with an overhead door that descended from above until it met with the other door ascending from below. Deeply engaged in conversation, I was pulling the top elevator door shut when I turned away momentarily; but the two doors continued to close. Suddenly those extremely heavy doors met and slammed shut, crushing the longest finger on my right hand between them.

When the warehousemen opened the doors, I discovered that the nearly severed finger had burst open and then been flattened between the tip and the first knuckle (a disgusting sight to say the least!). As I was rushed to the hospital, the finger swelled rapidly and turned completely black. The emergency physician stitched and dressed it as best he could, but informed me that a finger that badly mangled would most likely never regain its normal function or feeling. His prognosis was that the injured part would die from lack of circulation and need to be amputated in order to avoid the possibility of blood poisoning. He advised me to return for further evaluation within a few days.

As a right-handed person, I realized that a partially amputated finger on that hand would not only be unsightly, but would hamper me in writing as well as in the performance of other everyday functions. Then the Holy Spirit reminded me that, because of my position as a redeemed child of Almighty God, I was not obligated to accept the inevitability of any medical prognosis. I had been granted perpetual access to the Great Physician Himself and thus to all His restorative power! When I realized my blood-bought position in Christ, I cradled the injured hand in the other one and took my stand upon the healing promises in the Word. As I did so, the pain left immediately.

The next day, I drove some distance to join a group of area pastors for our monthly fellowship meeting. When I told them of my mishap, they gathered around me and prayed for a miracle of restoration. Within a very few days the finger had returned to its normal condition. Every mangled blood vessel and nerve connection had reattached itself, the site had healed over rapidly and the finger functioned normally once again.

Needless to say, when I later presented myself to have the stitches removed, the surgeon stood back in amazement when he saw that a complete restoration had taken place. Today there is only a tiny, nearly invisible line on that finger to forever remind me of my loving God's unlimited ability to make *all* things new.

*   *   *

CHAPTER TWELVE

THE DEAD RAISED

**"Why is it considered incredible among you people
if God does raise the dead?"** *Acts 26:8*

This question posed to King Agrippa by the Apostle Paul
was an excellent one. Like King Agrippa, Christians
occasionally need to be reminded that our Lord's well-deserved
title is *God Almighty*! This all-powerful God, the One Who created
vast galaxies from nothing but His Word alone; the One who
orders the individual functions of the universe by His power—*this*
God is immeasurably beyond our realm of human comprehension.
Why then, whenever He raises the dead, do scoffers (and sadly,
even some Christians) dare to mock the validity of such a
miraculous act? The following accounts genuinely occurred in my
own ministry and are recorded here without embellishment. I hope
the reader will be as blessed by their re-telling, as I was
overwhelmingly blessed and privileged to have witnessed and
actually been part of them!

*　　*　　*

The Miracle of the Flies

For several years I had been away from the ministry of
evangelism and been engaged in a counseling practice in the
Boston, Massachusetts area. Among the various commitments of
my business, I was frequently involved in teaching seminars.
During these seminars I taught unusual psychological techniques to
psychiatrists, psychologists and medical doctors as well as lay
people who worked in ancillary medical positions. I had attained a

high level of success in my lay profession and was content to remain there as a means of helping others. However, the Lord had other plans for me.

The Holy Spirit awakened me one night and instructed me to close my counseling practice and return to my true calling—reaching the nations with the Gospel message. Immediately, I surrendered to His will and began mentally planning to resume full time ministry. I told the Lord that I knew I could sell my practice to a good friend and fellow psychologist and promised to do so at the earliest opportunity. The Holy Spirit replied that He didn't want me to *sell* my practice, but to *give* it away. Somehow I knew that this was a test for my depth of commitment, so I agreed. The next day, I took my friend to lunch and initiated the transfer details.

Though I was then poised to follow the Lord's directive, I found myself facing a real dilemma. I had summarily disposed of my family's only means of support, but I had been off the evangelistic field for such a significant period of time that I had lost contact with many of the pastors with whom I had previously conducted crusades. I seriously wondered how I could go about obtaining meetings; but I knew that the same Holy Spirit Who had called me would also provide the methods through which I could fulfill His call.

Shortly thereafter my pastor invited my wife and me to accompany him and his wife to a ministers' retreat a short distance away. One sunny afternoon during the retreat, I joined him and three other pastors in a game of golf. One of our golfing partners was introduced as a pastor from Bath, New York who then invited me to conduct two weeks of services for him. I readily accepted and within a few short weeks was conducting a crusade in his church.

We had nearly completed the first week of the services when, on a very cold November afternoon I went to the church to pray. As I entered the side door, I climbed the few steps to a landing just outside the sanctuary. Before entering, I stopped momentarily to stare out the window at the beautiful sight of sparkling snowflakes slowly descending and spreading a white carpet over the ground below.

I glanced downward momentarily and saw on the windowsill ten (why I counted them, I'll never know) dead houseflies—really big ones. Most of them were lying belly-up, and their desiccated bodies bore mute witness to the fact that they had all been dead for quite some time. Ignoring them, I continued to gaze out the window as I found myself entertaining questions about my future. I had walked away from a lucrative occupation to follow the leading of my heart, but was it really God's will for my life? I began to ask God to give me some sign that I could never doubt, one that would definitively assure me of my calling. Having done that, I went inside the sanctuary and began to seek God for an anointing on the evening service that would complete that first week with even more outstanding miracles.

As I left the sanctuary, I stopped one more time to gaze out the window at the snowfall that had continued throughout my prayer time. As I stood there pensively, I slowly became aware that a swarm of annoying flies was buzzing around my head despite the cold air on the landing outside the sanctuary. Looking down at the windowsill, I was amazed to see that not even one dead fly remained there! Suddenly, I realized that God had raised those ten dead flies as a confirmation to me that I was indeed following the correct path to future ministry.

That very night, the Lord set in motion a further fulfillment of the sign He had given. After the service, the pastor told me he had a special plan for the following Monday, which would be our only free day during the next week. He would say only that he had a special surprise for me. On that Monday, we drove over seventy miles together to Orchard Park, where he introduced me to Thomas "Tommy" Reid, Pastor of The Tabernacle there. Following a wonderful time of fellowship, Pastor Reid invited me to minister at The Tabernacle, which I accepted with gratitude.

That series of meetings was marked by a pronounced manifestation of God's presence, and I was subsequently invited to minister at The Tabernacle on a regular basis. Pastor Reid then introduced my ministry to the pastors of several large churches both stateside and in Canada. Consequently, many of those pastors invited me to minister in their churches. His faithful support at that beginning stage was instrumental in bringing about the subsequent growth of my ministry. As of this writing, our relationship has spanned a period of thirty-seven years. I treasure his and Wanda's enduring friendship and the many times I have had the privilege of ministering with them at The Tabernacle. Thank you, my dear friend, Tommy, for the invaluable help you have provided by promoting this ministry over the years!

*   *   *

A New Heart

The late Jack Brizendine, another dear pastor friend of mine, once invited me to minister at his church in Battle Creek, Michigan. The Presence of the Holy Spirit was evident nightly as signs, wonders and miracles influenced many people to respond to the invitation to accept Christ as Savior. I wish today that I had kept a record of those great miracles as well as numerical records of the many people who were saved and healed during the services.

Reports of the meetings reached every sector of that great city—even into a room on the cardiac ward of a local hospital where a brother in Christ lay stricken with severe heart disease. When he heard about the miracles that were taking place at the church, the man declared emphatically, "If I can just get to one of the services, I *know* God will heal me!" His physicians refused to sign release papers; so one night he took matters into his own hands and prepared to make good on his intention.

While he was in the process of dressing for the service that night, one of his nurses entered the room. He informed her of his intention to leave and, horrified, she stated emphatically that if he were to go he would most likely die because his heart would not be able to take the stress of such extreme exertion. When the nurse became convinced of his determination to leave the hospital, she summoned the man's cardiologist, who came to his room and reiterated the fact that he would most likely not survive the trip. When his patient could not be dissuaded, the doctor insisted that he sign a form releasing the hospital and staff from any and all responsibility. The form also contained an ominous warning that the consequences of leaving the hospital would almost certainly be the man's death.

Of course, I had not been informed of the foregoing events, so the man's presence in the congregation held no significance for me. When I extended a call for those people who needed a miracle to form a prayer line, there were many responses. The resultant prayer line extended around the perimeter of the sanctuary and filled every aisle. The man who had left the hospital against all medical advice did not inform anyone of his perilous condition. He simply took his place toward the back of the prayer line to await his turn.

As the healing line progressed, the gentleman finally reached a point on the center aisle, a few pews down from the back of the church. At that juncture his heart, already stressed to the maximum, simply stopped beating altogether. Seeing him collapse, I leaped over the platform railing and ran down the center aisle. People who surrounded the man had broken his fall and placed him in the pew. When I reached him, the man's face was pallid and covered in perspiration; his lips and fingernails were cyanotic (that is, had turned blue due to lack of blood), and there was no pulse and no visible sign of respiration.

At that point, I was unaware that the man had actually died. Nevertheless, I didn't pray for his healing. Instead, I was prompted by the Holy Spirit to rebuke Satan and command him to release the man and let him go! Within seconds, his breathing became normal and color returned to his face and extremities. His pulse returned to a normal rhythm; he stood to his feet and began to exuberantly praise the Lord.

Once again, the man reclaimed his place in the prayer line. When he finally reached the platform, he shared the entire story with the congregation. We learned of his determination to leave the hospital and of his conviction that he would be healed at the service. Then, the man electrified the audience when he declared that, when he collapsed in the aisle, he had died and had found himself traveling somewhere in space on his way toward heaven. At that point, he said, he had heard my voice commanding death (Satan) to release him and let him go. In addition however, he also stated that he had heard me issue a command that he return to his body and be healed. As the reader knows, those were not *my* words. Therefore, it is my firm conviction that the Holy Spirit took the faith that prompted my words and translated them Himself into His own words that would bring back life and bestow healing and restoration. This theory of mine appears to be substantiated by the following scripture.

> **"In the same way the Spirit also helps our weakness;** *for we do not know how to pray as we should, but the Spirit Himself intercedes <u>for</u> us* **with groanings too deep for words; and He who searches the hearts knows what the mind of the Spirit is, because He intercedes for the saints** *according to the will of God.* **And we know that God causes all things to work together for good to those who love God, to those who are called according to His purpose."** *Rom 8:26-28 (Emphasis mine.)*

That man returned to every subsequent service and gave his testimony; how God had raised him from the dead, totally healed his heart, and given him back his life.

*   *   *

The Lord's Response to Kali's Challenge

Over ninety million false gods are worshiped in India, but the government outlaws only one. Kali is her name and she is known as the Goddess of Death. To become one of her followers, one must prove his devotion by killing someone by means of strangulation. (Not exactly the sort of god one would be eager to serve, is she?) Although Indian law throughout the country bans the worship of Kali, she is freely worshiped in the remote region where we had gone to minister. Her shrines were openly displayed along the roadsides, and I was to face her personally before our ministry in that remote area had been completed.

The Holy Spirit had made a way for our party of five ministers to hold a ministers' conference in Siliguri, a city located in a far northern province of India close to the border with Nepal. Four hundred and fifty ministers had come from all over India to be taught and ministered to that week during the three daily services and excitement was running high. The Lord had moved upon a wealthy, politically influential local woman to sponsor the conference and she had leased a large tent for the services.

Our sponsor had asked if I would preach and conduct a healing and miracle service on the last night that would also be opened to the general public. If I would agree to do so, she guaranteed that she could arrange for every civic leader and person of prominence in the city to be there for that service. Of course, I gladly accepted her invitation and looked forward to it with keen anticipation. However, because demonic oppression, sickness and death were rampant in that area of the country, Kali wasn't about to tolerate any challenge to her authority. I ran headlong into her resistance the afternoon before the miracle service when I went to the tent to pray for that service.

Because the weather was oppressively hot, large industrial-size fans had been placed on the platform to provide some semblance of cooling. The grids on the face of the large floor fans were *very* closely spaced to avoid accidental access to the rapidly whirling blades. Nevertheless, as I reached toward one of them to adjust the angle of the airflow, my necktie somehow was drawn through the grids and into the powerful blades, and I found myself being strangled by the knot. The situation was serious because I was unable either to cry out for help or to free myself from the fan's stranglehold. This was an obvious attempt by Kali to challenge my God, kill me and prevent the service and its miracles from taking place.

Fortunately, my desperate prayer for deliverance was answered when some workmen in the tent became aware of my predicament and wrenched my shredded tie from the fan blades, thus releasing me in time to save me from strangulation. That afternoon the only true and living God proved to Kali just Whose was the greater power!

*   *   *

A Night of Triumph Over Sickness and Death

That night, we found our sponsor to be a woman of her word. A large section across the entire back of the tent had been reserved for the local dignitaries whom she had invited, and it was completely filled. None of the people seated there appeared overly enthusiastic about being in the service, to say the least. Hindus all, they openly displayed their boredom during the sermon; but that was destined to change dramatically!

Because there was an inordinate prevalence of epilepsy among the people in that area, the Holy Spirit prompted me to

138

challenge that affliction first. When I invited those people who were suffering from epilepsy to come forward, a large number of people responded. Among them was one four-year-old boy who suddenly fell to the ground and died. I checked the boy and found there was no sign of pulse or respiration. In addition, we observed a very strange phenomenon—the brown pupil of his eyes immediately became milky-white in color. This was a definite sign of death, even though medical science tells us that it usually takes some period of time after death for that condition to develop in the eyes.

I told the congregation what had happened and then directed my attention again to the dead child. When there was no response after the first prayer, I knew in the Spirit that demonic forces had issued a challenge to God and to me, His messenger. I prayed a second time and again nothing happened.

At that moment, I sensed the Holy Spirit rise up powerfully within me. I reached down, picked up the little fellow by his upper arms and, with Divine authority, commanded the spirit of death to release him. Then I commanded the child to live in Jesus' Name— *and he did!* Instantly, the boy began to breathe and the color of his eyes returned to normal. The Christians present erupted in praise; the remaining epileptics were also simultaneously delivered and a wave of healing swept through the congregation.

I had been so intensely involved in dealing with the demons of epilepsy and death that I hadn't once glanced toward the section where the Hindu dignitaries were seated. When I did look in their direction, it was obvious that not one of them had remained in a state of boredom! Large numbers of them had begun to make their way down the center aisle, some to accept the Lord and some to report their healings or to receive prayer for their afflictions.

That night, the Holy Spirit had proven Himself more than equal to Kali's challenge. She had met far more than her match when the epileptic lad came back to life! Due to his miraculous resurrection, many Hindus had committed their lives to Christ; and many others, Hindus as well as Christians, had received their healings. We rejoiced while our interpreters interviewed countless people around the altar and as we heard the testimonies of those who had been healed from all manner of infirmities.

*   *   *

Attention Cat Lovers!

This incident always makes me chuckle and I daresay will do the same for the reader. One fateful evening, my daughter Heather's pregnant cat "Kibbles" was in labor and the delivery seemed imminent. Heather's mother was out and Heather needed to leave for her birthday party at a friend's house. As the only responsible person on site, I was summarily appointed to the position of midwife (or the more masculine-sounding *midhusband*, if you please). The delivery room (a large cardboard box) was brought into the living room in order for me to supervise the blessed event. I dutifully watched over Kibbles as she took her good old time delivering her brood.

When the long awaited time arrived, Kibbles delivered her first kitten. The attentive mother began to clean up her baby; but she abruptly stopped and I was dismayed to find that the little one was struggling to breathe. Kibbles sniffed its tiny body, retired to the other side of the maternity ward and left the doomed newborn to its inevitable fate. The kitten's feeble attempt to live produced only short gasps every few seconds. Within minutes all effort to breathe ceased and the kitten died. It lay there motionless while four other healthy kittens came into the world. As the various ones emerged, Kibbles hurried to remove the umbilical cord, lick the fur clean and nurse her brood. For the better part of an hour the dead kitten lay unnoticed and untended to by its mother, who instinctively knew her assistance would be useless. "Poor little dead kitty," I thought. "You never had a chance to live beyond those few brief moments."

140

I found myself growing progressively angrier at the alien spirit of death that had caused this innocent little animal to die. Suddenly, the Spirit of the Lord came over me like the wind on the Day of Pentecost.[48] I reached down into the "maternity ward," picked up that cold, lifeless body and lifted it up on the palm of my hand to the Life Giver. In desperation I cried out, "God, if I'm still Your prophet, cause this little kitten to live *now!*"

Immediately, that precious little creature took in a great gulp of air and began to breathe! (Somewhat *purrfectly,* I might add.) When I laid the kitten back into the box, Kibbles hurried over and began the cleanup process, licking and purring at the same time. I cried for joy, not only because the kitten was alive and well; but because I recognized the fact that my Heavenly Father had taken the time to encourage this disheartened prophet that his cries were still being heard—even a relatively insignificant one concerning the life of a *kitten.* How much more so then would He hear the cry of His child when faced with a greater need!

We named the kitten *Lazarus.* (Remember Lazarus, the man whom Jesus raised from the dead?)[49] Some weeks later however, we were amused to discover that our Lazarus would need to be re-named *Lazarina!*

*   *   *

---

[48] And suddenly there came a sound from heaven as of a rushing mighty wind, and it filled all the house where they were sitting. *Acts 2:2 (KJV)*
[48] When He had said these things, He cried out with a loud voice, "Lazarus, come forth." The man who had died came forth… *John 11:43-44*

141

CHAPTER THIRTEEN

EXTRAORDINARY EXPERIENCES

In the truest sense, *all* miracles are unusual and fall totally outside the realm of human capacity to comprehend. On the other hand, some miraculous manifestations defy the standard classifications and are so exceptional in nature and scope that they demand a chapter of their own. Accordingly, I have presented some of them here in a separate category of their own.

*   *   *

Back to the Future

During a time of ministry with Pastor Tommy Reid at The Tabernacle in Orchard Park, New York, a strange and miraculous event occurred, the like of which I had never heard of nor witnessed before that day, nor have I ever done so since. This incident defies any attempt to categorize it and is one of the most unusual and memorable experiences of my long ministerial career.

The schedule that first Sunday, called for me to preach in both of the morning services as well as in the one that evening. Before the opening service, my wife and I shared breakfast with Pastor Reid, his wife, Wanda and another minister who was visiting the Tabernacle that day. The other brother present was, at that time, the president of an organization that was engaged in a nationwide Christian outreach ministry to foreign students who were attending American universities. Many of those young people had been saved under this ministry and had returned to provide a Christian witness in positions of influence within their respective countries. He was a delightful and interesting man who was engaged in an important work and we enjoyed our brief time of fellowship with him.

Shortly before preaching time during the first service, the Holy Spirit instructed me to set aside my planned topic and use the following scripture as my text instead: **"Like an eagle that stirs up its nest, that hovers over its young, He spread His wings and caught them, He carried them on His pinions."** *Deut. 32:11*

I had never preached a message based on that text, though I had briefly alluded to the passage in other sermons in the past. However, I couldn't even remember where the particular verse was located in the Bible, and I was due in the pulpit within a very short while! (It certainly would have been just a tiny bit easier for me if the Holy Spirit had at least mentioned the reference! I guess our convenience is not as great a concern for Him as is our obedience.) Frantically I searched through the concordance in the back of my Bible but, as is the case with most of those truncated concordances, that particular scripture wasn't referenced there. I asked various ministers seated nearby if they knew where that scripture could be found but with no success. One of the associate pastors hurried to the church office, looked up the reference in an unabridged concordance and brought it to me. No sooner had I opened my Bible to the passage (*Deut. 32:11,12*), than Pastor Reid was giving my introduction. I laid my Bible on the pulpit and began to preach a sermon with only the text before me.

My position that day is a classic example of a situation in which the speaker has been abruptly thrust into a position of utter dependence upon the Holy Spirit's ability to guide and direct literally every thought. A large congregation was waiting expectantly to hear the Word of the Lord, and I knew only that I had been directed to preach a sermon with which I was totally unfamiliar. Perhaps young preachers (and some older ones as well) who are reading this account would do well to let my predicament serve as a prime example of the Holy Spirit's faithfulness. It's a wonderful thing to be able to know His voice and trust Him at such times. He will never allow Himself to be accused of abandoning anyone who is willing to completely obey Him no matter what the situation may be!

True to form, the Lord was certainly faithful that morning. His thoughts flowed freely as I explained how a mother eagle knows when it's time for her eaglets to leave the nest and learn to fly. In order to motivate them, she removes all soft materials, such as discarded feathers and animal pelts from the comfortable nest. This exposes the rough twigs and branches from which the nest had been constructed. Having totally discomforted her brood, she takes the eaglets onto her pinions (the bony frontal area of the wings) and flies out over the edge of the high place where they have always been at home. At first, it probably seems like great fun to the eaglets—until the mother eagle abruptly drops her wings from under them and they find themselves plummeting toward the earth at a speed hitherto unknown or even dreamed of! Then, when they've abandoned all hope of survival, the mother eagle swoops underneath her brood. The floundering eaglets grasp her pinions and soar with her again. The same routine is repeated until the eaglets learn to flap their own wings and fly—and fly they do! (I suppose the whole process could appropriately be dubbed the "*Fly or Die Method of Flight Instruction.*")

The Lord so inspired the sermon that, when I had finished; I realized all the material had not yet been exhausted. I announced that I would complete the message during the following service; and most of the people remained to hear the conclusion. The same heavy anointing marked the second service as had been experienced during the first one; and I finally completed my divine assignment. When I left the platform that morning, the minister I had met at breakfast approached me. His face was ashen and he was visibly shaken when he asked to speak with me and then recounted the following story.

Fifteen years before that time, he had been ministering in the Philippines as administrative assistant to a missionary stationed there. He had loved his job and the missionary under whom he served. He said he had never aspired to do anything other than to be the *Elisha* to his *Elijah*. He had been perfectly content to remain

145

in the background of the other man's ministry and felt that this would be his lifetime assignment.

[May I digress momentarily and remind the reader that it is often a humble servant such as this man was that the Holy Spirit will choose to fulfill a ministry of greater prominence in the world. God Himself once said by way of rebuke to one of His people, **"But you, are you seeking great things for yourself? Do not seek them..."** *Jer 45:5.*]

His story continued, and my new friend told me that at a certain point during his time in the Philippines, the Holy Spirit had begun to deal with him. Despite the joy and satisfaction he had always found in his work, he found himself becoming increasingly distracted by a pronounced sense of uneasiness. As the feeling grew, he felt strongly that the Lord was directing him to leave his ministry in the Philippines. He was reluctant to do so and began to question the Lord despite the persistent sense of discomfort. Desperate for an answer, he had diligently sought the Lord for confirmation and clarification.

The man's face assumed an expression of awe as he related the rest of his story. One day when he was deep in prayer, he experienced a totally supernatural event he would never forget. He found himself suspended in time and space and, while he remained in this state he heard an entire sermon based on the text of the present morning's sermon. He shook his head with amazement as he related it in his own words.

"In the Philippines, *fifteen years ago*, I heard the *identical* sermon you preached this very morning here in Orchard Park, New York, and I heard it *in your inimitable voice!* It was that sermon that awakened me to the fact that my discomfort was indeed borne of the Holy Spirit; and He was directing me to move on to another ministry into which He would lead me. Like the eaglets, I had become far too comfortable and the Lord had begun to stir my nest—a terribly uncomfortable experience. The Lord convinced me that to leave my ministry in the Philippines was His will, and so I reluctantly obeyed. After my return to the States, He then led me to my present ministry which has much greater potential for worldwide impact than I could have ever foreseen had I stayed in the Philippines."

To say I was stunned at the man's story would have been a gross understatement. Having read this amazing account, the reader can understand why, despite having functioned for years in the supernatural realm, this is one experience I will never forget!

*   *   *

A Visual Manifestation of God's Presence

A short time ago my wife and I held a series of services with Pastor David Hernquist in The Bronx, a borough (county) of New York City. We had a wonderful four days there and on the last night, I prayed for believers to receive the Baptism in the Holy Spirit with the evidence of speaking with other tongues. Following the prayer, approximately thirty-five eager people received the infilling of the Holy Spirit in that one powerful service!

After the rigorous schedule of that past week (my wife and I had ministered in five services on Sunday as well as the ones on the past three weeknights), we were too tired to go out to eat; so we requested our driver to take us for sandwiches to take back to our room. As we pulled into a tiny strip mall, a car pulled out directly in front of the driveway, so we took that only vacancy even though the sandwich shop was at the other end of the mall. My wife preceded me to the shop and I followed a few moments later. As I approached the small pizza parlor directly in front of our van, I greeted the four young men who were standing on the sidewalk. After a few remarks of greeting, I began to witness about Jesus. All of them listened intently, but one man, who appeared to be the leader of the group impatiently interrupted me and asked, "What was that light about?" Mystified by the question, I asked what light he was referring to; and the young man replied, "When you walked toward us a few minutes ago, there was a bright light around your head—what *was* that?"

The other three then joined in excitedly, "Yeah, we saw it, too; your face was glowing!" One man added, "It was brightest around your head and face, but it was around your whole body!" (Then the Holy Spirit reminded me of a similar incident from the Bible concerning Moses after he had come from the Presence of the Lord;[50] and I realized the significance of this present-day experience.)

I told the young men that this remarkable event had been a supernatural sign given by God. He had manifested His own Presence in that unusual manner so they would believe the truth of my words concerning Jesus and their need for salvation. Then I went on to explain the simplicity of inviting Christ to come in and take control of their lives. I felt they might be hesitant to indicate such a personal decision in the presence of their friends, but encouraged them to do so when they were alone that night. As I left them, I breathed a silent prayer and committed them to the Holy Spirit's loving care.

While I will probably never know during this lifetime whether or not they ever followed through, it was powerfully impressed upon me that the Lord had certainly given those young men ample (and visual) proof of His personal interest in each of them. Perhaps in Heaven someday I will be privileged to meet one or all of them!

*   *   *

---

[50] "…Moses did not know that the skin of his face shone because of his speaking with Him. So when Aaron and all the sons of Israel saw Moses, behold, the skin of his face shone…" *Ex 34:29b, 30a*

A Collective Miracle Experience

Out of the varied experiences of healing and conversion we witnessed during a miracle crusade in Defiance, Ohio, one particular event stands out as being distinctively unique in nature and scope. On that night, the service was packed as hundreds of people gathered in a high school auditorium and the Presence of God was electrifying.

During the early part of the service while the congregation was standing in worship, I prophetically declared that many people were going to receive the Baptism in the Holy Spirit at some point in the service that night. At that very moment, the *entire congregation simultaneously* fell back into their seats under the power of God and most of them began to speak in tongues, many of them for the very first time! Although I have seen similar circumstances of mass reaction to the Holy Spirit's Presence since that time, that one instantaneous reaction involving *everyone* present has never been repeated in my experience. It was truly a unique and wondrous event!

*   *   *

The Bible tells us that following the exodus from Egypt, the Israelites under the leadership of Moses, traveled through the desert for many years. In that harsh desert environment, it was imperative that miracles of provision become the order of the day. Just imagine the logistics of providing food and water for two to three million people in that barren, infertile wasteland. Add to that the necessity for providing sustenance for their numerous flocks and herds of animals; and it reveals the awesome logistics required for that monumental undertaking. The following incident illustrates one small example of a miracle of provision, one of many similar experiences in my own life. While nowhere as dramatic as the various incidents during the biblical Exodus, it nevertheless illustrates how innovative the Holy Spirit can be when any of His children have a need.

149

*   *   *

The Shampoo Incident

Donna and I once founded a church in Chicago and our family sacrificed extensively so the work could flourish. Many times we went without adequate salary so ministry bills could be paid as the church rapidly expanded. Personal finances were always scarce at that time and one day the supply of shampoo for our family of eight (my mother was with us then) was getting low. As my son Brent and I drove along Chicago's Grand Avenue to buy much needed household supplies, we saw a profusion of plastic shampoo bottles scattered across our traffic lane. At the same time, we noticed an open parking place just ahead. As if that weren't enough, a traffic light held back the traffic behind us. (God thinks of everything!) As we quickly parked and began to pick up bottles, a police car appeared and stopped directly behind us.

The officer turned on the flashing lights to block traffic and began to help us pick up the scattered containers. Gathering the bottles in our arms and carrying them to the car made for slow going and, just as I breathed a prayer for some sort of container, a new (still folded) plastic garbage bag blew across the street and directly into my path. (Sort of reminds one of the scripture that tells us God knows our need even before we ask, doesn't it?) In a matter of minutes the three of us had gathered up twenty-nine large bottles of *Alberto V/O Five Shampoo!* Our need had been abundantly supplied by God's "good measure—pressed down, shaken together, and running over"[51] supply. We even had enough to share our bounty with others.

Consider the logistics involved in this one minor instance of divine provision. A truck carrying a load of shampoo bottles for return to the manufacturer had "somehow" lost a few along the

---

[51] *Luke 6:38a*

way. The bottles' only defect was that the labels were off kilter. Twenty-nine bottles "fell off" just as I approached and a perfect parking space was vacated on that very busy commercial street exactly when and where I needed it. At that very moment, a police car was passing by and the officer was inclined to stop, block traffic and even assist us. Last but not least, the wind then delivered a bag for which I had prayed. Coincidence? I hardly think so!

It can never be legitimately said, "This is too small a matter for God to bother with!" Be assured that He who feeds the sparrows (and also provides shampoo!) knows precisely what His children need and when they need it. [52] He's just waiting for them to trust Him and *ask*.[53]

*   *   *

A Nor'easter Averted

I had scheduled a one-night miracle service to be held at an auditorium in a New Jersey city. On that night, I would encounter a most unusual miracle. I have witnessed other instances of God's triumph over nature's power (some of which appear elsewhere in this book); but this particular incident was unique in nature because it involved the mighty Atlantic Ocean and its well-known violent storm systems.

My plane landed in the midst of turbulence and was most likely one of the last to do so that afternoon. When my host picked me up at the airport, he said a major storm was moving rapidly into the area from the nearby Atlantic Ocean; and menacing black

---

[52] "Are not five sparrows sold for two cents? Yet not one of them is forgotten before God." Indeed, the very hairs of your head are all numbered. Do not fear; you are more valuable than many sparrows." *Luke 12:6-7*
"...for your Father knows what you need before you ask Him." *Mt 6:8b*
[53] "Ask, and it will be given to you; seek, and you will find; knock, and it will be opened to you." *Mt 7:7*

151

clouds above us provided mute testimony to the accuracy of his prediction. He was fearful that the evening's service might have to be postponed because weather forecasters were broadcasting ominous warnings of severe weather over that entire region.

For weeks before this time, opposition from certain religious leaders had been mounted against the meeting. They had done everything in their power to prevent it, but they had been unsuccessful and I had come to hold the service—only to be confronted by a fierce and imminent storm. I must say Satan gave it his best shot, but once again the Lord proved that He has indeed made His people "more than conquerors."[54]

When we are moving in obedience to the Holy Spirit, there is a quiet peace, an exceptional calm assurance that takes command of our thinking at such times, and I experienced the same peace throughout that period of opposition. I knew the Lord had instructed me to go to that city and I could rest in the fact that nothing ever takes Him by surprise. He knew well in advance that the destroyer, having failed to thwart the service through the storm of religious opposition, would attempt to stir up a storm in the natural realm. Granted, not all storms are of satanic origin; but some are—and I was convinced that this one was.

I attempted to reassure my host that the storm would not come ashore and we would indeed be able to hold the meeting that evening. Having said that, I quietly rebuked the storm[55] and declared that it had no right to hinder the service; therefore, it must return to the sea. Within a very short time, the storm veered off course and went back toward the ocean. Shortly thereafter, the

---

[54] "Yet in all these things we are more than conquerors through Him who loved us." *Rom 8:37 (NKJV)*

[55] "And there arose a fierce gale of wind, and the waves were breaking over the boat so much that the boat was already filling up. Jesus Himself was in the stern, asleep on the cushion; and they woke Him and said to Him, 'Teacher, do You not care that we are perishing?' And He got up and rebuked the wind and said to the sea, "Hush, be still." And the wind died down and it became perfectly calm." *Mark 4:37-39*

skies cleared and the sun broke through. We had witnessed firsthand an example of the unerring accuracy of God's Word: **"He caused the storm to be still, so that the waves of the sea were hushed."** *Psalm 107:29*

That would prove to be only the beginning for that remarkable night. The following incident took place in that service as well as others related in other chapters of this book.

*   *   *

The Divine Bill-Payer

By all accounts, the meeting that same night was a successful one. Following the ministry of the Word, many people came forward for salvation and many others were healed by the power of God. But the most unique miracle of all took place at another unusual point in the service—offering time. Shortly after the offering had been collected, I received a word from the Lord and announced to the congregation, "There's a man in the service tonight who has put all the money he had in his pocket into the offering plate. That man also has an invoice in his possession tonight—an amount that he would have been unable to pay even if he had not given in this offering. The bill is for *exactly two hundred eighty-four dollars and seventy-six cents.* Would that man please stand up?" (In my experience, seldom has *exact* wording been so crucial!)

We waited for a few moments to allow the man in question to search through his pockets and wallet. Finally, a man stood to his feet, bill in hand, and I called him to come forward. The statement was a legitimate printed one and the total amount owed was precisely the same amount the Holy Spirit had given to me.

Then I turned to the audience and gave the following painstaking instructions. "The Lord has directed me to take another offering to reward this man for his faithfulness, but not everyone is to participate in this offering. The only ones who are to give are

153

those to whom God speaks clearly and reveals an exact figure. I don't want anyone to give because they empathize with this man's plight and have a heartfelt desire to help him. Only those who are certain that the Holy Spirit has spoken an exact amount are to respond, and then they are to be careful to not give even a penny more or less than that amount." Having said that, I prayed and sent the ushers out to receive the people's love gifts, after which they were to count the offering and bring me the total. While I don't think I even need to reveal the result of their count, I will anyway. It was *precisely* two hundred eighty-four dollars and seventy-six cents! Anyone who is aware of human nature and has worked with large crowds of people can attest to what a great miracle that was—that not even one person in that vast audience disobeyed the instructions given or failed to accurately discern the voice of the Holy Spirit!

This unusual miracle clearly illustrated that one can never give in faith without our Heavenly Father seeing the extent of their sacrifice. Moreover, He is intimately aware of our needs, and He possesses infinite resources to ensure that our bills are paid in full—to the very penny. What a joy it was to present that offering to the grateful brother whose need the Holy Spirit had prophetically revealed to me. I don't think his joy was any greater than mine or, for that matter, than that of the people in the congregation that night!

*   *   *

A Feat of Superhuman Strength

When my wife and I built our first home, we found it necessary to do much of the interior work ourselves in an effort to economize as much as possible. Over time we accomplished many tasks—everything from installing electrical wiring, plasterboard and tile to building kitchen cabinets, wallpapering, painting and staining hardwood floors and woodwork. However, my greatest challenge was installing the hot water heating system. At that time, heating a home with a hot water system required the installation of a cast iron furnace to feed the baseboards throughout the house. (Looking back, I'm amazed at the youthful audacity that took on such an intricate and demanding task!)

Winters in Northern Maine are brutally cold, and it was on just such a day that the furnace was delivered. When I arrived to begin connecting everything, I saw that the deliverymen had set the furnace just outside the basement door opening. Because the trench for the foundation footing had not yet been filled back in, the six-hundred-pound furnace had eroded the loose ground around the trench and had slid partway into the channel, where it had stopped just inside the doorway, tilted at an odd angle. This meant that, not only did the furnace need to be moved across the basement floor to the concrete slab prepared for it in the utility room area, but it would have to be righted first.

Without thinking (obviously!) I leaned my weight against the side of the furnace's great bulk in a foolhardy attempt to accomplish the monumental task by myself (we couldn't afford to hire a helper). As impossible as it sounds (and *was!*), I lifted that massive piece of equipment and jockeyed it across the floor and into position on the slab as easily as if it had only been the weight of a large cardboard box! It was only afterward that I realized just how physically impossible that incredible feat had been. Dumbfounded, I stood back and gazed in amazement and disbelief at what the Lord and I had accomplished together. Of course, *He* had done the heavy lifting all by Himself—He had just allowed me to push a little and *think* I was doing it! To this day, whenever I think about that incredible experience, I am as amazed now, as I was that day.

*　　*　　*

155

God Doesn't Need to Use Satan's Tools to Accomplish His Will

I once returned home from a crusade and my wife informed me that one of our elderly friends from the local church in Lynn, Massachusetts was in the hospital, gravely ill with cancer. Such news was shocking to me because the last time I had seen Dan he had appeared to be in good health. My wife told me that, until recently he had been unaware of his illness; however, doctors had recently discovered it and found that the disease had spread throughout his body. Dan had shortly thereafter lapsed into a coma and his physicians had given him little time left to live. My wife added that, even though he was in a coma, whenever Dan spoke, he called my name.

Needless to say, I rushed to the hospital to pray for my friend. When I approached the nurse on the oncology floor, I explained that I was clergy and asked to be directed to Dan's room. She replied caustically that I wouldn't be allowed to visit him. Being well aware that members of the clergy are allowed into a patient's room at any time, I sensed that the woman's attitude was being motivated by the enemy in order to prevent God's will from being done. I ignored her objections and found Dan's room on my own. When I entered, I found that my comatose friend was indeed in deplorable condition. His complexion was ashen, his breathing was shallow and needles and tubes protruded from various locations on his frail body.

As I approached the bed and prepared to pray, the nurse I had previously encountered entered the room and proceeded to make herself totally obnoxious—noisily clanging implements and tossing items around. Ignoring her attempts to disturb the scene, I placed my index finger into Dan's palm and wrapped his inert hand around it as I spoke into his ear. "Dan, this is Burt Seavey. I heard that you were calling for me. I just got back in town and I've come to pray for you. I know the doctors say you can't hear me; but I also know that even though your mind is unconscious, your spirit is always awake and you can hear me on that level." I asked him to squeeze my finger if he could hear and understand me, and he did so.

It is my firm conviction that, even though Christians often do die as a result of illness, the Lord doesn't need to use Satan's methods to call His own people home. [56] With this in mind I told my friend, "Dan, you don't have to die of cancer. You are a son of God, and when it's your appointed time to be home with the Lord, He will take you there—and He can do so without using sickness or pain." Having said that, I laid my hands on him and began to rebuke the demonic presence commonly known as cancer. Immediately, Dan opened his eyes, gave me the familiar smile I was accustomed to seeing and began to talk with me. When the nurse saw what had happened, she dropped the utensil she was holding and literally ran from the room. (Come to think of it, she never did return—wonder if she ever fully recovered from the shock?)

Following this Divine intervention, Dan was totally alert and free from all pain. His physicians performed a battery of tests and it was determined that no sign of cancer could be detected anywhere in his body. He was subsequently released from the hospital. Sometime later, the Lord accomplished His will without using sickness of any kind. He came in Person one night and took his faithful servant home to be with Him as he slept peacefully in his own bed!

*　　*　　*

---

[56] This is a subject I cover in depth in my book, "Why Doesn't God Heal *Me*?" Christians don't need to die from sickness, which is Satan's work. When God is ready for them, He simply calls them home. (See: *Ps 104:29b*.) An expanded edition of this book will soon be available. Contact the author for information.

On a Similar Note—Gene's Miracles

Some years later, while I was pastor of a church in Chicago, a similar incident took place. Gene was an older man, the big, outwardly abrupt, gruff-sounding father of our church pianist. He attended another church in the area but had developed a cordial relationship with me. He believed in and was fascinated by miracles but he had never witnessed one. It had always been his desire to personally see the Lord heal someone and he had often expressed this longing to me. Although healings regularly took place in our church, Gene never seemed to be visiting on those occasions. Gene was a man of many construction skills and, when our church became involved in renovating a large supermarket building in Chicago to use for our church facility, he often volunteered his time to assist me. As we worked together, we engaged in many stimulating conversations.

At one time, Gene had proudly shown me his favorite tool, a large pocketknife he used for many things and always kept *keenly* sharpened. One day, when I was working on a scaffold and my friend was involved in some project on the ground-floor level, I heard a sharp cry of alarm and glanced quickly in his direction. He was grimacing in pain and grasping one hand tightly in the other. The pocketknife lay on the floor at his feet and copious amounts of blood were pouring from his injured hand and onto the floor. Not waiting to climb down, I leaped from the scaffold and saw that a severe gash at the base of his thumb was bleeding profusely. Immediately, I grasped his hand and began to pray and, as I did so the flow of blood stopped dramatically and we watched the wound close up—so thoroughly that no mark remained where it had been! Except for the blood that remained on our hands, there was no sign that an injury had occurred. Gene had certainly witnessed his own miracle and we rejoiced together.

Sometime after this incident, I came home after a crusade in another state to find that my friend had suffered a severe stroke and had lapsed into a coma from which he was not expected to recover. Even though in a comatose state, he had been repetitiously calling my name and my wife had promised the family that she would send me as soon as I returned home.

Needless to say, I went to the hospital at once to pray for my friend. When I arrived at the bedside, I could tell by the man's appearance that his condition was indeed grave. Gene had always been a vital, muscular man, one who was accustomed to being in command of every situation; but now he was very agitated and appeared shrunken and vulnerable as he lay in that hospital bed. I grasped his hand in mine and said, "Gene, it's Burt Seavey and I've come to pray for you."

His body visibly relaxed as I continued, "I know your spirit is awake despite the coma you've fallen into. I want you to squeeze my hand if you can hear me." He responded by gripping my hand firmly. As I had in the previous story involving my friend Dan's experience, I told Gene the Lord doesn't need to use sickness for a means of bringing his people to Himself. I then began to pray for a miracle. At that very moment, I sensed the Presence of the Lord very strongly. Suddenly I knew in my spirit that this was indeed the Lord's appointed time to call my friend home; but I was equally convinced that He didn't intend to use sickness in order to do so. At the same time, the Holy Spirit made me aware of the fact that Gene wanted very much to go and be with his Savior; but he was clinging to life out of concern for his wife and his several unsaved (adult) sons who occasionally needed his firm hand to guide their sometimes-unruly conduct.

Having received this word from the Lord, I told Gene that I would pray for his faculties to return and that he would emerge from the coma and be able to meet with his family and assure them that the Lord would take care of them when he was gone. I also said that, when he had done this, he could feel released to go to heaven in peace.

When my prayer was finished, Gene opened his eyes, smiled and spoke with me briefly. I told his waiting family they could visit with him and I then left the hospital. When I arrived home nearly an hour later, my wife informed me that Gene's daughter had called in the interim to tell us that her father had met with them and then simply closed his eyes and quietly slipped away to be with the Lord. I knew then that Gene had witnessed his second miracle and he was now rejoicing face to face with His Heavenly Father and beloved Savior!

*　　*　　*

Our God as Teacher

Our ever-resourceful Lord never ceases to astound me with the infinite variety of methods He uses to display His ingenuity! One evening in Caribou, Maine, He amazed me yet again. A gentleman in his sixties came into the prayer line with an unusual request. He had never learned to read and he wanted very much to be able to read his Bible. Being thoroughly convinced that our God can do anything, I thought, *Why not?* I prayed a simple prayer and told the man to believe that he had received his miracle. He went away praising and returned the following night wearing a triumphant smile on his face. Looking very much like a cat that has swallowed a canary, he stood and asked if he could give his testimony. I called him forward and asked what the Lord had done for him.

Still smiling broadly, the man came to the platform and said, "Last night I couldn't read *anything;* but this man prayed for me and now I can read!" He promptly opened up his Bible and began to read clearly—and from the difficult language of the King James Version, at that! What was even more surprising was that the Bible was the *only* book he was able to read. No other written material was legible to him. When he was asked to read a newspaper headline, he was totally incapable of doing so. I have

160

no idea why the Lord chose to answer his unusual request in such a literal manner, but I'm sure He had His own reasons.

"How unsearchable are his judgments, and his ways past finding out!" *Rom 11:33*

*   *   *

"Tornado Heading This Way!"

Everyone knows that the states throughout the vast flat plains section in our country are particularly vulnerable to tornados. During one service in Southern Illinois, a fully occupied church and I nearly became the victims of just such a catastrophic storm. Shortly before the ministry time, a state trooper informed the pastor that a powerful tornado had been spotted a short distance away and was on a direct path toward the church. We were advised that evacuation was not possible at that point and it was imperative that we move the congregation to the basement immediately. The pastor asked my advice as to how we should deal with this imminent threat. I responded with a prophetic prediction that the tornado would change course and completely bypass us.

The pastor was hesitant and unwilling to take a chance on the accuracy of what he considered to be my "opinion." As a precaution he moved the congregation to the basement auditorium where we continued with the service. We experienced a great move of God that night and observers later told us that, just prior to the point of impacting our building, the tornado had abruptly veered aside and continued on a harmless path through the adjoining unoccupied countryside!

*   *   *

Time and memory will not enable me to enumerate the multitudes and kinds of miracles that I've been privileged to

161

witness throughout the United States and around the world. Healing miracles alone often occurred by the hundreds, and sometimes even by the thousands in a single service. This shouldn't be surprising to us, because all miracles are performed by the power of God; they are merely channeled through yielded human vessels. God has certainly not changed and He is still performing miracles today! Scripture summarizes Jesus' own earthly ministry by saying:

> **"And there are also many other things which Jesus did, which if they were written in detail, I suppose that even the world itself would not contain the books that would be written."** *John 21:25*

That certainly can't be said of my own humble ministry, but if all the miracles, healings, signs and wonders that I *have* witnessed throughout my life were recorded, it would probably fill several volumes. I have a suspicion that there are record books of such things somewhere in heaven's library that I will someday be privileged to peruse. They will no doubt contain many events I've long since forgotten, some I wasn't able to observe at the time and some miracles that came to fruition after the fact, long after I had gone on to other places of ministry. In the words of the popular Christian song, "I can only imagine" how those accounts will read—and I can hardly wait!

CHAPTER FOURTEEN

MIRACLES OF HEALING

Throughout the years, I have witnessed a multiplicity of healing miracles. Some of them happened during specific crusades and have been detailed in the chapters pertaining to those particular crusades. Still other healings occurred as the result of or in conjunction with other manifestations of the Holy Spirit (i.e. deliverance, prophecy, etc.) and have also been dealt with in those chapters. However, in this chapter I have endeavored to chronicle the stories of some outstanding healings that involved mainly the operation of a gift of healing and/or gift of miracles (sometimes both).

*　　*　　*

My Mother's Miracle

As indicated by the sub-title, this miracle was not mine personally nor did it come about as an outgrowth of my own ministry. However, I have chosen to begin this chapter with this astounding account because my mother's illness and subsequent healing made such a profound impression on my life. It truly set the stage for my future ministry because, though I didn't fully understand divine healing at the time, seeing my mother healed in such a miraculous way led to the early development of my faith. Having witnessed this incredible act of God, I could no longer doubt that miracles were real and I subsequently developed a thirst to see them in my own ministry to the sick. For those reasons, it is appropriate to include it here.

During my teenage years, Mom developed an aggressive case of osteoarthritis that progressed rapidly with crippling consequences. The vertebrae of her spine developed huge calcium deposits and the entire spinal column twisted into an "S" curve.

Her neck was bent until her head rested on one shoulder, and she was unable to move her body without the aid of a steel reinforced corset that extended from armpit to tailbone. Needless to say, my mother lived with constant, excruciating pain, though she seldom complained. It was my duty to transport her for frequent medical treatments. The treatments themselves caused so much pain that I couldn't bear to listen to her anguished outbursts and had to leave the office until the sessions were over. The condition was considered incurable and the prognosis was that Mom would be confined to a wheelchair within a very few years.

My family and I were new Christians at that point and were attending a nearby Baptist church that did not believe divine healing was valid in the modern era. Because the only access to the sanctuary was up eight very steep steps, it was necessary for us to carry her up to the entrance. Having her body lifted and carried was very painful for her, so attending Sunday services was always an agonizing experience. In spite of this, Mom insisted on going to church every week, if at all possible.

On one fateful Sunday, the pastor's message contained a recitation of the many names and descriptive titles attributed to Christ. One of the titles on the lengthy list was "The Great Physician," which was not further elaborated upon beyond that brief mention. Nevertheless, the term captured my mother's rapt attention and, as she considered the meaning of that Name, she distinctly heard a Voice within her spirit that promised, *"In three weeks, you will be healed!"*

Overjoyed, Mom shared her news with the family as soon as the service ended. Although we couldn't explain this strange experience, we cautioned her not to expect anything to come of it. Despite our doubts, Mom firmly believed the Lord had spoken to her and that in three weeks' time she would indeed be well. Needless to say, every day in the ensuing weeks, we looked for some sign of improvement; but there was nothing to indicate any change in her condition. In fact, when Mom retired that third

Saturday night, she was in more pain than ever before; but she still believed God had spoken and would keep His word to her.

That following Sunday morning, Mom rose early to prepare for the church service. Usually, the process required the necessity for another member of the family to assist her in sitting up and being strapped into the corset before she could rise to her feet. On that fateful morning, however, Mom threw back the covers and stood to her feet unassisted. Amazed at the apparent "impossibility" of what she had just accomplished on her own, she called out to the family and joyfully proclaimed that she had been healed. Despite our limited belief system at that time, none of us could deny that a miraculous healing had taken place in Mom's body! The English language does not contain adequate words to describe the extent of our joy that day; nor can I ever fully express my gratitude to God for healing my mother in such a phenomenal way. The profound affect of that one miracle on my own future life and ministry is impossible to calculate.

Because she had personally received irrefutable proof that God still heals the sick today, my mother's life thereafter was set aflame with faith. In addition to faithfully witnessing for Christ as she had since her conversion, she then began to pray for the sick with astounding success. Because she had never learned to drive a car, Mom thought nothing of taking several buses to the farthest reaches of the city in order to pray for people who were afflicted with any and all types of illnesses. Her favorite prayer challenge was always the cancer case. To the best of my knowledge, my mother never prayed for a single cancer victim who was not subsequently set free from this devastating disease! In future years, she would go on to establish a neighborhood church in Brooklyn. Eventually she moved with our family to the Chicago area where she continued her ministry. It was her lifelong habit to pray with sick people wherever she encountered them, until the day came when she was called home to be with her Lord. What wonderful stories of victory we will be able to share the next time we meet!

*　　*　　*

"It's Not There!"

She was only a small woman, but she had a very big need. Barbara was a young woman who attended one of my Chicago crusades and requested prayer for a serious and ultimately fatal condition. As the result of fluid retention in her skull cavity caused by an inoperable tumor, her brain had become dangerously enlarged. In order to manage her condition and siphon off some of the excess fluids, doctors had surgically inserted a shunt into the brain. This inflexible plastic tubing extended beneath the skin and down the back of her neck, where it was then dispersed throughout her body. As a result, she was unable to bend her head or neck in any direction so it remained in an upright position at all times.

Following prayer for her healing, Barbara's pain abruptly ceased and she knelt at the altar, threw back her head, raised her hands and began to exuberantly praise the Lord. When she did so, she suddenly realized that she was able to bend her neck backward with no resulting pain or restriction whatsoever. At this point, she laid her hand on the back of her neck and felt for the shunt. Imagine her amazement when her probing fingers were completely unable to locate that rigid, restrictive apparatus! Everyone around the altar joined in with her joyful praises and an ensuing examination by physicians failed to locate either the tumor or the shunt. Both had simply vanished!

*　　*　　*

A Skeptical Baptist's Miracle

Many years ago, it was my privilege to minister at the annual convention for the Knoxford Praying Band Church, a vibrant church in Knoxford, a small town in New Brunswick, Canada. Although the population within the community limits was small, the church drew people from throughout the surrounding areas and their convention was always well attended by people from outside the area as well. In fact, that first Sunday morning the church was filled to capacity for the opening service.

Among the many visitors that morning, one man and his two teen-aged sons were seated in the second pew. Unknown to me at the time, the three were members of the local Baptist church who had come to prove to themselves that we "holy rollers" possessed no authentic experience beyond salvation and were simply people of emotional extremes with no legitimate biblical foundation.

In the midst of my sermon, the Holy Spirit arrested my attention and I stopped, pointed to the father and said, "That growth inside your nose has just vanished—check and see!" He quickly did a nasal inspection and began to cry because the obstruction had indeed disappeared. (He later informed me that the growth had been there for a long time and he had been afraid to have it surgically excised for fear he would find out it was cancer.)

Before the conclusion of the service, both young men and their father had been baptized in the Holy Spirit with the evidence of speaking with other tongues. Someone later reported to me that the following day the man had been seen on the main street excitedly relating his miracle to a group of eager listeners. Ultimately, he had been responsible for bringing a large group of people to the services and some of them were then filled with the Holy Spirit as well.

*   *   *

Healed Through an Anointed Prayer Cloth

We were just concluding two weeks of power-packed meetings with our very good friend, the late Pastor Dewey Herron in Roanoke, Virginia. After the final service that night, a gentleman approached me and requested prayer for his eighteen-year-old nephew, who was paralyzed in both legs and confined to a wheelchair. Since his nephew lived in New Jersey, it had been impossible for him to attend the meetings in Roanoke, but his uncle desperately wanted to see him healed. He wanted to know if it was possible for someone to be healed at a distance.

I explained the effectiveness of prayer cloths when someone was too far away for the laying on of hands. I told him I would pray over a prayer cloth and he could send it to his nephew. He explained that his nephew was a born again Christian; but he was concerned that, since the young man was Baptist by denomination, he probably wouldn't receive the cloth in an attitude of faith. I instructed him to enclose the cloth in a letter that would explain how God had used the Apostle Paul to perform extraordinary miracles through the use of prayer cloths. [57] We then prayed over a cloth and asked the Lord to give healing faith to the nephew. The next morning Donna and I went on to a church in Roanoke Rapids, North Carolina to begin a crusade there with Pastor Melvin West.

Imagine my surprise the following Friday evening when I saw the man from the previous crusade walk into the church in North Carolina. He had driven two hundred miles and a grueling four and a half hours, but he walked in with a huge smile on his face. He said nothing before the service, but there was no hiding his joy afterward when he reminded me of the prayer cloth he had requested for his nephew and then reported what had happened. When his nephew had opened the letter, the prayer cloth was masking the text; so he had moved it away in order to see the words—but he never got to read any of them. As soon as he touched the prayer cloth, he leaped from the wheel chair and instantly began to walk! Since the man hadn't had a chance to read

---

[57] "God was performing extraordinary miracles by the hands of Paul, so that handkerchiefs or aprons were even carried from his body to the sick, and the diseases left them and the evil spirits went out." *Acts 19:11,12* (NOTE: The author would be happy to send a prayer cloth to any reader upon request.)

168

what the cloth was for, his is a miracle that no one can claim was a "psychosomatic" one. Apparently, explanation and permission aren't always necessary when God has a job to do!

＊　　＊　　＊

Grandma's Love Finds a Way: Donny's Miracle

The late Pastor James Martin in Fremont, Ohio had invited me to minister for a three-night meeting that ultimately stretched to three weeks of a literal heaven-on-earth visitation. For the duration of those weeks, the pastor purchased fifteen minutes of daily radio time. On each program I preached, described the miracles that were happening and invited people in the area to attend, which many of them subsequently did.

That powerful radio station covered a wide area of the state. Within that radius there lived a tiny, four-year-old boy named Donnie, who had been stricken with cerebral palsy in infancy. The disease had advanced rapidly throughout Donnie's short life and had left him with slurred speech, frail body and both legs entirely encased in heavy braces. His limited ability to walk was painfully hindered by the braces and he was unable to run at all—a painful limitation for a small boy. (His grandmother later confided to me that Donnie would often sit at the picture window and cry as he watched healthy young boys run and play in a park across the street. Sometimes he would ask why he couldn't be like them.)

Though his grandmother was not saved and the family lived a hundred miles from the church, she heard one of our daily broadcasts and decided to bring little Donnie to be prayed for, hoping that God really could still heal today. It couldn't have been an easy task for her to make that long trip with a small boy in the car; but love will always find a way.

169

On the night they attended, when I gave the invitation for the sick to come for prayer, Donnie's grandmother hurried forward and positioned the boy at the very front of the long line of people. My heart broke as I watched the child slowly come across the platform toward me. The braces afforded limited flexibility at the knees and as he "walked," he threw each little leg awkwardly to either side in a wide arc.

When Donnie stood before me, he seemed so very small in comparison to my six foot three inch frame that I decided to kneel in front of him so he wouldn't be frightened by my size. As I knelt, I looked into his beautiful, hopeful eyes and gently asked what he wanted God to do for him. Of course I knew the answer—Donnie wanted to run and jump and laugh and talk normally! (Needless to say, there had been very little to laugh about in his young life up to that point.) His halting speech was barely understandable as he replied that he wanted "to be like other boys." There was such innocent trust reflected in those eyes that despite myself, I began to cry as the compassion of Jesus swept over me and I gathered the boy's little body into my arms.

Through my tears I asked, "Donnie, do you believe Jesus will heal you tonight?" He replied immediately and emphatically, "Yes!" With full assurance of the Holy Spirit and faith in the authority of God's Word behind me, I assured Donnie that Jesus loved him very much and was indeed going to heal him.

[Allow me a bit of irony here. Theologians teach all about a God of love; but at the same time would have been quick to inform Donnie that to believe God could or would heal today was theologically incorrect. After all, every properly trained theologian *knows* Jesus doesn't do that anymore! Perhaps I should have explained to this child the doctrinal position of so many denominations and said, "Donnie, the *only* reason Jesus healed people when He was on earth was because He wanted to build a big church and that was the best way He could get it started. Since the church has already been established and we have the Bible now, Jesus doesn't need to heal anymore; so sick little boys like you just have to stay that way."

How sadistically cruel such a statement would have been—and how woefully *incorrect*. In my opinion, characterizing our compassionate Lord in that manner is not only insulting but dangerously akin to blasphemy! Thankfully, Jesus Christ is and forever will be the same as He was within the pages of the Bible[58] and He is *still* touched with the feelings of our infirmities.[59]]

Kneeling there with Donnie in my arms, I attempted to pray through my tears; but Jesus' own compassion for the sick overcame me and I was unable to form the words—so I prayed *tears*. And God translated them into a river of healing that flooded over Donnie and instantly reversed every trace of the disease that had ravaged his tiny body. In a moment of time he was totally healed!

Suddenly I felt Donnie's small arms forcefully push me nearly off balance and out of his way as he began to do what he had always yearned to do—*run*. Wearing a huge grin, he made three complete circuits around that large auditorium. Above the shouts of praise erupting from the congregation, the metallic clicking sound of the braces could be heard as Donnie joyfully demonstrated the handiwork of the Lord. When he finally paused long enough to speak, he did so with perfect clarity.

While Donnie was running his three laps around the church, I came down to the congregation's level to watch the gleeful display from a more advantageous position. Suddenly, from the platform behind me I heard a tearful voice crying out to God for salvation. Glancing behind me, I saw Donnie's grandmother on

---

[58] "Jesus Christ is the same yesterday and today and forever." *Heb 13:8*
[59] "This was to fulfill what was spoken through Isaiah the prophet: 'HE HIMSELF TOOK OUR INFIRMITIES AND CARRIED AWAY OUR DISEASES.'" *Matt 8:17*

her knees in repentance and grateful surrender to Christ. What a fitting response to such an awesome miracle!

Donnie's was only the first miracle that wonderful night. When the rejoicing over Donnie had quieted somewhat, we resumed the prayer line and *many* more people received their healings as well. Following the service, Donnie's grandmother asked my advice concerning the proper course of action she should take. Since neither of Donnie's parents were believers, she was uncertain whether she should immediately remove the unneeded braces herself, or if she should wait until after they had returned home and told the parents of the evening's events. I advised her not to usurp the parent's rights, but to explain what had obviously taken place and allow them to observe Donnie's condition for themselves. Following that, they could then make the obvious decision and remove the braces.

A short while afterward, while conducting services with Pastor Moses Veigh in the nearby city of Findley, Ohio, I was surprised to see Donnie's grandmother among those greeting me after the service. She had learned from a radio announcement that I was preaching at that current location and she had again traveled a considerable distance to give me an update on Donnie's progress.

The grandmother reported that when Donnie's parents were told of Donnie's miracle, they had promptly removed the braces. Medical examination had borne out the fact that he was free of cerebral palsy. Since that time, Donnie had begun to live a perfectly normal life, doing everything four-year-old boys like to do and talking incessantly. She said, "He chatters on and on like a little magpie, and sometimes we want to say, 'Donnie, please be quiet for awhile!' Then we remember the days when he couldn't speak clearly at all, and we let him talk as much as he wants to!"

With tears running down her cheeks she continued, "I remember the times when Donnie would sit and watch the other children playing in ways he knew he'd never be able to do. Then came that wonderful night when God healed him. Now he runs and jumps and does all the things normal children do. I just had to see you one more time and thank you for praying!"[60]

Throughout the years since that time, I have been privileged to witness thousands of miraculous healings; yet Donnie's miracle continues to stand out above many others in my mind and will always be counted among my most cherished memories.

*   *   *

"Not Any More!"

During a miracle service in Siliguri, a city in the far northern area of India, after confronting the powerful local entity, Kali, the Hindu goddess of death, we witnessed the miraculous resurrection of a small boy from the dead. (This outstanding miracle has been related in detail, along with my encounter with Kali in Chapter Twelve of this book.) Immediately after that supernatural demonstration of Holy Spirit power, scores of Hindus were converted and healed, some of them simultaneously!

Due to the language barrier and the joyful confusion of the testimony time that followed, I was unable to learn the details of most healings among that sea of rejoicing people. However, one tall, stately Hindu woman wearing a magnificent *sari* stands out vividly in my memory. This sixty-five-year-old woman had been totally deaf in both ears since the age of five. As she prepared to answer the questions posed by one of our workers, her younger sister (who was standing behind her) imperiously interjected a condescending comment. "It's no use talking to *her*," the sister said. "She can't hear a word you're saying. She's totally deaf!" Without turning her head around the "deaf" sister replied, *"Not any more I'm not!"* Though demonic forces had held her in

---

[60] Please read *Luke 17:12-19*

bondage for sixty years, the Holy Spirit had set her free in a moment of time from both spiritual darkness *and* physical infirmity!

*   *   *

A Baby's Crossed Eye

I was still a student in Bible College when my older sister gave birth to her first child, a daughter whom Elaine and her husband had named Beverly. She was only a few weeks old the first time I saw that beautiful baby girl. (If my readers will bear with this proud uncle, I will state unequivocally that Beverly subsequently grew up to be a beautiful young woman who chose to serve others throughout her career as a psychiatric nurse. Her beauty is not only on the outside, but inside as well.)

As I admired the innocence of that tiny infant face, I observed for myself what my mother had already told me—that one of Beverly's eyes was noticeably miscast in the direction of her little nose. At that time, my sister was a devoted Christian and minister's wife, but neither she nor her pastor husband were believers in divine healing, so I was reluctant to ask their permission to pray for Beverly's healing. One night, while my sister prepared the evening meal, I held my niece in my arms and prayed earnestly while I walked throughout the house.

Sensing a healing anointing, I gently laid my big hand over the baby's little face and asked God to make the crossed eye normal. God heard that prayer and when I opened my eyes, I looked down into two perfectly re-aligned eyes. Needless to say, they have remained that way to this very day. Whenever I have been with Beverly since that time, I've never looked into her eyes without remembering that fateful moment when the God of the universe took the time to stop by and lavish His healing touch upon one Bible student's infant niece.

174

*   *   *

"Is You the Healer?"

The services at The Lighthouse Tabernacle in Patterson, New Jersey had been wonderful and many people had already been healed from various diseases. One night as I was leaving the auditorium after the service, Pastor William K. Wilson stopped me and said that one more person was waiting to be prayed for. I scanned the now empty auditorium and saw no one; but Pastor Wilson explained that she was hidden from view, but a blind woman was kneeling in prayer between the pews near the front of the church.

I sat in the pew behind the woman, tapped her shoulder and asked softly, "What do you need from the Lord?" When that motherly looking African American woman looked up in my direction, I saw that both eyes were covered with the distinctive milky-white film typical of cataracts and I realized she was totally blind. Following the sound of my voice, she asked excitedly, "Is you the healer?"

When I responded truthfully, "No, I'm not," her face fell. In a voice quivering with disappointment she said, "I was so sure you was the healer 'cause your voice sounds just like the preacher's." I explained that I was indeed the preacher, but that the *Healer* was Jesus (a critical distinction in my view). She smiled as she caught my meaning.

When I asked what she needed from the Lord, the woman's yearning reply was, "O, that I might receive my sight!" I asked her to close her eyes and, laying my thumbs gently on her eyelids, I prayed a short, simple prayer. When she opened her eyes, she screamed joyously, "I can see! *I can see!*" I shared her delight and chuckling, said, "If you can see, touch my nose." She did so in such a forceful way that I began to laugh out loud and she joined in. Then I asked her to point out individual lights in the high ceiling above us, and she did so with total accuracy. When I asked her to describe the colors in my tie, she pointed and correctly identified each color. (Can you say, *wild tie?*)

As we left the church that night both of us were weeping for joy. I was so grateful that this humble servant of God hadn't been overlooked. Occasionally I'm asked if I ever get accustomed to seeing miraculous things take place. My response is always the same: "*Never!* Each time is like the very *first* time!"

"The LORD'S loving kindnesses indeed never cease, for His compassions never fail. They are new every morning; great is Your faithfulness." *Lam 3:22-23*

* * *

Arthritic Hand Restored

During a crusade in Portland, Oregon a woman came forward for prayer. She was the victim of crippling arthritis that had left one hand totally useless. That hand was frozen into a grotesquely misshapen claw that could not be straightened. Having witnessed the healing of a similar condition at one point in my earlier ministry, I used the same scripture in this situation as I had at that time. Quoting the scripture contained in the story in *Mark 3:1-5*, I repeated Jesus' command to the man with the withered hand[61] and said to the woman before me, "Stretch out your hand." Without hesitation, she complied. Instantly the hand returned to normal and she simultaneously regained the ability to clasp and unclasp the fingers and move the hand freely with no residual pain or stiffness.

* * *

---

[61] "...He said to the man, 'Stretch out your hand...'" *Mark 3:5*

Healing Obedience

The two-week crusade with Pastor Melvin West in Roanoke Rapids, North Carolina was drawing to a close as we began the final service. The Lord had visited us mightily and miraculous events had been seen in every service. In addition to healings of all sorts, several people had been delivered from demons. (One outstanding account of exorcism during those meetings is related in detail in Chapter Twenty-One of this book).

I normally ask pastors to refrain from telling me any details, either positive or negative, about the internal affairs of their churches or the lives of the church members; and I had done so with Pastor West. (My reason for doing this is because I want to be totally reliant upon the Holy Spirit for whatever information He chooses to reveal to me prophetically.) However, this pastor's deep concern had caused him to let slip into our conversation that one of his members was desperately ill with hemorrhaging in her stomach. Physicians had been unable to stop the bleeding and had resorted to weekly blood transfusions in an effort to keep the woman alive. She had been restricted to eating strained baby food only, but most of the time wasn't even able to tolerate such innocuous meals. Meanwhile, she had steadily weakened and her weight had fallen dramatically as her condition rapidly grew worse. The prognosis was bleak and the woman was not expected to live very much longer.

In a situation such as that one, the best and only hope one can offer is Jesus. He is and will forever be the Hope of the hopeless. He is not only King of Kings and Lord of Lords; He's also the Great Physician. We can safely trust in His Word: **"...I, the LORD, am your healer."** *Ex 15:26*

Somewhere in the middle of my sermon that evening, the Holy Spirit interrupted and directed my attention to the woman whose condition the pastor and I had discussed earlier. Since during the previous meetings I had been prophetically calling out sick people as the Lord revealed their individual needs, I thought it was important that the afflicted woman and the pastor not feel that I was misrepresenting this specific knowledge as being prophetic in nature. Therefore, I made it clear to all present that I had learned of the woman's illness through the pastor and not by revelation. Furthermore, I stated that my knowledge of the situation was irrelevant, since Jesus alone was the One responsible for changing desperate circumstances such as hers.

When I asked the woman if she wanted to be well, she quite naturally replied in the affirmative. I then inquired if she would be willing to do *anything* the Lord asked her to do; and again she agreed. Following the Holy Spirit's directive, I asked her to stand and move out into the aisle and with great effort she complied. My next words surprised even me and, had I been depending on my own reasoning faculties at that point, it's likely I would have balked at saying them. Thankfully, the Holy Spirit is in control at such times and I said, "The Lord wants you to run to the rear of the church, touch the door and then run to the front and touch the pulpit. You are to do this three times and you will be healed. *Thus says the Lord!"*

Needless to say, this appeared to be an unreasonable request on God's part and on mine! *Run?* The poor woman was so weakened she could barely *walk;* and the Lord was telling her to *run?* When God makes an unusual request such as that, it illustrates the words of this scripture:

"O the depth of the riches both of the wisdom and knowledge of God! How unsearchable are his judgments, and his ways past finding out! *Rom 11:33*

One could also call to mind the strange command of the prophet Elisha when Naaman the leper came seeking healing. When Elisha sent that powerful dignitary to dip seven times in the River Jordan, that didn't make sense to the natural mind either; but his *obedience* led to his miracle.[62] We mortals would do well to bear in mind that God's instructions don't have to make sense to us—they simply have to be obeyed!

As irrational and impossible as the command seemed to be, the desperately ill woman struggled to obey. As she moved slowly up the aisle, it's unlikely her feet were ever lifted from the floor. She literally shuffled as she laboriously made her way toward the back door. When she reached her goal, she touched the door, turned and then painfully returned to the front where she touched the pulpit and repeated the sequence.

By this point the woman looked terrible—her ashen face and ever-faltering step wrenched every heart, including my own, as we watched the laborious progress of her determined act of obedience to the Lord's command. It didn't seem possible that she possessed the strength to accomplish the journey one time, let alone three—but she *did!* As her hand touched the pulpit for the third and final time, the power of God descended like a lightning bolt from heaven! With joyous abandon, the woman began to praise the Lord and dance energetically across the front of the church, while the congregation roared its approval. (I'm sure you would have danced, too, if you'd been dying and God had set you free from your affliction and infused you with new life!) What a glorious way to end a crusade!

Some months later, I was passing through that city and stopped to visit the pastor. He took me for a drive during which he stopped at the home of one of his church members. There he introduced me to a pleasantly plump lady and asked if I recognized her. When I replied negatively, the pastor smiled and revealed that this was the woman whose miracle is related above. In the

---

[62] "Elisha sent a messenger to him, saying, 'Go and wash in the Jordan seven times, and your flesh will be restored to you and you will be clean.'...So he went down and dipped himself seven times in the Jordan, according to the word of the man of God; and his flesh was restored like the flesh of a little child and he was clean." *2 Kings 5:10,14*

intervening weeks her appetite had returned, she had completely regained her strength and had resumed her normal activities. Excitedly, she told me she had returned to her doctor, who had been unable to find any evidence of her near-fatal infirmity.

*   *   *

Doomed to Die

My good friend, Pastor John Brown had once been pastor of my family's home church in Revere, Massachusetts. Following his tenure there, he had gone on to pastor Central Assembly, an Assemblies of God church in Tulsa, Oklahoma. When he invited me to Tulsa for a crusade, I was delighted to accept an opportunity to reconnect with my friend and to minister in his new church.

Over lunch one day during the course of the meetings, John asked if I would go with him to the hospital to pray for a member of his church. The man had fallen victim to cancer and had grown progressively worse until he was now in a comatose state and near death. John was aware that it is a strain for an evangelist to make hospital calls during an ongoing meeting, because word spreads and it becomes difficult to refuse others who are also seeking an appointment for personal ministry. Therefore, I knew the man and his situation had to be of intense concern to my friend. I felt the inner prompting of the Holy Spirit to go with him, and I agreed to make an exception in that one case.

When we arrived at the hospital, we were disappointed to learn that the man had been taken out of his room to undergo various tests. When we had waited a long while and he still hadn't returned, we were forced to leave. We made another attempt the second day but it was a repeat of the first. Our third visit appeared to be headed in the same direction, when suddenly the porter wheeled the man's bed into the room. There he lay, totally inert and deep in a coma. We were told that his body was not only riddled with cancer, but that his kidneys had also ceased to

180

function and the relatives had been told the man had only a very short time left to live. At that point, there was absolutely nothing that modern medical technology or expertise could do to save him. (Thankfully, as believers we never have to be irrevocably influenced by the dire opinions of medical science. We are subject to a much higher law—the law of *life* in Christ Jesus!)

Wanting to be alone with the patient, we asked one of the man's daughters to stand at the door and maintain our privacy for a few moments while we prayed. The woman's body was substantial enough to have qualified her for the NFL and she was determined to protect our prayer time. When the sick man's chief oncologist attempted to enter the room, the woman politely refused. Greatly annoyed, he asked the reason and was told bluntly, "Because the men of God are in there and are praying for my father." As he stormed away, the doctor's disdainful comment was, "Prayer won't do any good—he's only going to die *anyway*!"

As we prepared to pray, I spoke into the comatose man's ear and told him that God had sent us to lay hands on him and pray for his healing. Pastor Brown and I then prayed a brief prayer. Suddenly the entire bed began to shake with the power of God and, for the first time in several days, the man opened his eyes and looked at us with full comprehension. His ashen face became flushed with healthy color and he smiled and began to praise the Lord. We rejoiced with him briefly and then left to prepare for the evening service. I've often wished we could have stayed to see that doctor's face when he returned to find the man not only conscious, but also smiling and talking animatedly with his elated family!

Later in that same year, I returned to Tulsa to hold another week of healing services with Pastor Brown. At the conclusion of the first meeting, several people came forward to greet me. One heavy-set gentleman asked if I recognized him and I didn't. He then laughed and revealed that he was the dying man in the hospital. His cancer had entirely disappeared and he was now in the best of health. The man's family was with him and they told me that, because his enormous hospital expenses had depleted their resources, they had been forced to celebrate the previous Christmas without gifts for the family. But the entire family smiled as the man's wife declared, "We didn't even mind, because God gave us the greatest Christmas gift we could ever have received. Daddy himself was home to celebrate with us!" Hearing this, I was overjoyed to know that because of my obedience to the still, small voice of the Holy Spirit, a loving family had been preserved from a tragic loss.

*   *   *

Brand New Skin

During a ministry time with Pastor Joseph Dunets at Evangel Temple in Portland, Oregon, we were privileged to witness a mighty outpouring of the Holy Spirit. People were saved and miracles took place every night of the crusade. One night in particular however, stands out in my memory because one rarely sees a torrential downpour such as was falling that night. In fact, instead of discussing the storm during the weather segment, the local television station covered the unusual amount of rainfall during the breaking news segment of their nightly news broadcast. The scene outside my hotel room window looked like the biblical description for the beginning of Noah's flood. As the hour for the evening service approached, I began to think that if anyone managed to make it to church, it would be a miracle. To further compound the situation, that downtown church had very little parking space of its own and people were often forced to park many blocks away and walk a considerable distance in order to attend the services.

When I walked into the auditorium just before the service was to begin, I was amazed to find that nearly the entire main floor was already filled with people. By the time the service had been in progress for a short time, the entire auditorium was filled to capacity. To me, this was proof positive that people will tolerate many adversities (even extreme weather conditions) in order to be where God is demonstrating His miracle-working power.

That night, a woman in need of a very special healing miracle was seated a few rows back from the front of the auditorium. Her skin was afflicted with a condition that had the appearance of fish scales that covered nearly the entire surface of her body. When I prayed for the release of healing power over the congregation, the woman rested her infected hands in her lap, bowed her head and closed her eyes. Suddenly, she felt a sensation akin to warm oil being poured over her head and then flowing down over her entire body. When she opened her eyes and looked down at her hands, she saw that they were covered with soft, healthy new skin! A pile of flaky skin cells filled the lap of her garment. We rejoiced with her and with the others who had also been healed during the prayer. The following night, the woman gave additional testimony. When she had undressed for bed the previous night, she discovered that the inside of her clothing was filled with the same scale-like material and her entire body was covered with brand new skin! It was apparent to all that the *only* rain that night hadn't fallen outside the church—the Holy Spirit had also poured His healing rain onto all the faithful seekers inside the building who had braved the elements in search of their own special miracles.

*　　*　　*

Healed from Ileitis

We once conducted miracle services for several years in the Chicago, Illinois suburb of Oak Park. A respected reporter for the now defunct Chicago News came to our meetings, along with his photographer whose pictures of the miracles that night accompanied the long article subsequently written about what they had seen and heard. One outstanding miracle was that of a man who had received his sight after forty years of total blindness in both eyes!

Following publication of the article, a husband and wife read it and were persuaded to attend a service and observe first-hand the sorts of happenings that had been reported in the newspaper. Although they were not saved, they believed in God's power to affect miracles. The couple was desperate to find a cure for their only child, a daughter who lived some distance away in Sheboygan, Wisconsin. The woman, who was in her mid-thirties, had endured many years of excruciating pain caused by an intestinal condition known as *ileitis*. This condition is known to bring on sudden, severe attacks and had been the cause of countless emergency ambulance trips to the hospital as well as many surgeries. Despite a drastically restricted diet and many powerful medications, the illness had persisted and progressively worsened, until the young woman's body had become extremely weakened and greatly emaciated.

Excited and encouraged by what they had witnessed in the service, her parents had called their daughter, reported on the miracles they had seen and urged her to attend a miracle service, hoping that she would be healed. The young woman came the following week and did indeed receive an instantaneous miracle when I prayed for her. Not only did the pain vanish, along any further need for treatment or medication, but the condition itself never recurred. The parents and their daughter promptly received Jesus Christ that very night! The parents remained tireless workers and faithful supporters of this ministry and the host church for some years, until they retired to join their daughter at her new home in Arizona. Because of that one demonstration of God's power and love for them, the couple continued to serve the Lord until He called them home to be forever with Him. I have since lost touch with the daughter, but assume she is still serving the Lord to this day.

*   *   *

Put It To Work!

During one service in Lima, Ohio a man came forward and requested that I pray for him to receive the gift of healing as recorded in scripture:

"To another faith by the same Spirit, and to another gifts of healing by the one Spirit..." *I Cor 12: 9*

Normally I don't make it a practice to pray for anyone to receive one gift in particular. However, in this instance, the Holy Spirit impressed me that I should do so because He had implanted the desire for this gift in the man's heart. In obedience to the Spirit's prompting, I prayed that God would grant His servant's sincere request.

After the prayer, the man thanked me and started to return to his seat; whereupon I promptly grasped his arm and said, "Wait a minute! What did you just request prayer for?" The man replied that he had asked to receive the gift of healing. My answer was, "When I pray for someone to receive something from God, I believe it will happen. We've prayed, so let's believe you have already received the gift of healing."

Turning to the congregation, I asked anyone who was currently in pain to raise their hand. One woman promptly responded and said she had been afflicted with migraine headaches for quite some time and was never completely free from some degree of pain. At that point, she had been suffering with constant migraine headaches for the last three months and was in severe pain at that very moment. When the woman came forward, I addressed the man whom I believed had received the gift of healing and told him to lay his hands on the woman and pray for her healing. The man looked shocked, but did as instructed.

As soon as the short, faltering prayer was over, the grateful woman began to cry for joy—for the first time in years she was totally free from pain! The man who had never before done such a thing, had now successfully prayed for someone to be healed and experienced the instantaneous result. Though I never had occasion to meet the man again, I hope that night proved to be only the beginning of a powerful healing ministry that blessed the church for many years afterward.

*   *   *

An Unusual Deafness Case

In one of the churches I once pastored, I prayed for an older woman who had been totally deaf in one ear for sixteen years. There was no immediate evidence of healing, but I sensed the Lord had set the process in motion and said so. The next day the woman reported that she could hear perfectly when she rose from her bed that morning. She went on to say that a small, round, black object had fallen from the afflicted ear and onto the pillow sometime during the night. We never learned what unknown material had formed the obstruction and her physicians had never detected the presence of anything like it in the past, either in her ear or any other. All we did know was that when prayer caused the offending object to be dislodged, the woman's hearing was totally restored and remained so throughout the duration of my pastorate in that church.

*   *   *

"That's Impossible!"

During my most recent trip to Korea, my hosts were rushing me out of the church because reservations had been made for lunch and we were running behind time after the morning service. On my way out of the auditorium, I greeted a man in a wheelchair who had not come into the prayer line that morning. Impulsively, I leaned over, laid my hands on both knees and

186

prayed for his healing. After the prayer, I took his hands and told him to stand up and walk.[63]

Immediately, the man's solicitous wife cried out in alarm and my host interpreted her words for me. "That's *impossible*, Brother; he'll fall down! You don't understand—both of his legs are paralyzed and he *can't* walk!" The man's eyes never left mine as he quickly rose to his feet and triumphantly pushed his wheelchair out into the great entrance hall where he paraded it up and down using his "new" legs! (I didn't look back to see, but it wouldn't have surprised me in the least if his wife had fainted from the shock!)

As we walked together, I observed another man who was also in a wheelchair and seated off to one side of the hall. As we approached him, I instructed the man who had already received his miracle to pray for the other man. When he did so, the man was also instantly released from his infirmity and began to walk about with *his* wheelchair! (I'm sure lunch that day was all the more delicious for having been delayed by these two miracles!)

---

[63] "Jesus said to him, 'Get up, pick up your pallet and walk.' Immediately the man became well, and picked up his pallet and began to walk." *Jn 5:8*

CHAPTER FIFTEEN

EXPERIENCES WITH SPEAKING
IN FOREIGN LANGUAGES

**"These signs will accompany those who have believed:
...they will speak with new tongues..."** *Mark 16:17*

I didn't always believe that the practice of speaking in tongues was scriptural. In fact, as related in Chapter Two, at one time I ridiculed those who believed such "nonsense." If I should live to be Methuselah's age (nine hundred sixty-nine years!) I will never forget the night (detailed in Chapter Three) when the Lord overwhelmed my objections and sovereignly filled me with the Holy Spirit as evidenced by speaking in a language not my own. It is true that most of the languages spoken by those who have received the Baptism in the Holy Spirit are probably not presently used here on earth. In fact, sometimes they may be heavenly languages completely unknown to us.[64] That having been said however, on occasion I have come to sense exactly how the disciples must have felt on the Day of Pentecost when those who had gathered outside the upper room understood their initial experience of speaking in tongues. I have personally experienced that same awesome Day-of-Pentecost phenomenon on several occasions in my own life.

*　　*　　*

A Stunned Rabbi

Some years ago, I attended a conference in New York City. I was not the speaker—it was a time of rest for me. I had been on the road for quite some time in continuous evangelistic services

---

[64] "If I speak with the tongues of men *and of angels...*" *1 Cor 13:1a (Emphasis mine.)*

and desperately needed a short time for physical and spiritual refreshment. At that time, our ministry was in the process of purchasing a large gospel tent and all the necessary equipment to furnish and transport it. The tent, sound system and portable electric organ had already been purchased, but we still needed a large amount of chairs and our funds had been totally depleted.

After the service I went forward and knelt at the front pew to pray. My primary concern that afternoon was the need to raise enough money to purchase the chairs, and I hadn't any idea how or from what source the Lord would supply it. While in prayer, I suddenly found myself no longer praying in English. The Holy Spirit began to intercede through me in a language I didn't recognize from previous experiences in the spiritual realm. This burst of prayer was a brief one, but the words were spoken with a great deal of authority and left me with a deep assurance that I would soon possess that for which the Holy Spirit had interceded.[65] For the reader who is unfamiliar with this manner of prayer, I submit the following words from one of the Apostle Paul's epistles:

> **"In the same way the Spirit also helps our weakness; for we do not know how to pray as we should, but the Spirit Himself intercedes for us with groanings too deep for words; and He who searches the hearts knows what the mind of the Spirit is,** *because He intercedes for the saints according to the will of God."* *Romans 8:26, 27 (Emphasis mine.)*

At that moment, even though there was no tangible proof, I knew by faith that we already possessed the funds to purchase the necessary equipment. Having been given that sense of calm assurance, I stood, went to the back of the church and began to greet others who had gathered there. Before long, a born-again, Spirit-filled rabbi joined our group. His appearance was exactly as

---

[65] "For if I pray in a tongue, my spirit prays, but my mind is unfruitful." *1 Cor 14:14*

one would expect—full beard, *yarmulke* and traditional prayer shawl. He wore a serious look of concern as he introduced himself and directed this question to me, "Where did you learn to speak Hebrew?"

I didn't understand the reason for his question and, although he didn't appear to be a jocular sort of person, I assumed his remark had been spoken in jest. Smiling, I replied, "The only Hebrew I know is *shalom* (peace) and chicken soup!" His expression didn't change nor did he respond with a matching smile. With all seriousness he replied, "I'm not joking. Where did you learn to speak Hebrew?" I reiterated the fact that I couldn't speak *any* Hebrew and I asked what possible reason he'd had for asking that question. He replied, "When I knelt beside you, I distinctly heard you praying in high Hebrew." Because he had captured my undivided attention, I then asked the meaning of my statements in that language. His tone was one of concern and he slapped the palms of both hands on either of his cheeks as he replied, "*Oyvey!* What you said to God, I would *never* say to God!"

By this time, he not only had my total attention—he had also succeeded in scaring me half to death! I was well aware that opponents of the tongues phenomena had claimed for years that certain sources (always unnamed and untraceable) had reported having translated blasphemous words uttered in tongues during (always unidentified) Full Gospel services. To my knowledge and that of more accomplished historians than I, no proof of time, place or accurate translation has ever been submitted. Despite the fact that I knew this to be a false assertion, I certainly didn't want to be guilty of saying anything that was blasphemous or even remotely disrespectful to my Lord!

To my request for the exact translation of my words, Rabbi Ibrahim replied, "There's no exact translation because the Hebrew language, unlike English, has different ways to express utmost urgency. The closest I can come to your statement is, 'God, you *must* hear me! *You have no choice!*'"

191

Greatly relieved, I shouted, "Praise the Lord!" Though I realized my words had appeared to be presumptuous, I knew the words had been entirely appropriate, because the Holy Spirit had uttered them. I explained to the rabbi that before I had spoken in tongues, I had been praying for a specific ministry need. When the Holy Spirit had then prayed through me, He had been interceding in my stead, and I had been given full assurance that the need would soon be met. Since the Holy Spirit *is* God, He has the right to speak authoritatively before the throne. Therefore, because He spoke God's perfect will in the matter, the Father did indeed have *no* alternate choice! Such is the amazing power of praying in tongues.

By way of epilogue, I am pleased to report that within a month we had received the full amount needed for the chairs through an unexpected source. God never fails to keep His word!

*   *   *

A Conversion Through Tongues

The second incident took place in Canada, at a church in Connaught Heights (near Vancouver, British Columbia). We were approaching the end of the sixth service in a two-week series. The meeting was nearly over when the Holy Spirit captured my attention. In that particular church, a large balcony ran across the rear of the auditorium and down one side of the building. I turned toward that side of the auditorium, pointed to a specific section of the balcony and began to prophesy: "Up in this section, there's a young woman who is 18 years of age. Next week you are planning to join what you think is an occult group, but you are being deceived. It's not only an occult group—it's a satanic one, and they haven't revealed their true identity to you." (Surprise, surprise—Old Slewfoot was concealing his identity again. *Imagine that!*)

192

The prophetic word continued, "Once you're in this group, you will be trapped and they will not let you leave. Please come down here and be delivered from the evil spirits they've communicated to you." In response, the young woman immediately stood to her feet, came down the steps and hurried to the platform.

Within a few minutes I had led her to the Lord and, when I began to deliver her from demonic forces she fell to the floor under the power of the Holy Spirit. I've made it a practice to never deal with demonic spirits when physically exhausted unless they first attack me, and, since I had been working hard throughout the meetings and was very tired, I knelt beside the woman and began to pray silently for an increase in physical and supernatural strength before undertaking the deliverance. As I prayed, the Holy Spirit took over and I burst out in tongues—in a dialect I'd never spoken before. The demon cried out and the girl was immediately delivered.[66] When I then prayed for her to receive the Baptism in the Holy Spirit, she began to speak in tongues. The entire congregation rejoiced over this and with that we closed the service on a victorious note.

*   *   *

The Miraculous Aftermath

When I entered the church for the next service, I was told that the pastor had requested to see me in his office. There I was introduced to a sweet-spirited older man and his wife who related the following story to me.

Many years ago they had served as missionaries alongside another married couple in the African nation of Burundi. The couple's daughter had chafed under the privations and demands of

---

[66] "And demons also came out of many, crying out…" *Luke 4:41 (NKJV)*

missionary life. Her resentment intensified when she was sent to boarding school in another country where she was separated from her parents for long periods of time.[67] As the young girl grew into womanhood, her attitude became a root of bitterness that continued to grow over the years. Eventually, she had abandoned her faith altogether, and had come to hate Africa and to reject both her parents and her God. She had returned to Canada and was now in her forties, totally estranged from God and unwilling to attend any church.

Over the years, these former missionaries had maintained contact with the woman because of their close association with her parents. On many occasions, they had faithfully but unsuccessfully attempted to convince her to return to her faith. They had invited her to attend our current services so she could witness the miracles of God for herself. She had refused their invitation until the previous Friday night when she finally agreed to attend just that one service. The missionary went on to report that their guest had been unmoved throughout the entire service until they witnessed the events surrounding the demonized young woman in the previous account.

When I spoke in tongues to the demons, the words had been spoken in *Kirundi*, the language of the tribe they had lived among in Burundi. The language was familiar both to them and to their embittered friend. When she had heard this exchange with demons in a language I couldn't possibly have known, she had come back to the Lord! Hearing what effect those words had produced, I was eager to hear what I had said in Kirundi, and I asked the missionary for a translation.

"It's difficult to translate into English," he replied. "You commanded the demons to come out; but in doing so, you used an emphatic form of a command that only the chief of the tribe was allowed to utter. On rare occasions, the chief would delegate

---

[67] This was often standard procedure for many missionary organizations at that time in the early and mid-Twentieth Century.

another person to speak in his stead; but that was the only other way that particular command could be spoken by anyone else." The missionary then told me the words I had spoken could be roughly translated as, "You *must* come out—*you have no choice!*" We rejoiced together in the realization that the Chief *had* been speaking that night! Surely the King of Kings and Lord of Lords could also be accurately referred to as the "Chief of Chiefs," and He had spoken with all the authority vested in that position.

*   *   *

A Command in Latin

Another experience once happened during meetings in Syracuse, New York where I encountered a demonized young woman. As I prayed for her, I forcefully uttered several words in tongues. The demon screamed and promptly came out; and the woman was set free from the crushing bondage Satan had imposed upon her. At the conclusion of the service, I was in the process of greeting people when a teenaged girl approached me, followed closely by a very tall man who greatly resembled Abraham Lincoln. (No joke!)

The young girl explained that she was a Latin student and that when I had commanded the demon to come out of the woman, the phrase had been spoken in flawless Latin. I asked her for a translation and she complied with, "You *must* come out—*you have no alternative!*"

At that, the Lincolnesque gentleman who was standing nearby confirmed her statement. He said that as an attorney he had been required to study Latin in college and he understood it well. He went on to agree with her rendition and said it was precisely what he had been waiting to tell me.

Note that in the previous narratives there is a distinct similarity in the words used. Each time the Holy Spirit had spoken a *definitive command,* i.e.,

"You *must* hear me—*you have no choice!"*
"You *must* come out—*you have no choice!"*
"You *must* come out—you have *no* alternative!"

It's very clear that the Holy Spirit doesn't mince words and He is explicit in conveying what He means. When He declares that something must be done, it *must* be done. There can be no conflicting opinion!

*   *   *

The Holy Spirit Speaks the Navajo Tongue

A conversion that once took place in our Chicago church was also the result of a message in tongues. One of our members had brought a friend to the Sunday morning service and, though the woman appeared to listen intently, she offered no visible response to anything said or done during the meeting. This was not of particular note, since I knew nothing of her personality or religious background.

During the altar call, one of the elders stood and delivered a powerful message in tongues. When he had finished speaking, I eagerly anticipated the interpretation, which was not forthcoming. I firmly believe the Lord doesn't speak through His people in tongues unless He gives an interpretation so the hearers can understand His message. With this in mind, I encouraged the gifted ones in the congregation to seek God for the interpretation. I likewise inquired of the Lord, but received no answer. I thought His silence was strangely unlike the Holy Spirit, but soon went on to complete the invitation, to which no one responded.

As soon as the service was dismissed, our visitor hurried to the front, accompanied by the person who had invited her. From a closer vantage point, I realized that the woman's exotic facial features were typically those of the Native American Indian race. In broken English, she inquired how the elder who had delivered the message in tongues had come to speak Navajo. When I assured her that the man was of Croatian descent and neither spoke nor understood the Navajo language, she adopted an incredulous expression and told me what she had heard in her own native tongue.

She said the man had revealed her many sins, encouraged her to come to the Lord, and promised that she would then be "born again." With pure innocence she asked, "What does *born again* mean?" Inwardly, my spirit was leaping for joy when I realized the reason why the interpretation hadn't been given to the entire congregation—the message had been meant for only one person in the room and she had understood it perfectly! I then summoned the elder and gave him the joyful privilege of leading the woman to Christ.

*   *   *

The Lord Even Speaks Korean!

On one of our several mission trips to South Korea, my wife and I ministered an entire month in several cities throughout the country, preaching and praying for the sick. We were privileged to witness many healing miracles following the preaching of the Word. Since neither of us speak Korean, we were blessed to have the services of a marvelous interpreter, Dr. Won Bark Lee. After one service he brought me this wonderful report. While I had been ministering a healing prayer to one particular woman, I had spoken in tongues. To the woman's and the congregation's surprise, the words had been a series of encouraging statements in the Korean language of which I have absolutely no knowledge. I'm painfully certain of this because it took an entire month for me to master (I think) the phrase for "thank you!" There would have been no possible way that I could have expressed a complex (for me) prophetic message to this woman apart from the Holy Spirit's inspiration. What the Holy Spirit told her through me was, "Seek! There *is* a way! Stand firmly on the Word of God!" Our Lord is the Father of all language and communication—and I'm certain *He* speaks fluent Korean!

*   *   *

"*He* Wants You!"

In a church I once pastored, there was an older woman who attended fairly regularly but would frequently be inexplicably missing from services, sometimes for several weeks at a time. On one such occasion I was not overly concerned about her whereabouts, but was nevertheless pleased to see her back in her customary place one Sunday morning, though she appeared to be deeply troubled.

During a time of prophetic ministry in the service, the Spirit of the Lord came upon me in a powerful manner and directed my attention to this woman. I wasn't at all sure what the Holy Spirit had in mind, but I asked her to step out into the aisle where I went to meet her. No sooner had I begun to pray for her when I pointed upward toward heaven and spoke an emphatic phrase in tongues. Although neither she nor I knew the English words for what the Holy Spirit had said, the woman reacted by bursting into heavy sobs. I repeated the same phrase in tongues and she cried all the more. Rather than the emotion expressed from a broken heart however, her weeping appeared to be a grateful reaction to the comforting Presence of the Lord, and I knew He had ministered to her need, whatever it was.

(Only later would I learn that her engagement had been abruptly broken. Her fiancé had become enamored of a woman he had met on the Internet, subsequently abandoned his intended bride and moved to another state. Embarrassed and heartbroken, the woman had told no one but family of the situation and had been reluctant even to attend church.)

Immediately after the service was dismissed, a brother from the church who was a native of the African nation of Rwanda excitedly rushed down the aisle. He was eager to tell me that, when I had spoken in tongues, the words had been rendered in *Rwandese*, his own native language. I eagerly asked what I had said and he replied, "You said with emphasis, '*He* wants you! *He* wants you!'" He continued, "When you spoke the first phrase in tongues, I nudged my other Rwandan friends and said, 'Listen! Pastor's speaking our language!' When they paid closer attention, they clearly heard you repeat the same words."

Although I had spoken words I had never learned (and certainly can't repeat today), in her spirit that cruelly abandoned and deeply wounded sister had been made divinely aware of the very words she so desperately needed to hear. Despite the fact that her unfaithful fiancé no longer wanted her, she knew she was loved and wanted by her Heavenly Lover!

*   *   *

These experiences certainly illustrate one of the many purposes for speaking in tongues. To the critics who claim the practice serves no purpose and has no place in the present-day church, I submit that the scriptures obviously take an opposing view. The Apostle Paul found tongues to be necessary in his own life, so much so that he made the statement, "I speak in tongues more than you all;"[68] encouraged all the churches within his sphere of influences to make use of the practice;[69] and took the time to instruct the infant church at length about the proper use of tongues, both within one's personal life and during corporate worship.[70] Therefore, we must conclude that speaking in tongues must have

---

[68] *I Corinthians 14:18*
[69] *I Corinthians 14:5*
[70] *I Corinthians 14:1-33*

enjoyed an important place in the First Century church and should also occupy an equally prominent one in the present-day church as well. As the reader can see from the previous factual anecdotes gleaned from this one lifetime of experience, I can personally testify to that reality.

*   *   *

CHAPTER SIXTEEN

MIRACLES THROUGH PROPHECY

"...He awakens Me morning by morning, He awakens My ear to listen as a disciple. The Lord GOD has opened My ear; and I was not disobedient, nor did I turn back." *Isa 50:4-5*

"Surely the Lord GOD does *nothing* unless He reveals His secret counsel to His servants the prophets." *Amos 3:7 (Emphasis mine.)*

After all these years in ministry, during which I have given thousands of prophecies, I never cease to be amazed when I occasionally learn how the Lord brought about their fulfillment. Now and again, I meet someone who reminds me of the prophecy I once delivered to them and relates the circumstances of its fulfillment in minute detail. Although I may have long forgotten the people involved and the circumstances and content of those prophecies; God has a very long memory—and He's the One ultimately responsible for fulfilling them.

A Definition of Terms

The first story in this chapter of miracles will relate an experience that was to some extent, an example of a prophetic word; but was primarily a word of knowledge[71] *delivered* prophetically. In its primary definition, a "word of knowledge" is simply a fragment of necessary information previously unknown to the one who receives it. The Holy Spirit imparts this information either for personal enlightenment only; or it may contain information to be conveyed to another.

---

[71] For to one is given the word of wisdom through the Spirit, and to another the word of knowledge according to the same Spirit; *1 Cor 12:8*

Examples of Purely Informational Words of Knowledge

Three examples of purely informational words of knowledge in my own life come to mind. I will briefly mention them here simply as items of interest, since none involved a prophecy to another person; neither did they lead to a supernatural event.

- In the first experience, on the evening prior to a particular incident, I heard the words, *The SLA[72] Headquarters burned to the ground!* I had no idea why this thought had come to me; but the next morning, I turned on the television just in time to hear a news flash—"The SLA Headquarters in San Francisco burned to the ground last night!"

- The second experience took place while I was reading the local newspaper. One article related the tragic story of a young couple that had stopped their car to repair a flat tire. While the husband was busy replacing the tire, the jack had failed and brought the car down onto the wife's head, killing her instantly. As soon as I read the account, I turned to my wife and said, "That's not how it happened!" I went on to tell her that the man had killed his wife with the tire iron; positioned her body beneath the car and released the jack. Her head had been badly crushed which obliterated all signs of the tire iron injuries. I concluded, "This was no accident—it was *murder!* " My ever-optimistic wife (who would probably give even *Satan* the benefit of the doubt— *just fooling!*), replied that I'd heard too many murder stories in my life. I was completely vindicated when the husband was subsequently tried and convicted of murdering his wife in order to marry his secret lover.

---

[72] Symbionese Liberation Army, a violent radical group, active during the 1960's and 1970's.

- The third example of informational words of knowledge concerned a fund-raising method we repeatedly used at one point in my ministry. At that time, a gifted business manager and his wife were in my employ and frequently traveled with me. We often made it a practice to devote one evening of a crusade to a fund-raising banquet for missions. The purpose for the banquets was always announced in advance and they were invariably well attended.

Since I am not a fund-raiser by nature and was cautious of the offering time's potential for abuse; I have always been determined to conduct every fund-raising activity in a responsible manner—one that would present and meet the needs but not overtax the generosity of our donors. Every afternoon prior to the functions, my business manager's wife, Vivian (who was gifted in the word of knowledge) and I would seek God to determine the exact figure He had planned for us to raise that evening. Vivian's practice was to write the figure down, fold the paper and conceal it in her purse. When we three met before the banquet, she would ask what I had received from the Lord; then she would produce her folded note and read it to her husband and me. Invariably, our figures were identical! When that amount had then been pledged at the banquet, the total of the offering was announced and the appeal was ended. (That made for brief fund-raising sessions and I like to think our faithful donors also appreciated this approach!)

*   *   *

Prophetic Words of Knowledge

Very often the Holy Spirit imparts a word of knowledge as a means of forewarning another individual or preparing them for a future event. When delivered to another person, this gift is often linked with, and expressed through the gift of prophecy. Since this is the primary function of words of knowledge in my own prophetic ministry, I will devote the remaining and major portion of this chapter to miraculous instances that were the result of prophecy.

*   *   *

"You Won't be Back."

Midway through a two-week series of services on Cape Cod in Dennisport, Massachusetts, we were in the process of concluding the Friday evening service when I received a word that a woman present in the meeting would be unable to return the next week, and the Lord was calling her to commit her life to Christ that very night. I gave this revelation in prophecy, but no one responded to the call. Despite the lack of response I knew the woman was there and who she was.

After the congregation was dismissed, I smiled as I approached the woman and sat down in the pew in front of hers. She was a delightful elderly lady with beautiful white hair and a sweet disposition. We chatted briefly about the usual amenities and I told her how glad we were to have had her in the service that night. She said she had never before attended a Full Gospel service or seen a demonstration of the Holy Spirit's Presence and she had enjoyed it very much. To the best of my ability, I then attempted to explain that God sometimes reveals information to me about a particular person, information that He wants the person to be aware of. I went on to say that she was the woman I had mentioned previously; that she wouldn't be back to church the next week; and she needed to receive Christ that very night. After a brief explanation of the plan of salvation, she eagerly accepted Christ and her face lit up with joy.

She expressed her happiness and her gratitude for having found her Savior, and I was so glad I had obeyed the Lord and delivered His loving message. The woman then opened her heart and told me the following story. She told me she was eighty years

204

old and that she had lived in the same house and had faithfully attended the same church throughout her entire lifetime. She said she had outlasted every pastor who had served that church for the past eighty years, but not one of them had ever told her that she needed to be born again![73] How tragic that this dear soul had lived her entire life without personally meeting the One Who has been so clearly revealed within the pages of His Word—the very same Book all of her pastors throughout those eighty years had used as background for their Sunday sermons!

After service the following night, I talked with the friends who had brought my elderly friend to church the previous night. Excitedly they recounted that the woman had been bubbling over with happiness all the way home. With a joyful smile lighting up her face, she had kept repeating, "It feels just like there are joy bells ringing in my heart!" She had gone to sleep that night with the positive assurance that she was truly born again and, sometime during the night, her newfound Savior had come to escort her home to Heaven! I was profoundly grateful (and still am) that I had been faithful to deliver that crucial prophecy to a woman who had never been informed of her great need. That single opportunity had sealed her eternal destiny.

God is Interested in Individuals

The church that we had founded in Chicago had grown by leaps and bounds and we found ourselves in need of larger facilities to accommodate the growing congregation. Toward that end we were in the midst of renovations on a large building which had formerly housed a supermarket. At mid-afternoon, while I was busily tearing out walls, I answered the phone to hear the voice of my good friend of many years, Pastor Tommy Reid. He had been

---

[73] Please read *John 3:1-18*; "Jesus answered and said to him, 'Truly, truly, I say to you, unless one is born again he cannot see the kingdom of God.'" *John 3:3*

sponsoring monthly miracle services in the Buffalo, New York area with Evangelist Benny Hinn and the service was scheduled for that evening. However, Pastor Reid had encountered a serious problem. Brother Hinn had been scheduled to fly in for the service, but Springfield, Missouri had experienced a rare winter blizzard and the flight had been cancelled. The miracle service had been advertised extensively and couldn't be cancelled on such short notice. My friend asked if I would be willing to stand in for the speaker that evening.

As much as I wanted to help my friend, I explained that not only was I filthy from the work I was doing, but my home was at least twenty minutes away. Even if I could be ready and to the airport in time, it was unlikely that I'd be able to get a plane ticket to Buffalo at that late hour. Ever prepared, Tommy replied that everything had been taken care of and my ticket was already waiting at the "will call" desk.

Hurriedly, I called my wife and, by the time I ran into the house, my overnight case had been packed, my dress clothes had been laid out on the bed and the shower was running. Like myself, Donna was praying frantically that I'd make it on time for the only flight that could get me to Buffalo in time for the service. (The fact that the time zone in New York was already an hour later than Chicago made the pressure even greater.)

I'm afraid we broke the speed limit racing for the airport and, immediately after I boarded the plane, the door was shut behind me and we were airborne within minutes. When I deplaned in Buffalo, my driver whisked me off to the auditorium where the service was already in progress. I entered a side door and, within minutes of being seated on the platform, I was introduced and began to minister the Word.[74]

---

[74] "...preach the word; be ready in season and out of season..." *2 Tim 4:2*

That night, many healings took place, but I will concern myself here with one supernatural incident that involved a prophetic word I was inspired to deliver. During the time of healing ministry, the Holy Spirit suddenly shifted my attention to one particular section of the audience, roughly three-quarters of the way toward the back of the auditorium. I scanned the area, searching for the person to whom the Holy Spirit was directing my attention. The house lights had been dimmed, so it was difficult to see individual faces. Suddenly, an intense beam of light appeared to surround one woman's head. My first thought was that this must have been the person to whom I was supposed to prophesy.

Somehow, despite the supernatural halo, I didn't feel that the prophecy had been intended for that person. Perplexed, I moved slightly to one side, which gave me a different perspective on the halo's location. From that vantage point, I could clearly see that, directly behind the first woman, there was a shorter, much younger person—a fifteen-year-old girl. The glowing light conspicuously surrounded the girl's head and I called her to come forward.

I will not reveal here the personal content of the prophetic message, because it is possible that those present that night would remember the girl in question and I don't wish to cause her any embarrassment. Suffice it to say that, after I had whispered some particular details of a personal nature, I then delivered a lengthy prophecy. The young girl urgently needed to hear those particular words of correction, instruction and encouragement at that critical point in her life and she wept with relief and gratitude.

If ever I had doubted that our God is deeply concerned about every one of His children, such reservations would have been dispelled that night. Once again, the Lord demonstrated His deep interest in each of us as individuals by sending me that great distance to speak His will into that one young life.

*   *   *

"Don't Touch That Dial!"

Since my program *Impact!* was being broadcast on Chicago's Christian television channel at that time, I was once asked to join with other television ministers and appear on the air to help maintain enthusiasm among viewers during the annual fund-raising telethon. I've never been particularly comfortable with raising funds—in fact, I probably hold the world record for shortest offerings taken. At any rate, I had agreed to serve, so I was on duty early one afternoon when the light atop my camera signified that I was now on the air. Dutifully, I opened my mouth to say something about the station's need for pledges; but that wasn't what came out. This was before TV remote controls were in common use and, suddenly, I pointed my finger directly at the camera and said forcefully, "Don't touch that dial! I'm speaking right now to a fifteen-year-old girl whose life has reached a point where you think the only possible escape from your situation is ending your life. You've stayed home from school today to commit suicide and you've been flipping through channels trying to get up courage to actually kill yourself! But God loves you; He wants to save you and help you with your problems. I can help you find Him. The number is on the screen—so *call me now!*"

In less than three minutes' time, I was on the phone with the girl to whom the Holy Spirit had indeed spoken so definitively. She admitted that she was the victim of ongoing sexual abuse and had decided to end her situation by committing suicide that very day. Her first question was, "How did you know all that stuff about me?" She then went on to explain that, in the process of idly changing channels while she mustered the courage to kill herself, she had paused curiously on our channel. When she realized that the broadcast was a religious one, she had reached out to change the channel. At that very moment I had burst onto the screen and commanded, *"Don't touch that dial!"* Startled, she had paused and been stunned at the accuracy of the prophetic word that followed;

and it was obvious I couldn't possibly have known of her intentions.

We continued our phone conversation for some time while I outlined the path to salvation, and she eagerly accepted Jesus as her Savior. Over the course of the following months, she kept in contact, but although my wife and I offered to counsel with her, we never had the privilege of meeting her in person. However, I think of her often and thank God for the prophetic sensitivity to His Spirit that enabled me to spontaneously hear and speak His word into a desperate situation. Doing so not only saved a young life in this present world, but also rescued a soul for the eternal one yet to come.

*   *   *

The Flight Attendant and the Storm

Somewhere in South America I once changed planes enroute to a crusade in Argentina. While in the jet way waiting to board, I glanced inside the plane and my gaze fell upon a certain attendant who was directing people to their assigned seats. The Holy Spirit spoke very clearly then and said, "You will witness to her tonight." When I entered the plane, she pointed me to my seat and I wondered how it would be possible to speak to her at all since mine was a center seat; and this was compounded by the fact that flight personnel are always busy and not easily engaged in any meaningful conversation. I knew the Lord had spoken to me, but in curiosity I asked how He would arrange it. He didn't answer. I guessed that this was a "need to know" situation and I had been given all I needed to know.

We had been airborne only a short while when the hostess approached me and indicated for me to follow her. She led me to a vacant section at the back of the plane and seated me opposite the bulkhead where the jump seats for the flight personnel are located. Ordinarily, this would not be my favorite place to sit because any turbulence that occurs is felt more strongly in the rear section; but I knew God had arranged this private area for His purposes. My long legs were certainly grateful for the added space to stretch out and I settled in for the long flight. Not long afterward, we flew into a severe storm and the plane began to roll and toss violently. At that point, the flight attendant was required to return to the jump seat directly opposite me, where she strapped her harness and sat back to wait out the storm. If ever there was a captive audience, that was it!

As the turbulence grew more violent and the crash of thunder could be heard above the engines, my captive companion became obviously fearful and apprehensive. I began to reassure her and eventually broached the subject of salvation. As I did so, the Holy Spirit unfolded glimpses into her life that I could not otherwise have known. I told the woman what the Lord had said— that she had once been an active Christian; but over the years she had abandoned her commitment to Christ and had backslidden from the faith. Then I reminded her that her grandmother whom she dearly loved had prayed for her for a long time prior to her death and had never given up on her expectation that her granddaughter would someday serve the Lord again. Stunned and tearful, the young woman verified the truth of everything the Lord had told me.

Then the Holy Spirit gave me a wonderful revelation to share with her. "Your grandmother may be long dead, but her prayers live on; and the reason God told me to speak to you is the direct result of your grandmother's unceasing prayers which will be answered tonight." Within a very short time, I experienced the great joy of leading that "lost sheep" back to her Shepherd. Not long afterward, the storm abruptly ceased, and she went back to serving her passengers. (It's certainly true that the Lord calms storms; but sometimes He *creates* one to give one of His wayward children just enough time to come back home!)

Before we deplaned in Buenos Aires, my new friend thanked me profusely for being there at the right moment and for being obedient and faithful to share the word of the Lord and lead her back to Jesus. God's timing is always perfect!

*　　*　　*

Busy as a Bee

Australia is a truly wonderful country and is home to some of the friendliest people I've ever met. Both of my ministry tours there have been pleasant and productive ones for the Kingdom of God. The early portion of my first ministry tour was on the beautiful island of Tasmania, a short distance off the Southern coast of Australia. This particular anecdote proves that God has a wonderful sense of humor!

It happened in the last Sunday night service with Pastor Mark Crawford at his church in Launceston, Tasmania. The next morning I was scheduled to fly to the city of Adelaide on the mainland where I would be the speaker for the General Conference of my host pastor's denomination. The senior pastor in Launceston was planning to accompany me to the conference, along with several of his associate pastors. This was a large church and I had not been personally introduced to all the associates on staff; therefore I was unaware of the fact that one of the associate pastors had elected not to attend the conference because of pressing matters with his secular business.

After the sermon, many people gathered around the altar seeking further ministry and, following the prompting of the Holy Spirit, I began to call out individuals and prophesy to them. At one point, I asked one man to step forward to receive this prophetic word from the Lord: "I hear the Holy Spirit saying, *'Bizzzy, bizzzy, bizzzy!* You're too *bizzzy!'"* (I felt impressed to pronounce the word *busy* in exactly that prolonged manner and, as I did so, the congregation snickered noticeably.) Their reaction seemed a bit strange, but I went on to say, "In the United States we have a saying, 'Busy as a bee.' The Lord says that's what you are—*bizzzy* as a bee (again said with the same inflection). The Lord wants you to take more time to spend with Him. He has many things to communicate to you."

At this point, the congregation broke into open laughter and the man broke into tears. (Unbeknown to me, this man owned a very large bee farm where some of the most sought-after honey in the world is produced! International demand for rare leatherwood honey had produced rapid growth for his business and greatly expanded his business responsibilities.) Needless to say, having been thus admonished by the Lord, the man promptly cancelled his business plans and joined us the next day for the conference!

Many times the Holy Spirit uses terminology recognizable by the recipient of a prophecy, but unfamiliar to the prophet himself. In this case, it was the actual sound of a bee, followed by the terminology, "busy as a bee." Because the beekeeper knew I was not aware of his occupation, my use of these sounds and phrases captured his attention and convinced him of the validity of the prophecy.

I have also found that at other times, the Holy Spirit has been known to use carpentry and woodworking terms to a carpenter; plumbing references to a plumber and agricultural idioms to a farmer. We have examples of this in Jesus' own teaching ministry where Scripture records His frequent use of terminology familiar to His followers—fishing to fishermen and seedtime and harvest, sowing and reaping to farmers, etc. (To which we might also add: bizzzy bees to a beekeeper!)

The Missing Treasure

An elderly widow once called me with a unique request. She had heard that I could sometimes "find things for people." I agreed that the Lord had sometimes done such things through me and we made an appointment to meet. In my office, she explained that her husband of many years had passed away a short time before and had left everything to her in his will, including a large stock portfolio worth a sizeable amount of money. However, his will did not specify where he had hidden the documents, and ever since his death she had searched in vain. The woman desperately needed the funds and wanted to know if I could help her locate the securities.

When I sought the Lord, He spoke to me clearly through a prophetic vision in which I was taken to the woman's home where I had never been. I was shown a very narrow stairway leading up to an attic. At the top of the stairway, I saw a door that opened away from the staircase and into a small hallway that branched off at a right angle to the staircase. Against the far wall of the hallway, I saw a small antique trunk, inside of which I knew she would find the missing stock portfolio. A short time after our visit, the woman called and reported that she had indeed found the stocks in precisely the same location that I had seen in the vision!

The Word of God gives us scriptural validation for inquiring of the Lord through prophets when important items cannot be located. Two such incidents are referenced below which illustrate how separate prophets (*seers*) in the Bible provided information regarding lost valuables. [75]

---

[75] "But as one was felling a beam, the axe head fell into the water; and he cried out and said, 'Alas, my master! For it was borrowed.' Then the man of God said, 'Where did it fall?' And when he showed him the place, he cut off a stick and threw it in there, and made the iron float. He said, 'Take it up for yourself.' So he put out his hand and took it." *2 Kings 6:5-7*
"Now the donkeys of Kish, Saul's father, were lost. So Kish said to his son Saul, 'Take now with you one of the servants, and arise, go search for the donkeys.' He said to him, 'Behold now, there is a man of God in this city, and the man is

*　　*　　*

A Prophetic Declaration of Healing

In the early days of my ministry, I held a meeting in my wife's home church and hometown of Presque Isle, Maine. One night, a young woman in her early twenties came forward for healing. Her condition was internal, so there was no way to see any external evidence of healing; but I declared prophetically that she had been healed. Before she walked away, I discerned that she was having some difficulty regarding me as a prophet and doubted the word concerning her healing. (Personal prophecy was very rare in those days.) As proof, I told her that *precisely* at ten forty-five the following morning, a man would approach her desk and make a statement, the precise content of which I can't recall after all these years. I told her that, when she heard the man's statement, she would know that I was a genuine prophet and that she had indeed been healed.

The following night, the young woman stood to testify that her morning at work had been a busy one and she had totally forgotten about my prophecy to her the night before. Suddenly, at precisely the time stated in the prophetic word, a man had come to her desk and spoken the very sentence I had told her he would. "At that moment," she said, "I knew I was totally healed, and I've had no further symptoms whatsoever!" You can always be certain that God knows every minute detail of our lives, even before they've occurred!

---

held in honor; all that he says surely comes true. Now let us go there, perhaps he can tell us about our journey on which we have set out.' …[*the prophet declared in verse 20*] 'As for your donkeys which were lost three days ago, do not set your mind on them, for they have been found.'" *I Samuel 9:3, 6, 20* [*Author's note.*]

*   *   *

"My Parents Are My Problem!"

One night during my senior year at Zion Bible Institute, I went to the diner down the street from the campus at Three Corners in East Providence—a favorite watering hole for Zion students. (The food was good and it was cheap enough for financially strapped students!) Oddly enough, I was alone that particular night. A classmate approached my table and said he had been attempting unsuccessfully to witness to a sixteen-year-old girl seated at the counter. Aware of my prophetic giftedness, he felt that I was the one who should be talking with her. He brought her over to my table and I invited her to sit opposite me in the booth.

We talked for a short time while I attempted to discover what her spiritual problem was. Then she came up with a statement I'm sure no one has ever heard a teenager use before. "It's my *parents!* They just don't understand me!" Of course, you know I'm only kidding about having never heard that one before. It was probably the very first teenager's lament after the fall; and it's a difficult thing to dispute because the youngster saying it probably believes it to be true. (At the very least the youngsters have convinced themselves that it is!)

Suddenly, the Holy Spirit revealed to me the true nature of the girl's situation and I said, "Your parents are not your problem. Your real problem is that you're involved in a sexual affair with a married man and your parents don't approve! This sinful relationship is also the reason you won't accept Christ."[76] She lowered her head and began to sob as she asked how I had known such an intimate detail about her life. I told her that the Lord had

---

[76] "He said to her, 'Go, call your husband and come here.' The woman answered and said, 'I have no husband.' Jesus said to her, 'You have correctly said, "I have no husband"; for you have had five husbands, and the one whom you now have is not your husband; this you have said truly.' The woman said to Him, 'Sir, I perceive that You are a prophet.'" *John 4:16-19*

215

shared the real need of her heart with me because He loved her and wanted to save her in spite of her sin. Before long, she had prayed a salvation prayer and, when she left the diner that night, the joy of the Lord was reflected on her face.

*   *   *

To Heal a Church

A friend of mine, an African American brother who was pastor of a likewise ethnically oriented Baptist church, once invited me to preach their yearly conference and I was honored to accept his invitation. The opening service was held on a Sunday morning and the church was filled to capacity. People were even standing in the side aisles and across the rear of the sanctuary.

At preaching time, I thanked the pastor for inviting me and greeted the congregation with the usual introductory comments. However, as I opened the Bible to begin my sermon, the Presence of the Lord swept over me with a prophetic revelation that exposed a hidden agenda on the part of a group of people in the congregation. Through gossip and innuendo, they had planned to oust the pastor in order to gain control of the church.[77] I then pointed out one particular woman and told her to stand. As she did so, the Holy Spirit revealed that she had been the motivating force behind the conspiracy and served as its leader. In obedience to the Spirit, I spoke strongly and demanded that she come to the platform and repent to her pastor *immediately*. Sobbing convulsively, she literally ran to the platform, threw her arms around the pastor and begged for his forgiveness.

Once again the Holy Spirit directed my attention to the congregation and I said, "If I can reveal one person's part in this conspiracy, you know I can reveal the four men who are involved

---

[77] "The thoughts of the wicked are an abomination to the LORD: but the words of the pure are pleasant words." *Prov 15:26 (KJV)*

in it along with her. It would behoove those four men to repent willingly and spare themselves the humiliation of being publicly identified." Need I say that four crestfallen men quickly rose and ran to the pastor, repented and begged him for forgiveness. Come to think of it, I never *did* get to preach that morning—the remainder of the service was taken up with more personal prophecy and much rejoicing. The Holy Spirit accomplished far more in that short time than I could have done had I preached my sermon—He had single-handedly managed to clean up an entire church! (It would do well for the church of Jesus Christ to recognize the fact that we can accomplish far more by relying upon the Holy Spirit for guidance than we can by trusting in our own natural plans and abilities.)

In the following Wednesday evening service, I asked all those to come forward who had not received the Baptism in the Holy Spirit with the evidence of speaking in other tongues and who would like to receive this experience. Eighty-five people responded to the invitation, and within a few minutes, they had all received their infilling experience. That Baptist church then echoed with the voices of people who were joyously praising God in other tongues. What a wonderful night that was!

After the conference ended, the pastor told me the following interesting story. Several years before the present time, the former pastor had brought in an evangelist to conduct a week of meetings in the hope that his people would embrace the Charismatic experience. (I will not divulge the evangelist's name here, but will say only that he was then and remains today one of the world's best-known teachers in the Word of Faith movement.) At the midweek point of the services, the board called their own private meeting and subsequently shut down the meetings, dismissed the evangelist and fired the pastor!

Considering this church's past history of anarchy and resistance to authority, is it any wonder that the Holy Spirit found it necessary to move in such a powerful way during our very first

217

service? He alone realized the urgent need to expose the rebellious and divisive spirit that permeated the congregation and put a stop to the plot to drive out their godly, Spirit-filled pastor. However, the Lord did such a complete work there that, for the next two years, I was invited to return as their annual conference speaker. And what a time was had by all—this evangelist included!

On a humorous note: after a service during the second conference, one smiling woman emphatically commented (speaking in the black idiom, and accompanied by the requisite head and hand movements), "I done got you figured out!" I returned her smile and replied, "Then you've accomplished something even my wife hasn't been able to do. What is it about me that you've managed to figure out?" Her immediate response was, "You ain't nothin' but a *black* preacher, trapped in a *white* man's body!" At that, I laughed aloud and replied, "I *do* believe you're right!"

*　　*　　*

Things Aren't Always As They Seem

Following a prophetic conference in Florida, a minister friend of mine and I boarded a plane on our way home to Chicago. Although my friend was a Spirit-filled believer, the concept of personal prophecy was a new one to him, and this was one of the reasons I had asked him to accompany me to the conference. Throughout that long weekend he had observed many personal prophecies being given and, though he did not doubt their validity, yet he still entertained some reservations on the subject.

Our seats were located at the bulkhead, mine on the aisle and his in the center. A young woman in a business suit occupied the window seat and was busily working on papers, using an attaché case on her lap for a desk. She glanced up briefly only to see who would be sitting next to her, and then she returned to her work. Suddenly, I sensed the Presence of the Holy Spirit and knew He wanted me to prophesy to her.

Since we weren't yet seated, I whispered to my friend and asked him to switch seats. Knowing that I detest being in the middle seat because of my six-foot-three-inch height and large frame, he stared at me incredulously and asked why I wanted to switch my preferred aisle seat for a center one. I whispered that the Lord had a prophetic word for the woman in the window seat. Curious, he asked what the Lord wanted to say to her, and I replied, "I don't know yet; I just know He wants to speak to her through me." He shrugged, gave me one of those dubious looks to which I've become accustomed and complied. As I settled into the middle seat, the woman gave me a cursory glance and returned to her papers. Since she appeared to be totally engrossed in her work, it seemed unlikely that there would be any easy way to open a conversation without being rude.

As the plane reached cruising altitude, we gave our drink orders to the attendant. When the beverages were delivered, I passed over the soda the woman had ordered. For a brief moment our eyes met and she said, "Thank you," to which I replied, "You're welcome." (Not much in those lines to generate a conversation, is there?) Even though the paperwork remained on her tray, she took a short break to drink her soda. I took advantage of this brief interlude to ask if she was flying to Chicago on business or was she returning home. She said Chicago was indeed her home; then initiated further conversation by stating that her mother was a Roman Catholic, her father was a Muslim professor of Arabic studies at a local university and that she had opted to follow Islam instead of Roman Catholicism.

I thought it very strange that the woman would volunteer such personal information that had absolutely nothing to do with the simple question I had originally asked, but I saw my opening and said in return, "Then you must believe in Mohammed." When she agreed, I posed another question, "Then you believe

219

Mohammed was a prophet?" Again she replied in the affirmative, and I responded, "I'm also a prophet, and when I boarded this plane, God told me to prophesy to you." (I wish the reader could have seen her classic double-take at that statement!) The woman stared at me with a look of utter bewilderment and, in the silence that ensued; I asked if she would like to hear what God wanted to say to her. She hesitated for only a moment and then agreed that she would. (Most people are too curious to decline!)

The prophetic word was this: "Outwardly you appear calm, cool and collected—a professional woman who is in complete control of herself. But that's not how you are on the inside. In reality, you're a seething, boiling pot of emotion about ready to boil over. In fact, a friend recently wrote you a letter in which she stated that, if you didn't seek psychiatric help soon, you would lose your mind and end up in a mental institution."

With that, tears streamed down the woman's face and she asked, "How did you know that?" I replied, "Prophet Jesus told me that in order to show you that He loves you and wants to help you." She then put away her papers and, for the remainder of the flight, gave me her undivided attention while I revealed that Jesus was the Son of God; that He loved her and was concerned about her welfare; and He was inviting her to receive Him as her Savior.[78] Though she didn't immediately respond affirmatively; she indicated an interest in pursuing the matter and I left her in the Lord's keeping. I sincerely hope she followed through on her intention and that I will someday meet her again in Heaven

*　　*　　*

---

[78] "But if all prophesy, and an unbeliever or an ungifted man enters, he is convicted by all, he is called to account by all; the secrets of his heart are disclosed; and so he will fall on his face and worship God, declaring that God is certainly among you." *1 Cor 14:24,25*

God Has a Long Memory

It has always been a great joy to minister with my friend, Pastor Tommy Reid at The Tabernacle in Orchard Park, New York. Though I've held many wonderful services there, an experience on one particular Sunday morning proved to be another totally unique one.

The altar area was filled with approximately one hundred Sunday School teachers who were being honored that day and had come forward to receive Pastor Reid's words of appreciation and prayer of dedication. All of the ministers on the platform were standing as well when I heard the Holy Spirit say, "Pastor Reid will ask you to come and pray over one young man—but what he really wants is for you to prophesy to him. Do it, because I want to speak to him." A few moments later, Pastor Reid turned and asked if I would come forward and pray for a 21-year-old man in the group. The Holy Spirit said, "This is the one I spoke to you about."

Immediately the prophetic words began to flow freely as I prophesied of the young man's future ministry, the scope of which would resemble a great wheel with spokes spreading outward from a central hub. Each spoke represented one segment of a multi-faceted ministry. The Tabernacle was the hub and would serve as an anchor for the many different aspects of the young man's ministry assignments. The Lord indicated that, although he would repeatedly be sent out, he would always return home again to be refreshed and reassigned. The man wept while the Presence of the Holy Spirit ministered powerfully to him.

After the Sunday evening service, Pastor Reid introduced me to a woman he thought I should meet. He explained that she was the mother of the young man to whom I had prophesied that morning. It was indeed a pleasure to meet that mother and to tell her how proud she should be to have raised such a fine son whose ministry was destined to be an effective and far-reaching one. The woman nodded in agreement and smiled as she told the amazing story that follows. I will attempt to reconstruct it here as the woman related it to me.

"When you ministered here twenty-one years ago, I was nearly into my ninth month of pregnancy. You called me from the audience, put your hands over mine on my stomach and prophesied over my baby. In the words of the prophecy, you repeatedly referred to the child as my *son*. At that time, neither my husband nor I had been told the sex of our child; but the Lord knew he would be a son, and He had an important word for him. We saved the tape of that prophecy for the past twenty-one years and we listened to it again this afternoon. Every word on the taped prophecy was identical to the prophecy you delivered this morning!"

Needless to say, the three of us rejoiced together at the unerring foreknowledge of God. Because He sees the future, He can reveal details of our future lives and ministries whenever He chooses—sometimes even before we're born!

*   *   *

"By This Time" (And Not Before)

The Fremont, West Virginia area had been plagued with a three-month drought prior to our series of revival services there. Several nights into the meetings, at the end of one service the Holy Spirit swept over me and I delivered a powerful prophecy concerning the drought. The words came spontaneously, "By *this time* tomorrow night there *will* be rain! Thus says the Lord!"

When we left the building that night, my wife and I glanced up at the sky. The heavens twinkled with stars; not a single cloud was in sight and there was no indication of impending rain. As we drove toward our quarters, the weather forecast on the radio reiterated that there would be no rain in the foreseeable future. However, no matter what was observed or declared within the natural realm, we knew God had spoken—and He is never restricted by the elements or the predictions of mere mortals. He has his own ways of managing the forces of nature and His forecasts are always accurate.

At that time, I was a very young man and had never before prophesied a weather miracle, so I expected the fulfillment to come quickly. Accordingly, when I awoke the next morning, I immediately looked to see the weather outside, fully expecting to see dark clouds rolling in. Once again the sun was shining and no clouds appeared on the horizon. The weather reports throughout the day continued to repeat the same pessimistic message we had heard the night before. No clouds appeared throughout the day; the hot summer sun still shone brightly in a cloudless sky during the drive to church that evening; and the radio reports were unanimous in their monotonous prediction of ongoing drought conditions. [79]

The church building was a converted movie theater so there were no windows in the sanctuary; there was no way to look outside and watch for the prophesied rain. Before the sermon, I addressed the issue of the previous night's prophecy. I knew that, because there had been no sign of rain, that there were probably some doubts among the people. I reminded the congregation that the word of the Lord had declared the rain would come "*by this time tomorrow night.*" God was under no obligation to send rain earlier in the day because He hadn't promised to send it then. He *was* bound by His word however, to send rain by the same *time* this night. Ever true to His Word, He did just that—as we were dismissing the service, we could hear the unmistakable sound of heavy rainfall on the roof above our heads.

That night, we hurried to our cars in a drenching downpour. (My wife and I didn't own an umbrella at that time, but I found it interesting that no one in the congregation had brought one with them!) The rain was coming down so fast that you could truly say

---

[79] Read: *1 Kings 18:41-48.*

it was "pouring cats and dogs." I can verify that because I stepped over a "poodle." (I agree, that was a *bad* pun by anyone's standards! My wife says I should be *pun*ished. Where? In a *"pun-atentiary,"* of course.)

My puns may be bad, but the miracle of the rain was wonderful. To add to the miraculous nature of the rainfall, there were no clouds anywhere in sight. A glance at the heavens revealed only the presence of stars scattered across an ink-black sky. The downpour was so heavy that we were unable to drive the usual route over a dirt road to our lodging; instead we were forced to take a paved road on higher ground.

*　*　*

Judgment Must Begin at the House of God

The following incident occurred during the same series of meetings in West Virginia. The Spirit of the Lord had been powerfully moving in signs, wonders and healings every night that first week. Because of a prior commitment, the pastor wasn't able to be present during the Sunday morning service but had left others in charge of the meeting. During the fore service, a woman stood and, in a harsh and judgmental tone, she delivered what appeared to be a prophecy concerning finances.

Seated beside me, my wife felt my body stiffen, and knew instinctively that the Holy Spirit was prompting me to deal with the evil spirit prompting that illegitimate word. I stood to my feet and rebuked the offender sternly, "Sit down! That is not the Word of the Lord! How dare you prophesy out of your own desires!" (I later learned that the woman was indeed a false prophet who had been attempting to manipulate the people's financial contributions.)

When the pastor returned later that day, I explained what the Holy Spirit had revealed to me and told him how I had dealt with the situation. Not knowing the woman's name, I described her to him. He indicated that he really didn't know the woman well since she had only recently begun to attend the church and that he had no objections to my actions. (More about this at the end of our story.)

In the Sunday evening service (seven days into the scheduled two weeks of meetings), I ministered the Word as usual. A powerful time of ministry to the sick followed, but it suddenly became evident that for no apparent reason a spirit of heaviness and discouragement had descended upon the service. When I discerned this inexplicable heaviness, the Holy Spirit moved me to prophesy to the congregation. The precise words of the prophecy were, "Why are you downcast and discouraged? Lift up your heads and rejoice, for the Lord your God will *remove and replace the hindrance speedily!*"

As I finished speaking, the pastor rushed down the aisle, grabbed the microphone from my hand, and voiced his agitated objection: "What hindrance? There's no hindrance here! What are you talking about?" It was obvious that the prophetic word had touched a nerve! (Nothing in the words of the prophecy had referred to the pastor himself and, though I knew the hindrance spoken of had referred to him, I'd been given no knowledge of the reason behind it.)

The pastor's public rebuke to me continued, and he closed by threatening to cancel the remaining services if I didn't agree to preach what he wanted me to preach. I don't remember the exact wording of my reply, but I indicated that I was answerable only to the Holy Spirit and, if I would hitherto be hindered from following His directives, there was no point in continuing the services. The pastor snapped his agreement and we promptly left with our hosts without having been given our offering for the past week's ministry. (The offering had already been received, but never was forthcoming. I guess the pastor thought he could put it to better use than could this annoying evangelist!)

My wife and I had previously been invited to have dinner the following night at the home of a couple from the congregation. After dinner that evening, they had invited others from the church to come and surprise us with a baby shower (Donna was pregnant with our first child at the time). In addition to many lovely gifts, we were also presented with a generous check. Because they had somehow learned that our check had been withheld and we would be without income that week, those good people had contacted various other church members and collected another offering for us. There was no way those kind benefactors could have known that we young evangelists had no financial reserves whatsoever. We lived from offering to offering in those days, and we would have had no other way to obtain traveling funds to our next place of ministry. I'm convinced that God has a special reward for all such people who minister to the practical needs of God's faithful servants.

During the party that night, the General Superintendent of the pastor's denomination called and asked to speak with me. He asked me to explain the details of the previous night's events, but I politely declined. He asked if my reluctance was a desire on my part to refrain from hurting the pastor and I replied that it was. (I felt that God, and not I, should address any wrong done to me in His own way.) The official encouraged me to speak by saying, "You can't hurt the man any more than he has already hurt himself! The church secretary/treasurer was enamored by the pastor and she has been stealing money from her invalid mother's burial fund to give to him." He went on to say, that the mother had entrusted her savings to her daughter because she'd been unable to leave her bed and couldn't attend to her own financial needs. (It's interesting to note here that this was the same woman whom I had rebuked on Sunday morning, and the one whom the pastor had denied even knowing.) Hearing this, I then felt free to share the events of the previous evening.

The official's final statement provided complete vindication for my prophecy the night before. "For over a year," he said, "with the treasurer's help, the pastor has been stealing a thousand dollars a month from our denomination's missionary fund. We have just completed a three-month audit of his books; and today we have *removed* him from his position and will be *replacing him speedily.*"[80] The reader will note that those were the very words spoken in the prophecy.

*   *   *

"...Blessed be the LORD...according to all that He promised; not one word has failed of all His good promise..." *1 Kings 8:56*

*   *   *

---

[80] "...for you have rejected the word of the LORD, and the LORD has rejected you from being king over Israel." *1 Sam 15:26*

CHAPTER SEVENTEEN

PROPHECIES OF GUIDANCE, INTERVENTION AND FOREWARNING

In the classic sense, most prophecies by their very nature are predictive of future events. However, whether of past or future events, all prophecy is revelatory and contains details and information previously unknown to the prophet. Some prophetic utterances reveal unknown details, such as the root causes of an illness or problem; while in other cases a currently undiagnosed condition may be identified and healed through a prophetic word. Many times in my own ministry, healings and other miracles have followed all types of prophetic proclamations and some of these experiences have been included in other chapters.

One type of prophetic word however, falls into a unique category, hence the title of this chapter. In these cases, one can observe illustrations of the Holy Spirit's faithful attempts to influence the present or future course of people's lives in some important way.

*   *   *

Wisdom and Guidance for a Church Problem

On a foreign mission that spanned several countries and three continents, our prophetic team ministered in a church in Czechoslovakia. We found the people warm and receptive, though the atmosphere of the church seemed to be somewhat unsettled in ways we couldn't immediately discern. In the early part of the first service however, a member of the pastoral staff who was seated in the congregation abruptly stood and loudly declared that he and not the current pastor should be the church's rightful leader. Needless to say, this interruption caused the service to descend into utter confusion as many differing voices clamored to be heard above the others. Meanwhile, the pastor and members of our prophetic team unsuccessfully attempted to restore some semblance of order. Finally, a large contingent of people stood, gathered around the dissenting staff member and angrily left the building. Eventually the service resumed, though the situation had not been specifically addressed nor resolved. (Quite a disappointing opening night!)

We continued with the scheduled services and the Presence of God ministered to many individuals; but the pall of dissention continued to linger heavily over the pastor and his people. Families in the church were divided into opposing sides and a general sense of disunity prevailed. The pastor and his staff sought for an equitable solution to the impasse that would appease the rebellious man and his followers; but every attempt at reconciliation failed.

On the day of our departure, the pastor called a meeting of the pastoral staff (including the dissenting member) to discuss a possible solution to the problem facing the church. Our prophetic team was included in the deliberations and we were asked for our input as well. Various team members offered their best advice; but every proposal only served to produce further quarreling and disunity.

In the midst of this confusion, the Spirit of the Lord came upon me and I delivered a powerful prophetic word. Over the ensuing years I have tried unsuccessfully to recall the specific words of the prophecy, but the Holy Spirit had so dominated my thinking processes at the time that the words were spoken before I even knew what I was saying. I do recall the main directive to that church however, and if ever there was a Word of Wisdom, that was the perfect example. (I lay claim to *none* of what I said, however, for it certainly had not been of my own doing!) As the Lord began to speak through my voice, all dissention ceased and the room grew quiet and still as though in a state of suspended animation.

230

The essence of the Holy Spirit's solution to the divisive situation was that the current pastor should remain in his role and the dissenting brother should be appointed to the position of church evangelist. Immediately following this Word from the Lord, a sense of peace descended over the meeting, order was quickly restored and all parties congenially agreed to the arrangement. Through that one prophecy the future course of an entire church was determined.

*   *   *

Guidance for Undertaking an "Impossible" Task

The church building had been filled to capacity during each service of a crusade in Defiance, Ohio. Every night that week, overflow crowds had crammed into every pew and occupied all the temporary chairs set up during the services. The seating capacity of the building had long been insufficient to house the congregation itself, let alone accommodate the many visitors drawn there for special events such as our current crusade.

There were only two nights remaining when the pastor and I met in his office before the first service of those last two days. The next night's final service had been advertised as Miracle Healing Night. To accommodate the many additional people who were expected to attend that special service, the congregation had wanted to rent the local high school's large auditorium. The pastor had refused, citing lack of funds and the fact that approval by the school board would take at least two weeks. During our conversation in the pastor's office, I urged him to relent because I felt prophetically that the Holy Spirit was in favor of the proposal. I reiterated the fact that the church building would be unable to accommodate any further influx of people. Again he refused.

[I later learned that this pastor was a man of extremely limited vision. This had been amply illustrated during previous discussions concerning plans to expand the existing church

231

building. Two brothers in the congregation, the owners of a successful construction business, had generously offered to tear out the existing wall at the rear of the auditorium and build the entire addition at no financial cost to the church except for the construction materials—to be purchased at the wholesale contractors' rate! The church enthusiastically endorsed the project. However, when the pastor was asked the size of the proposed extension, the contractors were astounded to learn that his entire concept of expanding the church's capacity consisted in the addition of *only two rows of pews!* The two brothers explained that the expense of tearing out and extending the back of the auditorium to accommodate *two* rows would be the same as providing for *ten* rows; therefore, the pastor's proposal would not be cost effective. But such a practical concept was lost on the pastor who had adamantly refused to budge from his narrow perspective. Discouraged by the arbitrary limitations of such a restrictive vision, the contractors had refused to undertake the project and the congregation's plans for expansion had been abandoned.]

Just before I got up to preach that night, the pastor turned to me and said pessimistically, "All right. Go ahead and announce the move to the high school if you want to; *but it won't work!* There isn't enough time to get the school board's approval; and besides, we wouldn't be able to advertise the change of location to the public even if we *could* get the place, so *the whole thing just won't work.*"

Having thus gained his grudging approval, I told the congregation what the Holy Spirit had been saying to me; announced the new location of the following night's service; and stated that the Holy Spirit was capable of assuming full responsibility for gaining the school board's approval. This announcement met with the congregation's instant and enthusiastic approval. As soon as their applause had died down, a man at the back of the church promptly stood and stated that he could guarantee the use of the school's auditorium for our service. He identified himself as the school board's president and promised to contact the various board members by phone and secure their approval the following day.

Shortly after this exchange, another man stood and said he could arrange an interview for me on the television news broadcast the next day! In addition, he said he would sponsor an ad in the local newspaper to inform the public of the service in the new location! I didn't dare look to see the pastor's reaction to all of those astounding developments, but went directly into the sermon. The subsequent ministry time was further enhanced by a palpable atmosphere of faith and anticipation.

True to his word, the school board official did indeed obtain the necessary approval. The television news program on which I had been scheduled for a short interview drew such enthusiastic response from the public that people were calling the station with questions and the director kept signaling the news anchor to stretch the interview. As a result, the "short" time I had been given was greatly expanded until the remainder of the news time was taken up with my interview! (I was later informed that the station's switchboard had remained busy with incoming calls long after the program ended!)

Because of the newspaper ads and unexpected television exposure, even more people came that night than had been expected, and a capacity crowd completely filled that large auditorium for the final service. Just as the prophetic word had promised, God did indeed move in miraculous ways. The worship service was filled with an exceptional sense of the Holy Spirit's Presence; the sermon was enthusiastically received; several people came to the Lord; and many others received healing miracles. All in all, a fitting finale to a wonderfully blessed crusade![81]

---

[81] To read of an outstanding phenomenon that also occurred that night, see Chapter Thirteen, *Extraordinary Experiences.*

*   *   *

Guidance for a Lifetime Career

I was reminded of this story during my recent time of ministry at The Tabernacle in Orchard Park, NY (a community within the Buffalo area) and I asked for a written account of the details to be used in this book. The recipient of this particular word of prophetic direction was a dynamic woman, Mary Lombardo, the administrative assistant for Pastor Tom Reid. To conserve space, her experience has been encapsulated here, but is based upon her own words.

Following her graduation from Bible College, Mary had married and started working in the daycare center of her home church in upstate New York, Rochester Christian Center. Shortly thereafter, she had been asked by Pastor Stephen Galvano to serve as his administrative secretary. Although she enjoyed secretarial work immensely and was well equipped for the position, she had been reluctant to accept it because her entire purpose for having selected a bible college education had been to prepare for a career in some type of ministry. She had diligently sought God's will because she was uncertain whether or not He considered secretarial work to be a legitimate form of ministry. It was at that time of indecision that I came to minister at the church.

Following the Sunday evening service, Mary came to the altar to earnestly seek a word from the Lord concerning His will for her life. While I was praying with others around the altar, she received a vision in which her hands appeared to have been made of gold. The Lord indicated to her through this means that her administrative and secretarial skills were the gifts and talents He had given her and confirmed that it was indeed His calling into that form of ministry.

I was totally unaware of any of this divine exchange and, as Mary continued to kneel in awe of God's Presence, I laid my hands on her head and began to pray and prophesy. My words confirmed what she had just heard in her Spirit—that God had given her special gifts and she was to use them in service to the senior shepherd of that church. Following her own confirmatory vision and the prophecy that followed, she would never again question her unique form of ministry calling.

Mary faithfully served Pastor Galvano in Rochester for over seven years until the family moved to Buffalo, where the Lord opened a door for her to assume administrative duties for Pastor Reid. To this present day, she continues to pursue her calling with expertise, passion and dedication and, as of this writing, she has ably served in the same (albeit greatly expanded) position with Brother Reid for the past twenty-five-plus years.

*　　*　　*

"Jesus Will Reveal Himself to You"

My wife and I were driving home from vacation when I suddenly realized the fuel level was quite low and I turned off at the next exit. As we left the highway, we saw two service stations just ahead on opposite sides of the road. I started to turn into the more convenient one on the right, but the Holy Spirit stopped me and indicated that I was to go to the one on the opposite side. I've learned not to question Him, so I pulled over and began to refuel. No sooner had I inserted the hose when, from my position facing the roadway, I saw one car collide with another from behind. Both cars stopped and I ran over to offer assistance.

I quickly observed that the driver of the offending vehicle appeared dazed but unhurt, so I moved on to the other. Behind the wheel of the first car, the woman driver was sobbing and repeating, "Why did God allow this to happen?" She appeared to be uninjured, though the rear of the car was damaged and I could see she was greatly distraught. Sliding into the seat beside the woman, I sought to calm her until the police could arrive. Observing that a

Bible lay on the seat between us, I said, "I see you have a Bible with you. Are you a Christian?"

The woman then began to reveal that she was a follower of certain celestial entities and doctrines I knew to be elements of the New Age Movement. She went on to say that recently she had become greatly interested in Jesus Christ and had purchased a Bible to see what she could find out about Him.

The Holy Spirit impressed me to tell her that this intense desire to seek information regarding Jesus had been imparted to her because Jesus loved her and wanted to convince her of that fact. I then prophesied that if she would sincerely ask Jesus to reveal Himself to her, He would come to her in dreams over the next three consecutive nights. This would be a sign to her that He loved her and wanted her to commit her life to Him and disavow the New Age teachings. When the woman had sincerely promised to do so, I prayed with her. As soon as I finished praying the state police arrived.

While the officers filled out accident reports, I asked what had taken them so long to come to the scene. They responded that the police barracks was very close by, but they had been dispatched to the location of another accident and it had taken considerable time to return. Inwardly I rejoiced because had they arrived sooner, I would not have been able to converse at length with this seeker. The Lord had detained them just long enough to enable me to reach out and reveal His great love and concern for that one woman.

*   *   *

An Unhealthy Relationship

I recently heard an example of the ways in which the Holy Spirit has often used me to deliver prophetic guidance to someone whose circumstances I had not previously known. A nurse in my physician's office told the following experience to me while I was there for a routine checkup.

We had met for the first time two years before, when she had first started working in my physician's practice. At the time of our initial encounter, she and I had engaged in pleasant conversation during which I had inquired if she were a born-again Christian. She had enthusiastically replied that indeed she was. Though I knew nothing about her life, I sensed a strong prophetic anointing and knew I had a word for her that the Lord wanted me to deliver.

I revealed that her current pastor was a woman who had been exerting a pronounced negative influence in her life. In order for her to continue to advance in her Christian life, the Lord was directing her to quickly and completely distance herself from this destructive woman before she succeeded in destroying her potential for future ministry.

She said those words had made a profound impression on her at the time, so much so that she had begun to discern the pastor's ulterior motives and the unhealthy influence she had been upon her life. She had subsequently distanced herself from the pastor, found another church and seen her own ministry develop and grow.

Since joining her present church, she had been given full responsibility for the children's ministry. In addition, she had been allowed to organize and lead an entirely new ministry for the women of the church, something that particular body of believers had never done before. The weekly meetings had been enthusiastically received and she excitedly told me that even unsaved women were beginning to attend. She thanked me profusely for having been faithful to deliver the words that had helped to change her life dramatically and had freed her to grow into her present ministry.

*   *   *

An Ill-Fated Engagement

During a service in California in the very early days of my ministry, I delivered a prophetic word to a lovely young woman who was seated in the congregation. As usual, she and the details of her life were completely unknown to me. Her hands were folded in her lap and I would have been unable to observe an engagement ring had she been wearing one; but I spoke to her about her recent engagement to a young man who was totally unsuitable for her, especially in view of her Christian lifestyle. The prophecy warned of future devastation and heartache if the engagement was not terminated and an unwise marriage was entered into. After the service, my hosts commented that they had recognized the young woman, though she was not a member of their church. They knew her to be the daughter of another local pastor, but they had no further personal knowledge concerning her life, whether or not she was contemplating marriage or the identity of the fiancé.

The following day, another church member reported having seen the same young woman slumped dejectedly under a tree on the front lawn of her parents' home. She had appeared to be in distress and was weeping profusely. They had surmised that her obvious agitation was no doubt due to the difficult decision thrust upon her by my prophecy.

Several days later, my ministry partners and I were treated to an outing at a local tourist attraction. At some point during the day, we observed the same pastor's daughter in the company of a young man who was well known to our hosts. The young couple was smiling and talking animatedly as they walked hand in hand, their romantic relationship quite obvious to all observers.

Our hosts exclaimed that they now understood the gravity of the prophecy she had received. The young man's father was an extremely wealthy and prominent businessman in the area. It was common knowledge that his influence had rescued his son from frequent arrests, the result of several drunken driving incidents and a history of alcoholism and extensive drug use. It appeared that the young woman's fateful decision had already been made; and with a heavy heart, I knew that future disaster would be the result. I remember praying at the time that there would be a later change of heart and I have often wondered whatever became of that young woman who had been so clearly warned at that crucial crossroad in her life.

*   *   *

Forewarning for a Troubled Marriage

I once visited a church where I had only been once before. The service was enjoyable but something about the young couple in the pew in front of me repeatedly demanded my attention in the Spirit. There appeared to be nothing out of the ordinary about either one of them, but that unsettled feeling deep inside kept recurring. That particular sensing usually means something is amiss; and I instinctively knew that theirs was a marriage in deep trouble.

Immediately following the service, I approached the pastor, explained that I had a prophetic insight regarding the couple and requested his permission to minister to them. Since I had no knowledge whether or not their marriage had been the object of previous counsel, my desire was to deliver the Word of the Lord in his presence and that of any other staff members who may have been involved with their situation. He agreed and shortly thereafter the pastor and his two associates (husband and wife) accompanied the young couple and me to a nearby conference room.

As I looked into the young man's eyes, I said, "You are not without fault in this unfortunate marital situation, but you are not the primary reason this marriage is in imminent danger. I'll deal with your issues when I've finished speaking to your wife."

I faced the wife and the Holy Spirit laid her soul bare as our eyes met. His revelation knowledge instantly enlightened me and I said, "You have falsely represented to others that your problems with your husband are the major obstacle in your marriage; but that's not the truth. Your unhappiness and discontent stem from the fact that you are having an affair with a man from your past. He has recently returned from another state and you are seriously considering leaving your husband to continue the relationship with your lover on a permanent basis. I see the man in a vision; and in this vision I can see him in the act of strangling his mother nearly to the point of death. God is warning you that this man is not as he represents himself. Furthermore, the Lord is admonishing you to dissolve this adulterous affair at once; remain with your husband and children, and preserve your marriage."

The young wife broke down in tears and admitted that everything I had prophesied was the truth. Her former lover had indeed recently returned from Texas and had seduced her into believing that a life with him would be far better than marriage to her husband had been. She admitted also that the man had once become overwhelmed with rage and had attempted to strangle his mother. She agreed to break off the illicit affair immediately and begin to seriously work with her husband to solve their marital problems.

At this point, the Holy Spirit directed me to issue another prophetic note of caution: "Your problems can be worked out and this marriage can be saved. However, if you leave your husband for this man and fail to fulfill your promise to the Lord, you will find yourself in a desperate situation. Your lover will attempt to strangle you as he did his mother. You will find your life spiraling out of control; and in the end you will lose not only your husband and your marriage. You will lose your lover; you will lose your children; you will eventually lose your mind—and you will end up in a mental institution. Thus says the Lord!"

Then I turned to the husband and enumerated several (mostly minor) areas in his attitude toward and treatment of his wife that he would need to change. When I named each item as they were revealed to me prophetically, he readily acknowledged fault in those areas and agreed to work diligently to change each one. (I later became better acquainted with the young man and had occasion to observe him closely as he diligently attempted to change his behavior and restore his marriage.)

At the time I delivered the prophecy, I was unaware that the couple had previously been counseled by one of the associate pastors present, a woman who had been the victim of an abusive husband during a prior marriage. Because of her history of victimization, this pastor had always tended to side with the wife in situations of marital conflict; and she had previously done so in this case as well.

During a counseling session that following week, despite having heard the stern words of the prophecy and witnessed the wife's own confession of guilt, the associate pastor declared emphatically that she herself had not borne witness to anything I had said! Therefore, there was no need for the young wife to heed the prophetic word. She completely ignored the existence of the illicit affair; instead, she reiterated her contention that the husband was the sole problem area in the marriage and the wife needn't assume any fault for the situation. That was a perfect example of *personally tainted* counsel! It opened the door for the young wife to continue her sinful behavior, and she did so. Her adulterous involvement progressed until she eventually took the children and abandoned her husband in favor of the lover.

This sinful relationship led to an increasingly sinful lifestyle. The young woman soon became addicted to alcohol and drugs and her lifestyle became an increasingly violent one. As the children later reported to their father, the couple had sometimes engaged in sexual acts in the car with the children present. At other times, she had left the three youngsters in an unheated car during bitterly cold weather, while she and her lover frequented bars and crack houses. When police discovered the children's situation and rescued them, their father reclaimed them. (The state of Illinois rarely removes children from the custody of their mother; however, after reviewing the circumstances of the case, the state awarded sole custody of the children to their father.)

Despite having lost her children, the woman's downward spiral continued, until her lover ultimately did attempt to strangle her as he had his mother. At that point, she finally crashed into the wall the Holy Spirit had foreseen; and she was committed to a mental institution. Tragically, the words of the prophecy were fulfilled completely. The young wife had failed to listen to and heed the prophetic word she knew to be true. Her insistence upon finding encouragement in the counselor's contrary words had cost her *everything*, As a result of her disobedience, she had indeed lost her husband, her lover, her children and her mind! Such a needless tragedy!

Footnote: Sometime after these events, the husband re-married. His bride, a lovely Christian woman has been a wonderful wife and loving mother to his children. At last report, they were all serving the Lord and active in their church. The pastor/counselor, who had grievously damaged the situation because of her own past history of abuse, left the ministry sometime later following her husband's death from cancer. I have never learned the ex-wife's ultimate fate; but I sincerely hope she eventually repented and was restored to the Lord.

*   *   *

A Prophetic Warning for Repentance

In the very early years of our marriage, our first pastorate was of a church in a small town some thirty miles northwest of Baltimore, Maryland. When we had been there less than a year and the church had grown substantially, we called in an evangelist to conduct a week of meetings. The services were all marked by an overwhelming sense of God's Presence. During one service in particular, the entire congregation stood to its feet and burst into exuberant expressions of praise. At that point, the evangelist abruptly left the platform and went to the side of one young woman in the congregation, a member in my church who was in her early thirties, and began to prophesy with obvious intensity.

I could not hear his exact words from my position on the platform, but I simultaneously delivered a prophetic word to the same woman. The prophecies were nearly identical, as I later learned from the evangelist. The gist of both was that there was an extremely urgent need for repentance on her part. As both prophecies were being given, I had the distinct impression that this woman's very life depended on her obedience.

Suddenly, the young woman grasped her chest and, as she uttered a cry of pain, she bent over until her head touched the pew in front of her. When she straightened up, she seized her coat and purse and ran from the building. I remember thinking that she had made a terrible choice, for I knew in my spirit that life and death were literally hanging in the balance for that woman.

Considering the atmosphere of loud and exuberant praise that existed among the people at the time of the prophecies, I felt certain that not many people had heard what had been said and, if they had heard they could not have known the sense of dread I shared with the evangelist. The atmosphere of rejoicing continued even while the evangelist preached his message.

As we were preparing to dismiss the people, the woman returned and stood at the back of the church. She requested permission to speak and then addressed the congregation. The woman confessed that she had been circulating false rumors among the members concerning the pastoral leadership and she asked for our forgiveness and that of the congregation. Needless to say, we gave it instantly and the people nodded in agreement as well. She revealed that, when the prophecies had been given, she had distinctly felt the hand of the Lord squeezing her heart in His hands. Simultaneously, she had seen a vision of herself in a coffin and heard the words, *"By morning, if you don't repent!"* She said the reason for her abrupt departure from the service earlier had been because the first people to whom she had voiced her falsehoods had not been in church that evening, and she felt a need to go to their home first and repent.

Not satisfied with her collective confession and repentance, the woman remained at the door and, as the members left the church, she asked them individually for forgiveness. Rarely have I seen such a genuine display of repentance! Not long after that eventful night, the same young woman received the Baptism in the Holy Spirit and became one of our staunchest supporters and a faithful worker in the church!

*   *   *

Tonight is the Night

The following incident took place during a crusade in Caribou, Maine. Following a salvation message I had invited unsaved people to come forward to accept Christ and many people had come. Despite this response to the call, the Lord kept drawing my attention to one young man seated between two friends toward the back of the auditorium.

During the sermon I had found it necessary to reprimand the three and ask them to refrain from their disruptive behavior.

They had done so, but had retained their obviously amused and disdainful expressions throughout the message. It was obvious that all three were probably not serving the Lord, yet I felt a particular sense of urgency concerning the youth sitting between the other two.

Following the Holy Spirit's prompting, I sat in the pew in front of the young man and turned to personally address him. I told him it was imperative that he make a decision for Christ before he left the church that night. I pressed the point and could see he was under conviction and secretly wanted to respond; but he kept glancing toward his friends, unwilling to face their disapproval. With a growing sense of urgency, I told him that when he stood before God, there would be no one else standing alongside him; he had been given no assurance that tomorrow would come and he alone could determine his eternal destiny. I reiterated the Lord's word to me that his decision needed to be made that very night. Despite his obvious inner conflict, the youngster smirked and told me he would accept the Lord at some future time—at his own convenience. His flippant remark was, "I'm going to sow my wild oats first!" With that the three left, the young man basking in the approval of his companions.

During a later time of ministry at another church in the area, a young woman approached me after one service had been dismissed. I recognized that she was a Christian I had met at some time in the past and knew to have come from a very large family. Though she had served the Lord for years, most of her siblings had continued to be resistant to the Gospel. With a somber expression and many tears, she related the following story to me.

A short time after the previous crusade in Caribou, her younger brother (the young man I had unsuccessfully attempted to bring to a decision for Christ) had joined a group of friends for a night of drinking and joyriding. Driving much too fast, they had been involved in a devastating accident during which their car had collided with a huge tractor-trailer. The force of the impact had wedged their vehicle under the cargo box and decapitated the occupants. They had all been instantly killed with no time to repent and accept the Lord! I was then reminded of the urgency with which I had delivered my prophetic invitation and was deeply saddened at the realization that this young man had resisted his final opportunity for the sake of approval from his peers. I knew those same friends would not be at his side when he faced His Lord—and he would have an endless eternity in which to regret his rash decision.

*   *   *

A Very Different Outcome

During the same Caribou crusade on a different night, I had been seized by the same sense of urgency and had personally extended a salvation invitation to the teenaged son of a deacon in that church. He likewise had been seated with friends. But, unlike the young man in the previous narrative, he had hesitated only slightly before tearfully surrendering to the Holy Spirit's irresistible call to accept Christ. He had been genuinely saved that night and later received the Baptism in the Holy Spirit.

When I returned to the area sometime later, I was told that, following this young man's conversion, he had become active in the church and been chosen leader of the youth group there. Later that same year, he had attended a church gathering at a popular recreation area. Sometime during that day, his body had been discovered face down in only a few inches of water. The coroner's report concluded that his death had been accidental, caused by a previously undiagnosed heart malfunction that had rendered him unconscious. In that helpless state, he had fallen into the water and drowned.

The unexpected death of one so young is always overwhelmingly tragic for all concerned. However, because he had obeyed the Spirit's call that fateful night, the boy's parents could be filled with hope. In spite of their grief, they carried the expectation of someday being reunited with their son in Heaven!

* * *

An Alarming Forewarning

After one crusade at The Tabernacle in Orchard Park, New York I arrived at the airport only to be informed that my scheduled flight was overbooked and the desk clerk was calling for volunteers to reschedule on a later flight. To those passengers who were willing to wait for the next flight, they would refund their ticket price and give a fifty-dollar voucher toward a future flight. Never one to miss a bargain, I quickly volunteered and settled down to wait the mere forty-five minutes until the next flight.

Observing people has always been an interest of mine, so I occupied myself during the interim by watching people. (Take it from me, a lot of very interesting people pass through airport terminals!) Out of the group of passersby that morning, my attention was particularly drawn to two nearby airline employees, a handsome young man and a lovely young woman. They were working at separate stations a short distance apart, but I noticed that the man frequently directed smiling glances to his attractive co-worker who also smiled in return. Before long, he approached her and the two began to talk. At this point, I became aware of an overwhelming sense of foreboding and a future scenario unfolded prophetically within my spirit.

When the two parted, I approached the young woman. I was uncertain what her reaction would be—after all, I was a complete stranger. (No doubt she would think me *very* strange, indeed!). Despite the fact that my words constituted an uninvited intrusion into her life, I was driven by the urgency to warn her of the impending danger I had seen.

After introducing myself as a minister, I explained that sometimes God told me different things about people. Then I asked if she would allow me to tell her what God had said concerning her. (It has been my experience that most people are too curious to refuse the offer.) She looked dubious and somewhat apprehensive, but she agreed to hear me out.

I said that she and the young man to whom she had been speaking were friendly acquaintances; but they also found each other romantically attractive and he would eventually ask her for a date. I warned her not to accept the invitation because it would end badly. I said the young man would not have planned anything other than a pleasant evening, but at some point he would make sexual advances toward her and she would refuse. He would further press the issue and, when she continued to rebuff him he would be overcome with rage and rape her. Afterward, fearing exposure, the man would then strangle her to death.

Seeing the young woman's shocked and incredulous expression, I apologized for the ugliness of this revelation of future events. Nevertheless, I had been compelled to alert her to the seriousness of the situation. Once again I urgently warned her not to accept a date with that young man under any circumstances.

As I boarded my flight, I had no way of knowing whether or not she would heed it, but was relieved that I had delivered the warning. It was clear to me that the Lord had rearranged my flight times in order to allow the opportunity to deliver His message; and I prayed earnestly that the lovely young woman would take the situation seriously and avoid putting herself in the position of having caused her own tragic death. Through the years, I have often been reminded of that encounter and wondered about the outcome. Regardless of the outcome, I am certain of one thing—I had faithfully obeyed the voice of the Lord and discharged my responsibility, both to God and to the young woman in this true story.

*   *   *

A Closing Word of Instruction and Explanation

The overwhelming evidence of Scripture teaches that the *Gift* of Prophecy has been given to the Church at large and enables *all* Christians to share words of encouragement, edification and exhortation with individuals or with a body of believers. However, it's important to note that the pronouncements of one who functions in the *Office* of Prophet can be and often are far more extensive in scope and influence. They can foretell future events; prophesy direction into lives, churches and other ministries; and forewarn of dangerous situations or outcomes that affect Christians and non-Christians unlike. There have been countless instances in my life in which I have functioned in all of these and other areas of prophetic influence, the details of which have been too numerous to record here or even to retain in memory. The accounts I have given above and in other chapters of this book have been representative of instances when circumstances were such that I have been able to vividly remember them over the years.

*   *   *

CHAPTER EIGHTEEN

INSTANCES THAT REVEAL
GOD'S SOVEREIGNTY

We serve a sovereign God! The Word tells us that and we claim to believe it; but what does the word *sovereignty* actually mean to the average believer? The fact is that most Christians haven't the faintest idea of the immense scope of that word as it applies to God. Basically, the word *sovereignty* means, "to be in absolute control—to do as one pleases without consulting the masses"—thus the title *sovereign* is used when referring to kings and queens; and it was especially so in ancient times, when royalty could call for a subject's execution with no legitimate reason other than the ruler's own desire.

We've heard so much teaching about the "free will" of man that we have forgotten that God has His own agenda, one in which our free will sometimes has no place. There have been three times in my life when I have experienced the true meaning of God' sovereignty, and I will relate them here for the reader's consideration. I have already recounted my experience of having sovereignly received the Baptism in the Holy Spirit despite my objections; so I won't repeat that particular incident here. Suffice it to say that God Himself had His own timetable for my life and ministry and He wasn't going to allow my reluctance to delay His agenda for my life and ministry. Scripture specifically speaks to this issue: **"Our God is in the heavens;** *He does whatever He pleases."* Ps 115:3 *(Emphasis mine.)*

* * *

Here I Come—Ready or Not!

Some years ago, while based in the Chicago area, we conducted weekly teaching meetings in a friend's home in Indiana. (We later relocated to the area and moved to a rented building. Eventually we bought property and established The Oasis Praise and Worship Center in Osceola, Indiana.) The weekly attendance in the original house location grew until every room on the main floor was filled to capacity. Many of the people who attended these house meetings were from a large community church in the local area. They came because they were hungry to learn about the Holy Spirit and supernatural things; and many of them subsequently received the infilling of the Spirit.

One evening, one of the associate pastors from the hosts' community church was sent to find out what we were teaching in our meetings. When the he came forward during the ministry portion of the service that evening, I laid my hand on him and prophesied, "The Holy Spirit is going to light your fuse tonight!" At this, the man fell to the floor—all six feet, four inches of him. As he fell, he began to speak in tongues.

He lay on the floor for quite some time, speaking in his newfound heavenly language. When he rose to his feet, the expression of joy on his face was one I will never forget. Shortly thereafter, because of this supernatural experience, he was summarily discharged from his pastoral duties at that evangelical church. He subsequently founded a charismatic church in another community some distance away. True to His Word, God had sovereignly "lit the man's fuse" that wonderful night— without consulting him in the least!

*   *   *

Filled With the Spirit—Attitude and All

At the conclusion of my sermon at a Chicago church, I called for those who desired to receive the Holy Spirit Baptism to come forward for prayer. The altar area was filled with seeking people, but the Lord directed my attention to one woman in particular. Nothing about her physical appearance would have elicited the prophetic word that I gave to her.

"Although you have come to the altar to receive the Baptism in the Holy Spirit, the Lord is aware of your inner attitude. You have sought the Holy Spirit many times before this; but whenever you come to the place in your seeking where you must yield yourself completely to Him, you adopt *this* attitude (to illustrate, I folded my arms across my chest in a gesture of defiance and assumed an insolent expression). At that point," I continued, "You absolutely *refuse* to surrender to the Holy Spirit."

Immediately, the woman folded her arms, planted her feet in a resistant stance and adopted a disdainful facial expression. To further emphasize this insolent attitude, she nodded her head in agreement and said abruptly and with deliberate emphasis, "That's right!"

Undeterred by her attitude, I opened my Bible and asked, "Do you know the meaning of the word *sovereignty*?" The woman didn't change her defiant expression as she voiced a negative response. I then read the third verse of *Psalm 115*: **"But our God is in the heavens;** *He does whatever He pleases (emphasis mine).*" With that, I declared, "I've just read about the sovereignty of God. Now you are going to experience the sovereignty of God. *Be filled with the Holy Spirit!*" Immediately, the woman fell backwards, threw her arms above her head and began to speak in other tongues! *"That,"* I said to her and to the congregation, *"is the sovereignty of God!"*

When I spoke with the same woman after the service, the radiance of the Holy Spirit was evident in her face and reflected in the warmth of her words. She told me she had genuinely desired the Holy Spirit Baptism for a long time; but she had felt an inexplicable compulsion to refuse the infilling, even at the very point of receiving it. She thanked me for obeying the Spirit and allowing the Lord to illustrate His sovereignty—even over her own objections.

*   *   *

A Reluctant Conversion

I once was invited to preach at a campground somewhere in Pennsylvania, the name of which evades me now. In the midst of one sermon there, I left the platform, walked back for several rows and stopped to prophesy to a sixteen-year-old boy who was seated on the aisle beside his mother. The prophetic word to the mother was, "God has seen your faithfulness and the deepest sorrow of your heart. He has also heard your fervent prayers for your son to be saved. Because of your faith for your son's salvation, the Lord is about to grant your deepest desire. *This day*, your son will be saved!"

The young man smirked his disdain for God's words as well as for me. Then he folded his arms across his chest in the classic gesture of defiance and shook his head emphatically in denial. His stubborn attitude had no effect on me because I knew what the Lord had determined to do. I smiled at him and quoted *Psalm 115:3* with emphasis, **"But our God is in the heavens; *He does whatever He pleases!*"** Then I repeated the Lord's prophetic declaration, "Today, son, you *will* be saved."

I returned to my sermon and, needless to say, the lad maintained his rebellious attitude throughout the message. Outwardly, he hardly presented the appearance of someone who was even remotely contemplating a decision for Christ. However, I can truthfully say that outward attitudes have never moved me—only the word of the Lord moves me. Whatever He says will absolutely come to pass, despite man's best (or worst) intentions. No sooner had I given the invitation to accept Christ as Savior, when that same young man quickly responded. He immediately raised his hand, leaped from his seat and hurried down the aisle. We met at the altar and wept together while he sincerely repented of his sins and surrendered his life to Christ. From her vantage point on the aisle, his mother also shed tears of joy.

After the service, mother and son told me the following story. The boy had been incarcerated for a grand theft auto conviction. Once a month, his mother was permitted to take him out of jail for one day on a release program. On that particular day, she had chosen to bring him to our service. Her rationale was that, if he saw miracles take place, perhaps that would convince him of the power of God and of his own need for salvation. The Holy Spirit knew it would take a sovereign act of God to move the young man toward salvation—and that unlikely prophecy was precisely the instrument He chose for the boy to witness (and be involved in)!

Following their narrative, I invited the young fellow to join me for a man-to-man talk. We sat for a long time under a large shade tree as we talked and laughed together, while I instructed him in the way to live out this new life he had just entered into. Because the Holy Spirit moved sovereignly that summer afternoon in Pennsylvania, a new name had been inscribed in the Lamb's Book of Life and a young man had been delivered from a possible future life of crime!

*   *   *

Out of all the thousands of miraculous works I've seen thus far in my ministry, these three instances have been the only purely sovereign acts of God I have witnessed. That having been said, the reader should understand that occurrences of a sovereign nature are extremely uncommon. The Word teaches, and my own experience has borne out, that God much *prefers* to intervene in the affairs of mankind in *response* to man's free will choices. He does not *generally* impose His will upon us. I confess that I know very little concerning God's reasons for choosing to move in such sovereign ways. All I *do* know for certain is that, however rare and unusual these instances may be, our God has reasons that are known only to Him. Whenever He displays his sovereignty, He does so because "our God is in the heavens; He does *whatever* He pleases!"

> **"The secret things belong to the LORD our God, but the things revealed belong to us and to our sons forever..."** *Deut 29:29*

*　　*　　*

CHAPTER NINETEEN

CONFRONTING THE OCCULT

It has long been my earnest conviction that the present-day Church has been guilty of shirking its duty in opposing and confronting the errors of occultism in general and spiritism in particular. The Word clearly gives mature, Spirit-filled Christians the power to take on the enemy on his own ground, but the church at large has been reluctant to assume its rightful place in the so-called religious world by exposing and opposing error. This is not to say that I in any way approve of ill-advised attempts by the immature Christian to take on spiritual powers beyond their own depths of growth. It has been my experience that many such Christians have forged ahead in a spirit of bravado and been spiritually wounded because they were not adequately prepared. In fact, I caution new believers against this very thing until they are fully confident of their scriptural rights and indwelling power. Also, since fear is always the enemy when confronting occult powers, one must be fully convinced of the indwelling power of the Holy Spirit and free from all fear before attempting *any* voluntary confrontation with the enemy. That having been said, I invite the reader to vicariously share some of my own forays into the world of spiritual darkness.

*   *   *

Which Witch is Which?

During the period of my life when I was engaged in a counseling practice on the North Shore outside of Boston, I became a member of a professional group. The group, composed of psychiatrists, psychologists and medical doctors, met once a month at a function room in a downtown hotel, and featured a different guest speaker every month. (One month they even asked me to speak. I guess they couldn't find anyone else that time—

smile!) With very few exceptions, I found the meetings and the speakers as well to be boring, so after a year I stopped attending.

Some months later, I received a phone call from a good friend and fellow member of the group who asked if I would be attending the meeting that night. He said two very unusual and exciting guests had been invited to speak and he thought I would be interested in going. When I asked who the speakers were, he told me the members hadn't been informed of their identity; but the officers had promised that the meeting would be different than any other one we had ever attended. My friend prevailed on me to join him and, when he said we could leave and go for pie and coffee if the meeting wasn't as advertised, I agreed to go.

The guest speakers were not in the room during the brief preliminaries (probably to prolong the mystery). When they were brought in and introduced, they turned out to be a husband and wife team who were both practicing Wiccans—witch and warlock. It wasn't difficult to discern which witch was which (smile), because the former was female and the latter male. The warlock was a tall, handsome black man in his mid-thirties and his wife was an extremely ugly Caucasian woman in her mid-sixties. As if the contrast in age and physical appearance were not strange enough, their manner of dress added to the impression. The man wore black slacks topped with a short red velvet jacket over a bare chest. The woman was clad all in black and looked exactly like the caricatures often used to portray witches in cartoons. She was snaggle-toothed and sported a large hooked nose complete with a wart on the tip—*honestly!* The only items missing were the pointed hat and broomstick.

Our meeting room was long and narrow and we were seated around a very long, wide conference table, which could accommodate thirty people. When I saw the speakers and realized what they represented, I started to rise and leave the meeting but the Holy Spirit emphatically commanded me to stay. Though I couldn't imagine His reason, I obeyed and sat back down.

The warlock removed his robe, lit a bundle of very thin candles and called for the lights to be extinguished. As he passed the candles over his bare chest and under his armpits, he chanted a repetitious and meaningless refrain, impossible to duplicate here in print. I nudged my friend and whispered, "Everyone thinks he's chanting, but he's really moaning, 'Oooo, this hurts!'" My friend simply shook his head and smiled at my attempt at humor. Once again I prepared to leave, and again the Holy Spirit told me to stay.

Following the man's ritual, the lights came back on, as did his velvet jacket. He turned to a doctor seated to his right and began to psychically reveal personal details about the man's life. The doctor nodded in confirmation and appeared to be spellbound by the warlock's words.

I was seated almost directly across the table from where the warlock was standing and could closely observe every part of the performance. The Bible clearly states that God alone should be privy to such knowledge,[82] and I was sickened by this unholy incursion into God's exclusive territory. Then, prompted by the Holy Spirit, I moved into action as the warlock continued speaking.

I smiled "innocently" and, feigning an expression of rapt attention; I silently invoked the power of Jesus' blood and bound the demons who were operating through the warlock. Immediately, the man's eyes crossed and he began to adopt a sing-song manner of speech, while he flailed his arms aimlessly in the air and continued to repeat a series of nonsense syllables. The member who had booked the speakers quickly whisked the man from the room, but they soon returned and the warlock appeared to have recovered.

---

[82] "The secret things belong to the LORD our God, but the things revealed belong to us and to our sons forever, that we may observe all the words of this law." *Deut 29:29*

As he began to address the next person, a doctor across the table from me, I again assumed an interested attitude and prayed silently. "Get him again, Lord!" I said, gleefully. Instantly, the man's eyes crossed and he once again began gyrating and repeating the same meaningless phrase in the warbling manner he had used before. This time as he sang, he picked up the portable tape recorder and repeatedly attempted to plug the microphone *itself* into the jack opening! (He had really stepped outside the realm of reality.)

Seeing the man's irrational actions, his wife began to address the audience in an obvious attempt to divert them from her husband's bizarre behavior and regain their attention. As soon as she began to speak, her husband began to loudly object in the same warbling, sing-song voice, "Don't you listen to her—she's lying to you!" He repeated the phrase over and over; and once again, he was taken quickly outside the room and never did return. The witch attempted to resume the psychic readings, but again I bound the spirits and the meeting was hastily adjourned. There would be no more "revelations" or "predictions" given to their gullible audience that night!

Afterward, I spoke with the member who had booked those two stellar performers. Feigning ignorance, I asked him what had happened to cause such a reaction on the warlock's part. He looked around carefully so no one within earshot could hear his response. "Knowing your background as a man of God," he said, "I know *you* will understand. A bad spirit got control of him; a *really* bad spirit took over and he couldn't operate." I smiled and replied knowingly, "I *do* know what you mean."

When confronted by the power of the Holy Spirit, all occultists would say that a "bad" spirit had taken control over them. From a demonic viewpoint, the Holy Spirit would be the biggest, "baddest," meanest Spirit of all![83] When He comes on the scene, He puts an end to occult practitioners' shameful actions and makes fools of the whole lot in the process. The outcome of that night was certainly "one more for the Good Guys"—Father, Son and Holy Spirit, that is!

*   *   *

It is my unwavering conviction that God wants His Church to exercise *full kingdom authority* over satanic forces whenever and wherever they are encountered. Furthermore, I am firmly persuaded that the Church should not wait for an overt attack; instead, Christians should become the aggressors, by attacking Satan's territory and bringing it down under their feet. Too many Christians possess *church-anity*, whereas the awesome power of God resides in *Christianity*. If more Christians began to seriously read and apply the principles of the Bible, they would come to the realization that what Jesus did, *we* can also do—in His name! I've always maintained that my ministry is not an extraordinary one. It simply reflects one man's earnest attempt to follow the Holy Spirit's leading and live out the promises of God to the best of his ability. Signs, wonders and miracles have followed simply because of that determination.

Of course, I'll admit to experiencing a distinct sense of elation when an attack on Satan's stronghold results in seeing demonic forces scurry away like roaches when the lights are turned on! In the midst of such situations, I must outwardly maintain a serious, emotionless expression; but my spirit-man is leaping for joy because Satan is suffering another defeat.

Since the Bible says we have been given control over demons through the Holy Spirit Who lives within us, I contend that

---

[83] The seventy returned with joy, saying, "Lord, even the demons are subject to us in Your name." *Luke 10:17*

Christians should be more actively engaged in shutting down spiritist services and churches. (As stated elsewhere in this book, I will not use the term *spiritualist* when referring to such organizations. They are spiritual only in the sense that they operate exclusively in the area of the *human* spirit, and are often in league with *demonic* spirits.) The following is an account of one such encounter in a spiritist church. Although entirely true, the story is somewhat humorous so, while reading it, don't be afraid to smile! Fasten your seatbelts and join me in reliving a wonderful victory for the Holy Spirit, the Word of God and the blood of Jesus.

*   *   *

"There's a *Bad* Spirit in this Place!"

My wife and I and our five children once lived in beautiful, seaside Beverly, Massachusetts, in a sixteen-room, historic Colonial home built in 1845 by a sea captain named Joseph Wilson. We loved the house, situated just two doors removed from the ocean. Because the third floor rooms were unoccupied except for occasional guests, we had invited a young seminary student to live in one of the rooms free of charge in exchange for occasional housekeeping duties. Ruth was a delightful, Spirit-filled young woman who later went on to teach and minister alongside her husband.

My mother, who was a powerful woman of God and a pastor in Brooklyn, New York once came for a visit, during which one of our group conversations evolved into a discussion of spiritist churches and their activities in our area. We talked about their impact on those who were unsaved and vulnerable; and considered the responsibility of Christians regarding such satanic incursions into our territory. We were convinced that Christians had the right to stop such activities. Accordingly, I asked if they would like to join me in attending a spiritist church service and exercising the power of the Holy Spirit against their occult practices. Of course, both women enthusiastically agreed.

262

We determined that, if we exercised the authority of the Word of God and the power of the blood immediately upon entering the building, we would witness nothing, because they would be altogether unable to operate and would shortly have to cancel the meeting. Thus, we agreed upon an alternate plan of action. We would attend looking like average seekers. We would not appear disapproving or critical and would do nothing to reveal our true identity as infiltrating agents from God's forces. I advised my compatriots to look interested and curious, the way tourists would appear to be on their first visit. We would allow the spiritist reader (*a.k.a. fortuneteller*) to function as usual until I glanced in the direction of my companions and winked an eye. That would be the signal to begin *silently* bringing the power of Jesus' blood to war against the enemy.

On the day of the service, we three "innocent tourists" arrived and found seats midway down on the center aisle. Three spiritists had been scheduled to perform psychic "readings" for random attendees that afternoon, most of which would concern themselves with communications from deceased loved ones. [Spiritists and fortunetellers often play upon the hurts, regrets and neediness of gullible people; and it has been proven that people who seek contact with the dead have such a great longing for that communication that they will manipulate any charlatan's words to suit their own particular needs.]

The senior pastor of the church walked to the podium and opened the service. She selected a person from the congregation and began to deliver a message—supposedly from the person's dear, departed mother. The spiritist reader then delivered the following message, "Your mother forgives you for the disagreement the two of you had and says she still loves you and wants to communicate with you." (Since I can't remember their exact words, I have used a typical one here; because who hasn't had a disagreement with a loved one at sometime during their relationship?) Upon hearing the supposed "accuracy" of the spiritist's words, the daughter burst into relieved tears and enthusiastically confirmed the authenticity of Mama's message, supposedly delivered from somewhere in *The Great Beyond*.

At that point, I glanced over at my two co-conspirators and gave the signal, whereupon all three of us silently began to plead the power of the blood against the spiritist. Immediately, the woman pitched forward so violently that her face struck the podium. Feverishly mopping her brow, she said, "There's a *bad* spirit in here and I'm unable to contact the spirit world any longer." Her eyes then locked onto mine and she said, "There is a *very bad* spirit here!" With that, she sat down and signaled her assistant to take over the session.

The second spiritist assumed the pastor's place behind the podium and proceeded to deliver another nonsense message from beyond the grave, such as, "Your favorite Uncle Joe remembers you well and sends you his love. He says he remembers the afternoon you went on an outing with him. He wants you to know he's so happy here in paradise." At that, Uncle Joe's niece tearfully expressed undying gratitude to the spiritist for contacting her uncle. [Sometimes spiritists and psychics actually *do* contact spirits—*evil* spirits, who became familiar with the dead people in question at some point during their lifetimes. In those instances, spiritists are able to give names and describe past experiences.] We then allowed the reader to continue on briefly to the next person; and again she demonstrated her ability to communicate with spirits.

When we'd seen enough of her sickening charade, I directed a fleeting glance at my compatriots and gave them the signal to silently plead the power of Jesus' blood. It would not be an exaggeration to say that the woman immediately pitched forward, struck her face and fell over the podium, frantically struggling to recover her breathing. Glaring directly at me, she stated, "There really *is* a very bad spirit in here today, and I can't go on any longer." Chuckling inwardly, I wrote a quick note and passed it to Mom and Ruth—*Two down; one to go!*

Needless to say, the events that followed our confrontation with the first two women were repeated in exactly the same way with the third reader, a man. At that point, the pastor, who had recovered her faculties somewhat, stood and announced that it was impossible to continue; regretfully, therefore, she would be forced to adjourn the service. As she made the announcement, the pastor glared malevolently at me. Without breaking eye contact, she added, "Somehow a very bad spirit has gained entrance to our service today, and we are no longer able to maintain contact with the spirit world." Actually, what she had termed a *bad* spirit was the always-*good* Holy Spirit. In a spiritist practitioner's opinion, the Holy Spirit *would* be considered very bad for their activities, because evil spirits are rendered powerless whenever He is present!

*   *   *

Two "Tourists" Take on a Spiritist

Following our Sunday morning service at a church in Crystal Lake, Illinois, the pastoral staff treated my wife and me to dinner at a local restaurant. In conversation during the meal, I related the previous story and concluded with the declaration that demons have absolutely *no* power when believers exercise their God-given right to bring God's Spirit to bear against occult practitioners. Dave, the associate pastor was greatly excited by the prospect and expressed his desire for the two of us to attend a psychic fair being held that day at a nearby motel. I excused myself on the grounds that I had exerted a lot of energy in ministry that morning and was eager to get home.

When Dave left the table briefly, my conscience spoke clearly through a very familiar voice. "He's just a young man who's eager to practice the very thing you've been talking about.

Why don't you just go with him?" Knowing that my conscience would probably not let up, I reluctantly agreed to go. Incidentally, my conscience has a name—*Donna*—and looks and sounds uncannily like my wife. (*Smile!*)

When Dave and I arrived at the location of the fair, we were disappointed to learn that there was a two-dollar entrance fee. Neither of us was willing to support those occult activities, so we stood outside the open doorway to the function room. On a tripod at the door was displayed a large sign on which each psychic's picture and area of expertise were given. For example: *Clairvoyant, Tarot Card Reader, Spiritualist*, etc. The Holy Spirit had seen to it that the individual billed as a "spiritualist" was seated at a table on the opposite side of the room, directly facing the doors where Dave and I had taken up our position. We chose her as our target.

I took Dave aside, away from the woman's view, and told him that distance couldn't hinder the Holy Spirit's power in the least. Therefore, it wouldn't be necessary for us to pay the entrance fee, because we could exercise God's power from where we stood outside the ballroom. As we walked back to stand in front of the open doorway, I told Dave to assume a curious tourist's demeanor and innocently survey the entire room. The plan was to be careful not to look directly at the target of our warfare, because it wouldn't be necessary to look directly at her in order to accomplish our goal. The signal was the word *now*. When I said it quietly, we both began to silently plead the power of Jesus' blood; all the while, we gazed randomly around the room and didn't appear to be concentrating on the spiritist practitioner at all.

The results were nearly instantaneous—the woman appeared visibly shaken and began to choke and gasp for air. She fell forward over the table and frantically mopped her brow while she struggled to catch her breath. Within moments, several of her fellow psychics gathered around to assist her; but the woman remained in acute distress. Finally, she rose to her feet and,

266

assisted by her companions, she walked unsteadily toward us, her face flushed with the effort.

From the moment she raised her head from the table, the woman fixed her gaze on the two of us. As she came toward the doors, she continued to glare at us with an expression of absolute hatred until the moment she passed by, a few feet away from our position. Although we had given no outward sign that could have connected us to her weakened condition, the spirits within her were obviously well aware of what we had done; and their resentment and loathing were reflected in her eyes. Needless to say, she never returned to the fair, which concluded a short time later.

Consider how many spiritist services, séances and psychic fairs could be shut down if Spirit-filled believers invaded those meetings and prevented demonic powers from operating in their presence! If such Holy Spirit-inspired interference were to persist over long periods of time; we could reasonably assume that the majority of the gullible public would soon lose confidence and stop seeking those services altogether. How many people would continue to put their confidence in psychic and spiritist practitioners if they were unable to contact Dear Departed Mother, Precious Aunt Blanche or Generous Uncle Dunkle? And how many impressionable people would visit fortunetellers or tarot card readers if they were hindered from revealing secret desires or foretelling future events, real or imagined? Just think of the multiplied victories that could be won by "ordinary" Christians, if they dared to invade the enemy's strongholds with the awesome power of the Blood!

CHAPTER TWENTY

WHEN INANIMATE OBJECTS ARE INHABITED BY DEMONS

The media of our day seem to be obsessed with the subject of paranormal activity and reports of "ghosts" play a prominent role in television programming. In fact, several popular television shows, both fictional and so-called "reality shows" have been devoted to this topic. In general, the fictional programs are based on popular myths propounded by psychics, mediums and occult practitioners of all sorts. The reality-type programs are devoted to investigating the concept of "haunted" hotels, homes, cemeteries, etc. For the most part, investigators, psychics and the general public alike subscribe to the theory that these unexplained occurrences are the actions of restless spirits—the spirits of persons long since dead. This conclusion is usually arrived at because some traumatic event is known to have occurred at the location in question and it is therefore believed that the place is "haunted" by the "ghosts" (spirits) of those people involved.

While it cannot be disputed that some such unexplained events *have* occurred in the past (and still do), the notion that they are caused by the spirits (ghosts) of those who have died cannot be substantiated in either Old or New Testament scripture.[84] Therefore I cannot subscribe to the belief that such strange occurrences are *ever* the work of the dead people's spirits themselves, no matter what the circumstances of their deaths may have been. In many such instances, the unexplained activity can be attributed to the presence of demons. Sometimes evil spirits

---

[84] "...It is appointed for men to die once and after this comes judgment."
Heb.9:27

   "For the living know they will die; but the dead do not know anything..."
Ecc.9:5

assume the appearance of known dead people and thus are able to convince the gullible that their ghosts really do exist.

That having been said, there may nevertheless be some validity to the theory that not all such "psychic" phenomena are the result of occult or demonic activity. Certain traumatic events may have been somehow imprinted on the atmosphere of a particular location simply through some unknown process of energy transference[85] not yet fully understood by modern science. As a prophet, I have often been in places that carried an aura of tragedy and sorrow from sometime in the past, though no evil presence was discerned in those particular locations. Possible *natural* reasons behind these sensations of past tragedies are best left to future scientific investigation and are not a major focus of this book.

The fact that some phenomena *may* be the result of unexplained natural forces in no way negates the established fact that demonic entities *do* sometimes inhabit inanimate objects and buildings. Examples of these are well documented throughout the annals of Church History; and there are numerous recorded instances of early church fathers who have confronted evil spirits within various inanimate objects of worship as well as within the pagan practitioners and followers themselves. I have had numerous personal experiences with confronting evil spirits who had taken up residency in inanimate objects. Three such instances have been recorded here for the reader's consideration.

*   *   *

"It's Coming From the Attic"

I was once asked to investigate a "haunted" house whose owners had been victimized by repeated mysterious and

---

[85] Kirlian photography experiments involving electrical force fields were conducted and well documented during the 1960s and '70s. These scientific studies explored this possibility with some measure of success.

frightening circumstances. The family had purchased a beautiful 1880's house and had lovingly restored it to its former splendor. However, the fear generated by these so-called "hauntings" had nearly driven the family from their home and they lived in a constant state of apprehension. When I arrived at the house, I became immediately aware of a malignant presence there. I made it clear to the owners that I believed any unexplained event that caused anxiety and fear was the direct result of demonic activity and not the actions of some benign entity. I asked that I be given no advance description of past events so I could be free to follow the Holy Spirit's guidance alone.

The man of the house agreed to my request and, as he led me through the rooms, my sense of demonic activity was a general one. However, when we reached the master bedroom, it immediately became obvious that malevolent forces were concentrated there in one particular area of the room. As we advanced into the comfortably warm room, I suddenly encountered a distinct pillar of bone-chilling cold that had no discernible source. When I mentioned it to the man, he said that he and his wife had originally placed their bed against that wall because it was the farthest one from the windows. However, they had always been cold in the bed, no matter how many warm quilts they had used to cover themselves. In addition, they had been frequently awakened during the night by a moaning sound and the sensation of being slapped on their faces. Often their covers had been abruptly torn from the bed; and this combination of events had prompted them to move the bed to the opposite wall. The manifestations in the room had become somewhat diminished, but the cold spot on the opposite side of the room had never gone away.

As I stood in the center of the frigid area, I sensed that the origin of the demonic presence was centered in the attic directly above the spot. I described the appearance of an old trunk stored there and the Holy Spirit showed me that the trunk contained a knife somehow connected to the source of the mysterious events. I had not been told of an attic prior to this time, but when I told the man what I had been shown, he admitted that the family never went up to the attic anymore because of fear. He said that he had carefully inspected the area at one time, and had seen a trunk above that part of the bedroom. However, he assured me that he had searched its contents and had found no such knife inside the trunk or anywhere else in the attic. While there, he had been made aware of an evil presence and the bedroom manifestations had increased in intensity during the days that followed.

The man refused to accompany me, but I ascended the attic stairs knowing I would be able to find and destroy the source of the family's torment there. The attic was mostly empty except for an old trunk lying on its side over a frigid spot in the center of the room. It was obvious to me that the man of the house had hastily abandoned his previous search, because various articles of very old clothing were still heaped inside the trunk and scattered on the floor around it. I removed several pieces of clothing and other debris and, at the very bottom of the trunk, covered loosely in an old ragged cloth was a small cheese knife with a wooden handle and short, curved blade.

Instantly the Holy Spirit showed me that the present site of the master bedroom had, at one time during the past century, been the original family's spinster daughter's sewing room. Having lost her beloved fiancé through tragic circumstances, she had descended into a state of severe depression. Her grief had finally overwhelmed her to the point where she had sat in that room and attempted to slash her wrists with the very knife I held in my hand. Though the attempt had been unsuccessful, she had remained in a state of melancholy and depression for years until the time of her death. Unchallenged, the demonic spirits of grief, hopelessness and suicide had thereafter attached themselves to the intended instrument of suicide and had permeated the entire house.

As I continued to hold the knife, I rebuked the demons within the implement and forbade them to inhabit either the knife or the house ever again. When I returned to the apprehensive man waiting in the bedroom, he was shocked to find that the cold spot had completely dissipated and a sense of calm had spread throughout the room. I asked if I could take away what was now simply a humble piece of kitchen cutlery, so he would never again be reminded of the family's torment; and he readily agreed. Subsequent reports revealed that the family never again experienced another demonic manifestation

*   *   *

The Angry House

After the morning service one Sunday, a young couple from the church asked to see me. They had an important request concerning their two small children, a boy and a girl who were five and eight years of age. This couple had previously brought their children for prayer because they were unusually temperamental and vacillated between periods of calmness and sudden rages verging on hysteria. After prayer, the children had experienced relief from the violent mood swings; however, they were now unable to fall asleep most nights until long after midnight. The children shared a bedroom and, as soon as they were tucked into bed, they would become fearful and agitated and would cry until the parents took them from the room. Sometimes it would be hours before they were able to fall asleep and be returned to their beds. As a result, the entire family had been unable to receive adequate rest and they were exhausted and frustrated. The couple had come to suspect that there might be a demonic presence in the house that was influencing the youngsters; so they asked if I would come to the house and deal with the unwelcome spirits. I impressed on the parents the importance of not sharing their suspicions with the children lest they become unduly frightened; and we made plans to meet at the house during the following week at a time when the children would be at school.

The family occupied a very old house, one that had been in the wife's family for many years. Throughout most of her childhood she and her mother had lived there with the girl's grandfather; but it had never been a particularly happy home. Although she and her mother were Christians, her grandfather had been a bitter alcoholic who was prone to sudden moods of rage. As a result, the house had always been in a state of upheaval and strife; and the young woman had left home at her earliest opportunity. Upon the grandfather's death, the house had been left to her mother who lived elsewhere. She in turn had invited the young family to live there free of charge.

When I arrived at the house I was shown into the children's small bedroom. As soon as I entered, I became aware of a demonic presence that seemed to come through the floor and radiate upward. When I told this to the parents, they remarked that the basement below had always been a musty and foreboding place where no one wanted to venture. Instantly I had a picture in my mind of what the basement looked like. The room was basically a storm cellar with dirt walls and floor; but in one corner there was a crude concrete slab over a portion of the floor directly under the children's bedroom. The demonic force was centered in that area and I now knew why that location had been chosen for demonic habitation and I told the young couple what I had seen.

The Holy Spirit told me that sometime in the past, someone had been murdered in the basement. The body had been buried in the dirt floor and concrete had then been poured over the grave to conceal the crime. Because of the extreme violence with which the act had been committed, a demonic presence had attached itself to the site and taken up residence there. Since I was now certain where the demonic presence was centered and why it was there, I asked to be shown to the basement.

As I descended the stairs, the stench of evil confronted me and grew increasingly stronger as I walked toward the wall on the far side of the basement. However, it took only moments to confront the demon and cleanse the area through the Holy Spirit's anointing. As I spoke the words of rebuke, I knew for certain that the demonic presence had been banished from the house and been forbidden to ever return. Instantly, the prevalent aura and stench of evil dissipated and was replaced by an atmosphere of peace.

The man and wife had steadfastly refused to accompany me to the basement and had remained standing apprehensively in the doorway to the stairs. When I came back up through the door, I could see the expression of stunned amazement on their faces. They said that, within a short time of my being in the basement, the children had returned home from school and begun to play quietly in the completely changed atmosphere of the house. We then prayed together and committed the home into the Lord's care.

We can only guess at the havoc the demon had caused in the past; but it's highly likely that the ongoing strife in the wife's birth family could be directly attributed to its malicious influence. At the present time, the demon (as is true with any conquering force) had first sought out the most vulnerable family members to attack. By victimizing the defenseless children, he had been able to caused turmoil for the entire family.

I wish I could say that the concrete slab was subsequently broken up and the past crime revealed; but to the best of my knowledge that has never been done. Of one thing I am certain, however—the devil's malevolent influence was never again felt in that house to this present day.

*   *   *

The Church Building That Harbored Demonic Forces

A pastor friend once told me of the difficulties he had encountered in his efforts to shepherd his people. The congregation was mired in apathy and resistant to any attempt on his part to bring about meaningful spiritual change. He had become increasingly discouraged and suspected that his congregation had fallen victim to some type of collective demonic influence.

In response to my friend's invitation, my son Eric (also an ordained minister) and I met with him one afternoon in the empty church building to seek a word from the Lord. It was a lovely sanctuary and at first nothing seemed amiss. As we ascended to the platform, however, an aura of evil seemed to hover over the entire area. My son walked to one of the platform chairs beside the pastor's central one. He said the man who usually occupied that chair was not what he appeared to be and his presence in leadership had caused a spirit of sexual deviance to permeate the congregation. Aghast, the pastor exclaimed that the man in question was the associate pastor in charge of the Sunday School and Youth Group in the church.

Because the Holy Spirit was impressing upon me that the basement rooms were especially infested with malevolent spirits, we then went into the lower portion of the building. As we toured through the various rooms, the sense of evil remained, but was concentrated in one particular room. By the Spirit I knew that children had been molested in that room and the perpetrator had been the man revealed on the platform. The pastor had been totally unaware of the man's predatory actions but was determined to confront him at his earliest opportunity. Together we bound the demonic force within the room as well as the entire church and then returned to the sanctuary.

The pastor was visibly shaken by our encounters with evil forces and, as we sat together in a pew, he shared something he had not previously revealed to us. He said that never before had he pastored a congregation where sexual problems had been so prevalent. Among them were perversions of all sorts—from illicit affairs to instances of incest even within extended families. In fact, sometimes one sinful behavior in particular had often recurred within the same family throughout several generations. Several of his members, while not personally involved in sexual sin, had been victimized in the past and still carried the emotional scars.

My friend had prayed with and counseled his flock faithfully; but the situations had remained firmly entrenched and seemed impervious to his godly counsel; and he had never felt that lasting victory had been achieved. He was greatly encouraged and felt that permanent change could now begin.

*   *   *

CHAPTER TWENTY-ONE

DELIVERANCES FROM DEMONS

"The seventy returned with joy, saying, 'Lord, even the demons are subject to us in Your name.' " *Luke 10:17*

The ministry of demonic deliverance (exorcism) is one of the most misunderstood of all the operations of the Holy Spirit. Of course, most Christians are well aware that Satan is constantly oppressing the unsaved with demonic activity. However, many Christians today are unwilling to accept the fact that demons also sometimes work within the body of believers itself. As a result, there is widespread oppression in the church today and Christians are largely unaware of it. On the other hand, we have those of the opposite persuasion—the ones I like to call the "spooky spirituals" or "granola Christians" (*nuts, fruits and flakes*). These believe that demons are *always* directly responsible for *every* adverse experience that occurs in the lives of Christians and unbelievers alike. As a result of this doctrinal error, many unfortunate people live in fear of the enemy and are constantly attacking nonexistent demons within themselves and others.

This chapter will not deal with the doctrinal issues associated with the subject of demon possession and/or oppression. Since the intent of this book is to encourage the reader by simply sharing my own personal ministry experiences, we will not devote additional space herein to deal with this misunderstood subject. Suffice it to say that I have encountered more than my share of demons, many of whom have attacked God's own people through a variety of methods. Subsequent to each of these encounters with demonic entities, the demons were gone and the person and I were still standing, none the worse for wear. Despite the inevitable outcome of each confrontation,[86] evil spirits will still try to resist eviction through the use of vocal threats or acts of intimidation—and sometimes both. The first account in this chapter is a humorous example of this type of demonic challenge.

*　*　*

The Duel of the Dads

One long service and ministry time were over (or so I thought), when the pastor asked if I would pray with one more person, a woman seated in the front row. When I asked her the nature of her need, she immediately began to manifest a demonic presence. The demon, distorting the woman's voice and facial expressions, snarled at me like an animal and declared that I didn't have the power to cast it out.

Somewhat sarcastically, I responded to this challenge by asking, "Well, who are *you*?" My adversary responded arrogantly, "I'm a son of Satan." Perhaps momentarily reverting to my native Brooklyn vernacular, I replied firmly,[87] "Well, *I'm* a son of God—and *my* Dad can lick *your* dad any day in the week! Come out *now*!" And it obeyed—immediately! The moral of this story is: *When confronted with a demon, just remember Who your Dad is!*

*　*　*

The "Michelin Man"

Among my many encounters with demons, one of the most dramatic events occurred during a service in New Jersey where I was engaged in conducting a crusade. A young wife had received

---

[86] "Behold, I have given you authority to tread on serpents and scorpions, and over all the power of the enemy, and nothing will injure you." *Lu 10:19*
"…greater is He who is in you than he who is in the world." *1 Jn 4:4b*
[87] Speak softly, but carry a very big stick—the Cross!

Christ during an earlier service and had reported this to her husband, a gang member whose vicious and violent lifestyle had earned him many sworn enemies. This justifiable fear of imminent nighttime attack had driven him every night to place a fully loaded sawed-off shotgun under the bed while he slept.

The news of his wife's conversion had been received scornfully and dismissed as being of no importance to his own life. At that time, Joe was a former bodybuilder and winner of the "Mister New Jersey" competition. He had been stricken with a rare and incurable disease that had caused his previously fit, muscular body to bloat to such proportions that he was barely recognizable, hence the nickname "Michelin Man." His sinful lifestyle and bloated appearance had produced a state of constantly simmering rage and his wife and two young daughters lived in a perpetual state of fear and dread, never knowing what his mood and actions might be at any given moment.

In desperation, Joe's wife Beverly had begged him to attend one of the services and receive prayer for a healing miracle. Despite his scornful attitude, Joe's woeful physical condition drove him to reluctantly agree and he was in attendance one night when I called for people to come forward who were candidates for the Baptism in the Holy Spirit.

As the seekers were coming forward, Joe suddenly bolted from his seat and strode down the aisle loudly repeating a demand to receive the Holy Spirit. Instantly I recognized the presence of demons and, knowing the man had no idea what this appeal was about, I approached him and said, "Sir, you have a demonic problem and the Lord wants to set you free tonight."

No sooner had I spoken, when Joe began to snarl at me and growled, "I said I wanted this Holy Spirit thing you're talking about!" When I repeated that Jesus wanted to deliver and save him before he could receive the Holy Spirit, his features contorted with rage and he became violently aggressive. Arms outstretched, he charged directly toward me shrieking, "I'm going to kill you!"

When he was mere inches away, he came to an abrupt halt. As he raged on, Joe began to claw frantically at some invisible barrier that had been erected between us. As he did so, several burly ushers struggled to maintain a firm grip on him in order to protect me. I stood calmly with arms at my sides and commanded the ushers to release the demonized man because he would be unable to harm me. The men reluctantly complied and, just as I had declared, despite his persistent frenzied attempts he was unable to advance any further.

When I called on the Name of Jesus, Joe collapsed to the floor, writhing and blaspheming while I commanded the demonic spirits to depart from him. As one by one they obeyed, Joe's anger dissipated, the screaming ceased and his body relaxed. I then led him to Christ and prayed for his healing.

Immediately, Joe's entire countenance changed to one of joy and amazement and he slowly rose to his feet while he watched the progress of his healing taking place before his very eyes. His grossly bloated body began to shrink to its natural contours as it became normal once again.

As the healing progressed, Joe's facial features and the joints on his swollen fingers became recognizable. The congregation erupted in jubilant praise, but God still hadn't finished His work! The Lord then honored Joe's previous request, spoken in ignorance and out of spiritual desperation; and He gloriously filled him with the Holy Spirit. As Joe poured out his joy in unknown tongues, God also called him into a life of ministry!

Following his astounding night of miracles, Joe began to devour the Word and became an ardent and effective witness for Jesus. After a time of spiritual growth and preparation, he and his family traveled in evangelism for several years, preaching the Word and singing for the glory of God. Eventually, Joe and Beverly established a ministry to the poor in their city and founded a church. We have kept in touch occasionally throughout the ensuing years and I am happy to say that the former "Michelin Man," his wife and daughters have all remained steadfast in the faith and in dedicated service to the King of Kings. Joe and Bev's remarkable story will forever occupy a cherished place within my memory.

*   *   *

The "Church Demon"

Some years ago, we began a two-week series of services with Pastor Elsie Shryock at the Foursquare Gospel Church in Greencastle, Pennsylvania. The first three meetings on Sunday, Monday and Tuesday had been blessed by the Presence of the Holy Spirit in a marked way. The Lord's anointing had rested heavily upon me and on the entire congregation. Before ministering the Word of God each evening, I had spent a long time calling out sicknesses and various afflictions, operating freely in the gifts of prophecy, the word of knowledge and healings. Following each divine revelation, the individuals received their healings; and a spirit of praise dominated every service. As we continued to observe the Holy Spirit at work, we had no reason to believe that such an atmosphere wouldn't be maintained throughout the remainder of the services. We were in for a rude awakening, however.

Then came the night (which I refer to as "Black Wednesday") when an intense display of demonic activity was unleashed on the service. The foreservice followed the familiar pattern of the previous three nights and I began to call out symptoms and specific ailments as the Holy Spirit revealed them to me. People were being instantly healed while still seated in the pews and we rejoiced in God's wonderful Presence. Suddenly, in the midst of this divine visitation, everything came to a halt when it seemed as though the Holy Spirit abruptly lifted from me and departed from the service altogether.

Unable to comprehend what had caused this change in atmosphere, I bowed my head and silently prayed for God's wisdom and discernment. As I did so, the Holy Spirit turned me around physically until I faced the rear wall of the platform. My spiritual eyes then observed the reason for the Spirit's interrupted flow.

Standing before me was an eight-foot-tall demonic entity encased entirely in a black, hooded garment. His head was bent over mine and his shrouded arms were wrapped around my entire body in an attempt to cut off my sensitivity to the Holy Spirit. I looked up into the hood of the shroud where a face should have been, but no face was visible—only the presence of intense darkness and evil. (I was reminded of one of Satan's titles, *Prince of Darkness*.) The situation was evocative of hell itself, and indeed hell was represented in its full fury!

There was no time to explain to the congregation what I had seen in the Spirit. I placed my hands against the area of the entity's chest and propelled it backwards. Utilizing the authority of Jesus' Name, I commanded the demon to leave the building and I thrust it through the wall. Prompted by the Holy Spirit, I ran to the front door of the church, stepped outside into the cold, November night and commanded the demon to never, ever darken the doors of that church again! Obviously, my statement was a rhetorical one, because any spirit capable of passing through a wall could also enter a building without using a door! A spiritual barrier *was* required however, and that barrier was erected through my God-inspired command. When I spoke the words, the demon instantly obeyed, gathered up its shroud and hastily departed.

When I returned to the sanctuary, cries of "I'm healed! I'm healed!" rose from the congregation, accompanied by names of the various conditions from which they had been delivered. After the enemy's retreat, the anointing returned and remained throughout our remaining days in that church. (When the two weeks were over, we discovered that more people had been healed in that one meeting than in all the other services combined!) I guess you could say the Lord had more than met the enemy's challenge to that church—and to this prophet.

Later that night, Donna and I enjoyed a time of fellowship at the pastor's home. Because I was the only person who had visually witnessed the details of the encounter, Pastor Shryock asked me to describe my experience. I was hesitant to give details because many Spirit-filled Christians, even some who are involved in ministry, don't believe in the existence of demons or in demonic manifestations of any sort, especially in church. When the pastor saw my hesitation, she told me she already knew what the hindrance had been and was simply seeking confirmation from me. As I related the details of the incident, the pastor nodded in agreement.

When I finished my narrative, Pastor Shryock revealed the unusual events that had occurred in the Wednesday service prior to the opening of our crusade. When the congregation gathered for that midweek service, a spirit of hostility and division arose between various church members to such an extent that the pastor had felt compelled to cancel the upcoming services. She had explained to the congregation that to expose an evangelist to such an atmosphere of disunity and division wouldn't be fair. As she had spoken that night, a divine conviction of sin swept over the congregation, accompanied by a powerful spirit of repentance. One after another, various members began to openly confess to sins they had committed against their brethren and cries of genuine repentance were heard throughout the sanctuary. Then, as abruptly as it had begun, the spirit of conviction departed from the service and confusion spread rapidly throughout the congregation.

Suddenly, one woman stood and requested permission to address the issue at hand. She then described in great detail a demonic entity she had just been shown by the Holy Spirit. The malevolent entity had been clothed in a black shroud; it's head bent over the pastor's and its arms holding her body tightly. At that very moment of demonic manifestation, the woman reported that the anointing for reconciliation had abruptly ceased. In response to this revelation, the congregation had entered into a time of intense prayer and spiritual warfare. By the time the service ended, the members had received a measure of spiritual relief; and once again they began to anticipate the upcoming services. There was a general sense of hopefulness that God would perhaps bring further insight and deliverance through the evangelist. We rejoiced together that the people's hopes had not been misplaced. The Lord had indeed banished the evil spirit that had been assigned to destroy their church!

*   *   *

The Issue of Demonic Deliverance Among Christians

Before we proceed further, allow me to clarify an important fact concerning the term *demon possession*. Many Christians believe it is impossible for a Christian to be demonically possessed. I heartily subscribe to that belief, since one cannot truly be "possessed" by two masters (Jesus *and* Satan) simultaneously. While there are many instances in scripture where individuals are described as being tormented by demonic spirits, the term *demon possession* is never used. Neither does the term *possession* convey the true scriptural meaning of demonic activity, especially when it pertains to Christians. In actuality, a more accurate term would be *oppression*. That is, "to be tormented, driven by, under the control of or physically sickened by" an evil entity.

When a Christian does manifest symptoms of demonic activity, it is usually due to some sin or weakness of character in their life through which an evil spirit has gained access to their thought lives and influenced their subsequent behavior. Bear in mind that, when an oppressed Christian manifests demonic activity during the process of deliverance, whether it be vocal (growls, curses, threats) or physical (facial distortion, flailing, writhing, etc.), it isn't the person who is saying or doing those things. Rather, the demon that has taken control of their mind is trying to prevent the exorcism from taking place. When subsequently delivered from the offending entity, the person is freed from their bondage and the manifestations cease to occur.

Throughout my decades of ministry, the Holy Spirit has used me as an instrument in delivering many otherwise fine believers from various types of demonic oppression. It is important to remember that Jesus never castigated the tormented ones. Instead, He focused His attention on delivering them from demonic bondage and restoring them to normalcy so they could then live their lives in dedicated and fruitful service.[88]

*   *   *

Delivered From Asthma

The following story involves one young Christian's lifelong affliction. The boy was genuinely saved; he loved God deeply and served faithfully in the New Jersey church his father pastored. The congregation had just completed construction of a new sanctuary that seated in excess of one thousand people, and I had been scheduled to hold a two-week evangelistic campaign that began on the evening of Dedication Sunday. On one of the subsequent nights as I ministered to the sick, this seventeen-year-old youngster came for prayer. He had a severe asthmatic condition that had begun in infancy, and he was desperately in need of a healing miracle.

---

[88] Please read *Mark 5:1-20.*

When the young man came before me for prayer, I discerned that an evil spirit had caused the asthma. (This is by no means true of every mental or physical affliction, but sometimes demons may be the root cause, and only the Holy Spirit can discern when that is the case.) When I commanded the demon of asthma to leave his body, the boy fell to the floor and the demon began shouting out foul curses that I will not repeat here. Within a few moments, the demonstration ceased and a peaceful expression appeared on the lad's face. Not only had the demonic bondage been broken, but he had been totally healed from the asthma that had plagued him throughout the seventeen years of his young life.

After the service, the youngster's father steadfastly refused to believe that it had been possible for his son (or any Christian for that matter) to have been tormented by a demonic spirit. (Unfortunately, ministers are often rigidly bound by their doctrinal prejudices—and despite all evidence to the contrary, this pastor was so influenced.) After I had completed my ministry there, he repeatedly defended his viewpoint from the pulpit and frequently expressed his opposition to that aspect of my ministry.

As an apparent consequence of this man's refusal to believe the word of the Lord and the physical evidence apparent in his own son, he who had never exhibited asthma symptoms became seriously afflicted with the disease. Sunday after Sunday it became necessary to frequently pause during his sermon, turn his back to the congregation and struggle to recover normal breathing. His son, on the other hand, never again suffered any further symptoms of asthma! (Inexplicably, that same pastor invited me back to minister for another two weeks the following year. Again the Lord faithfully manifested His Presence through divine healings *and* deliverances from demons—some of them involving Christians.)

*　　*　　*

An Unlikely Arsonist

One midnight in Minneapolis, the telephone in my hotel room wakened me to hear a young woman's desperate plea. She told me her home was some distance away and she wanted to be certain that I would pray for her eighty-year-old grandmother if she brought her to the church. When I asked what the woman's need was, she replied, "My grandmother is a Christian, but she has attempted to burn down our church five times, and I believe she could have a demon." (Did the phrase *holy smoke* just come to mind? *Smile!*) I promised to evaluate the situation upon meeting the grandmother, and said I would pray according to what the Holy Spirit revealed. (Bear in mind that not all grandmas with matches are afflicted with demons. Sometimes strange manifestations present themselves in severe cases of dementia.)

The following night, the woman and her grandmother were present in the service. Grandma appeared to be a sweet, reserved person—that is, until I mentioned that I had discerned the presence of a demon. Upon hearing that, the woman went ballistic in every sense of the word! The demon threw Grandma violently down and she began to writhe across the floor, all the while screaming out blasphemies against God, Jesus, the cross and the blood. (He also added a few uncomplimentary observations about me, which placed me in very good company.) I lowered the microphone to the woman's mouth so the congregation could hear what the demon was saying through that tormented Christian lady. I did this in order that they could hear what was happening and be made aware that demonic demonstrations are real and must be dealt with.

The pastor was a very good friend of mine and later told me that he had considered asking me to move the microphone away so the congregation wouldn't be subjected to the blasphemous words. But the Holy Spirit had instructed him, "Don't touch him! He's My prophet and he's doing what I told him to do."

289

That pastor's hesitation was understandable given the climate of fear and revulsion that exists in most present day churches, however. It has been my observation over the years that few pastors and their churches are even willing to deal with demons. Those that will do so make it a practice to conduct the process in some back room and behind closed doors, where the congregation is not allowed to witness the process. (Perish the thought that the church service might not end at the usual time or that some member or newcomers might be offended!) Nowhere in Scripture are we told that Jesus ever used a back room or attempted to shield demonic manifestations from the general public. Whenever Jesus cast out demons, He did so in public places where great crowds of people were able to witness the awesome power of God in action! In fact, I'm sure some such public exorcisms encouraged others who were similarly afflicted to come for deliverance. I'm sure the same is true today as well.

When I had allowed sufficient time for the demon to demonstrate the vile methods sometimes used to influence an afflicted person's speech and behavior, the Holy Spirit directed me to proceed. I commanded the evil spirits to leave the woman and never come back. The demons were then prevented from voicing any more obscenities and they shrieked a different tune when they were forced to leave their habitation and never return. What a joy and privilege it is to set someone free from demonic bondage! No one was more pleased that night than Grandma herself, with the possible exception of the woman's pastor! (Smile.)

*   *   *

Let's Make a Deal

The following incident took place in the same church in Minneapolis. One night, a young woman perhaps in her late twenties or early thirties came for prayer. I don't remember how she described her need, only that as she did so I immediately discerned the presence of an evil spirit. (Of course, that doesn't mean the woman's own spirit was evil—only that a demonic presence had somehow taken up residence within her mind. When I exposed the demon's presence, it immediately threw her to the floor where she began to writhe like a snake.

I knelt beside the woman and began to seek the Holy Spirit's wisdom, insight and direction—and it was a good thing I did so. It is certainly true that demons usually speak loudly through their victims in order to intimidate not only the one who is performing the exorcism, but any others who are assisting or observing from the audience as well. However, in this instance, that was not the case. The demon communicated with me subliminally, not speaking in my ears, but in my mind.

Before I reveal the content of what the demon said, a description of the woman will enable the reader to visualize the scene. She had long blonde hair, large brown eyes and was exceedingly beautiful in face and form. The clothing she wore presented her in an extremely seductive manner. Revealing his intentions, the demon attempted to bargain with me on a sensual level. He named my hotel and room number and concluded with this vile promise, "If you will just leave me alone and allow me to remain in this woman, I will send her to your hotel room tonight and she will do whatever you want her to do. Just let me stay!"

That particular evil spirit shortly discovered that exorcism was not *Let's Make A Deal*, and *I* was not Monty Hall! Of course, no one else had heard the demon's words; but they certainly heard my reply. Indignantly, I yelled, "Demon, don't try to cut a deal with me—come out now!" With a loud scream,[89] the defeated spirit departed from the woman and she was instantly set free.

---

[89] "For in the case of many who had unclean spirits, they were coming out of them shouting with a loud voice; and many who had been paralyzed and lame were healed. So there was much rejoicing in that city." *Acts 8:7-8*

Like Mother, Like Son

God graciously poured out His Holy Spirit upon our crusade in Roanoke Rapids, North Carolina and wonderfully supernatural things had happened. Miracles of healing were numerous and several demons had already been cast out when the following incident took place. I well remember it because it proved to be one outstanding instance of demonic demonstration that I will never forget.

For more than a year, I had worked at fever pitch without a break and had already ministered extensively in the current series of services. It would not be exaggeration to say that by this time in the crusade I had reached the point of physical and emotional exhaustion. I say this because it is not generally wise to deal with demons when one's energy resources are depleted; and the following situation presented itself at just that unfortunate juncture for me.

On that particular night, the Holy Spirit revealed that a certain woman in the congregation had fallen victim to a demonic presence. I called the woman from the congregation to come to the platform for deliverance. When I prayed over her and commanded the demons to leave, I sensed that some demonic activity had ceased, so I told the woman to return to her seat. I felt a vague sense of unease at the time, but attributed it to the fact that I was very tired and my mind was somewhat clouded as a result. While in prayer the following day however, the Holy Spirit reminded me of what I had previously suspected—that the demonized woman had not been completely delivered. He commanded me to revisit the issue and finish the work I had started. I sincerely repented of my error and promised the Lord that, if the woman came to service that night, I would complete the deliverance.

Since the pastor said he had never seen the woman before, I wondered if she would even be there that night. But she *was* there, as the Holy Spirit had known she would be. When I again invited her to the platform, I apologized and explained that her deliverance the night before had not been completed. The Holy Spirit then began to reveal the identities of the demons that were still present and, when I exposed them, the woman's facial expression immediately changed to one of intense malevolence. The pupils of her eyes became vertical slits, identical to those of a reptile. She began to hiss at me with her mouth opened wide and her tongue darting in and out like a snake—the only thing missing were the fangs! (Such a sound is impossible for a fully opened human mouth to produce. A hiss can only be formed when the mouth is closed, the front teeth are together and breath is forced between them.)

In the midst of this demonic display, a sixteen-year-old boy who regularly attended the sponsoring church jumped to his feet from the back row and began to stride purposefully down the center aisle toward the platform. As he came, his arm was outstretched in a posture of prayer and he was yelling, "Be with her, O god, be with her! Strengthen her, O, god!" At the moment the boy stood, the Holy Spirit said, "A demon within him is responding to this woman's need for reinforcement against you. Stop him!"

The youngster came up behind the woman and, before he could touch her, I extended my arm over her shoulder, touched his forehead with one finger and cried out, "Jesus!" As I did so, the boy's entire body was literally lifted into the air and then slammed to the floor where he began to writhe in a snake-like manner. By that time the woman had already been delivered; so I asked the pastor to lead her to Christ while I took on the demons who were manifesting within the boy.

The Holy Spirit instructed me to first lay my Bible on the boy's chest. When I did so, he went berserk, screaming out

293

blasphemies against the Father God, Jesus and the Holy Spirit while he continued his serpentine writhing. At my command, the demons fled and the youngster was completely set free. Both woman and boy gave their hearts to Jesus that night; but that was not the end of the story.

The woman subsequently revealed that she had been a spiritist for quite some time. (Note that I use the term *spiritist* rather than the commonly accepted *spiritualist*, because such people are not at all *spiritual,* as we understand the term.) She had been attending another church where she'd been able keep up a façade of godliness without fear of detection. She then confessed that the demonized boy was her *son*! Although he attended the church where I was currently preaching, the presence of demons within him had gone undetected until that very night! When the boy had called on "god" to strengthen his mother, he had in actuality been summoning *his* god, Satan.

In this case, I can say with certainty that demonic spirits in the fullest meaning of the terminology had indeed *possessed* the two people in question. This had been possible because they had both been extensively exposed to evil spirits through their involvement with spiritism and neither of them had received Christ as Savior. The indwelling protection of the Holy Spirit had not been present, therefore; and their unregenerate human spirits were open and vulnerable to satanic habitation.

Such instances should serve as convincing proof of the present-day church's desperate need for the gift of discerning of spirits![90] Sadly, times have not changed much in the intervening years since that experience, and that gift of the Spirit is sorely needed today more than ever before.

This and the following two episodes, may seem fabricated and beyond belief to some; but I assure you that all of them are

---

[90] "…and to another the effecting of miracles, and to another prophecy, and to another the distinguishing of spirits…" *1 Cor 12:10a*

absolutely true and faithful to the facts as presented. I know this for certain because I was there and was intimately involved in each incident!

*   *   *

A Bizarre Demonic Manifestation

Night after night the Holy Spirit had been present and had performed wondrous supernatural acts during my ministry time in Lima, Ohio. At the conclusion of one evening service, several people came to kneel in prayer at the altar. I walked slowly along the altar rail praying for individuals as the Holy Spirit revealed their needs to me.

When I lightly touched one thirteen-year-old boy on the top of his head, I suddenly found myself forcefully demanding demons to come out of him. When I did this, all hell (literally!) broke loose in a physical display that was almost beyond belief! Without the use of his hands or arms, the boy arched his back, sprang to his feet from a kneeling position, and then was slammed to his back on the floor. He began to manifest demonic activity in speech and expression and, when the Holy Spirit revealed the identities of several demons resident within him; I cast out each one until the boy was completely delivered. The physical feat that preceded the deliverance was not the most astounding display we witnessed that night however—it was the demonstration that accompanied the deliverance itself. I had never seen the like of it before, nor have I since.

When I called out the name of each demon and commanded it to leave, the boy's bare arms, from shoulders to fingertips, actually *glowed* with an eerie green phosphorescence! As each demon was identified and then forced to depart, the color of the boy's arms returned to that of normal flesh. The entire process then repeated itself again and again with the exposure of each subsequent spirit until the deliverance was complete. Afterward, the boy joyfully testified that he had been set free from all *seven* evil spirits—to God be all the glory!

Incidentally, while this exorcism was in progress, some "sightseers" from the congregation ventured to the altar area to witness the strange event. When they observed this unusual phenomenon, they cried out in fear and hurried back to their seats. Such a timid reaction begs the question, *Why should Christians be afraid of any demonic display of power?* The Scripture clearly teaches us that the Christ Who is within us is far greater than any strange demonstration Satan could possibly devise!

*   *   *

"I'm Going to Kill You!"

Due to the sensitive nature of this material, I have omitted the name and location of the church where the incident took place, lest it prove offensive in any way to those who were involved.

While praying for the sick one night, the prayer line seemed to be growing increasingly longer despite the large number of people who had already received prayer. When I glanced around the church, I saw another young man suddenly rise from the back pew and make his way to the very end of the line where he waited for a considerable length of time.

When the young man finally stood before me, I immediately became aware of the presence of a homosexual demon, although nothing about his appearance would have suggested any sort of sexual deviancy. In order to avoid a publicly embarrassing situation for the young man, I asked the organist to lead the congregation in worship while I took the man into an office situated at one end of the platform. He sat down in a very low, beanbag-type chair and I stood facing him while I revealed what the Holy Spirit had told me regarding a spirit of homosexuality.

What followed occurred within a matter of seconds, a considerably shorter time than it will take to relate here. The expression in the man's eyes immediately changed to one of rage and demonic hatred. Without using his hands for support, he leaped to his feet in one quick motion and came toward me with arms outstretched as though in preparation for attack. In response, I simply pointed to him and spoke the Name of Jesus. The young man fell back into the chair as though he had received a powerful blow to the head. He continued to sit there, limp and docile, as I informed the demon that *I* was now in charge and not he. When I told the man to stand and follow me onto the platform where I would deliver him from the demon, he meekly complied.

The young man stood a few feet in front of the platform's cement block wall that surrounded the platform while I went to the microphone to tell the congregation (without revealing the nature of the problem) that the young man was going to be delivered from a demonic presence. When I said those words, all eight hundred people uttered a collective gasp of shock and disbelief! I turned rapidly toward the man in time to see him levitating—about eighteen inches above the floor! His entire body remained that way for several moments, frozen into a rigid, upright position and vibrating violently. (From her vantage point in the congregation, my wife witnessed the entire process. She later told me that the young man first had become rigid and then had risen straight up and parallel to the wall, where he then continued to hover in mid-air for several seconds.)

As though not satisfied with his initial display of power, the demon then threw the man forcefully backward until his body crashed into the cement wall. He rebounded and ran directly at me, shouting, "I'm going to *kill* you!" Once again, I pointed my finger at him and spoke the Name of Jesus; and he fell to the floor and proceeded to writhe like a snake while demons growled and screamed outrageous blasphemies against the Lord—and me.

As the young man continued his screaming and bodily contortions, the Holy Spirit revealed the presence of six other demons—*rage, murder, cancer, death, insanity* and *suicide*. When the identity of each one was called out, the entity thus exposed emitted an anguished shriek and came out of the man. When all seven demons had been evicted, the young man's spent body lay still and his appearance changed to that of an entirely different person. I helped him to his feet and he hugged me around the neck (this time with no intentions of breaking it!). While the man wept and expressed gratitude to God for his deliverance, the congregation broke into exuberant shouts of worship and praise.

Unfortunately, this spectacular public deliverance unleashed an unexpected firestorm of controversy the following day. Despite what he had witnessed with his own eyes, the young man's father (a deacon in that church) became infuriated at the implication that his own son had been the victim of demonic infestation. (I have a suspicion that the father was more concerned about his own reputation in the church than he was for his son's welfare!) The father claimed that his son loved the Lord very much. As proof, he cited that fact that the son had even moved into a small mobile home he had set up on a lot adjacent to the church and he attended every service held in that church. The son responded to this by saying that no one had ever asked him *why* he had abruptly moved out and gone to live near the church. Neither had anyone inquired why he felt compelled to attend every single service, even those directed to segments of the church congregation in which he was not involved (i.e., children's and women's services and even choir rehearsals).

When I met privately with the young man, he explained in detail the circumstances and events that led to his descent into demonic domination. At the time of this incident, he was eighteen years of age and, for a long time he had been plagued with tormenting thoughts and inexplicable periods of blind rage. Often he had fallen into trance-like states wherein he would be completely unaware of his actions. He told me that he had once

298

emerged from one of those trances and found himself in the process of strangling his mother, a godly woman whom he deeply loved. At that point, he had decided that, in order to avoid another diabolical effort to kill his own mother, he would have to leave his parents' home. He had subsequently bought the mobile home and parked it on a vacant lot adjacent to the church. In an effort to be freed from the demonic voices in his head, the young man had made it a practice to attend every service hoping someone— *anyone*—would be able to discern his problem and help him.

He then shared the following statement, which broke my heart. "I went into every prayer line conducted by every preacher who came through this church; and until you came, *not one of them* was able to discern the fact that demons were the reason I was driven to do evil things against my will." He concluded his sad tale with one of the most plaintive questions I've ever been asked: "*Why didn't they know?*" In reply, I could only shake my head with sorrow and frustration.

On a happier note, some months later I received a referral form from a Bible College where the young man had applied for ministerial training.

Two for One

It's certainly true that demonic forces are not responsible for all migraine headaches; but in the following incident, a demonic presence *was* definitely involved. During a service in Caribou, Maine, I once had the privilege of delivering a woman from a demon that had tormented her for eighteen long years. She came into the prayer line sobbing, in great pain from a migraine headache. She told of the misery she had suffered over the years from nearly incessant migraine headache attacks. Infrequent times of respite occasionally occurred; but these invariably brought only slight and temporary relief. Whenever she entered those periods of rest, she would entertain a glimmer of hope that her torment had come to an end; but then another severe attack would resume the cycle of misery.

Before undertaking her deliverance, I delivered a word of caution to the congregation. "When a demon leaves a person it will very often seek a point of weakness in someone else through which it can enter and continue its reign of terror.[91] Therefore, it's important that you pray and cover yourselves with the protection of the blood of Jesus." Having said this, I proceeded to bind and cast out the demon. Using the woman's own voice, the demon cried out with a loud scream and then fled. For the very first time in eighteen years, she was experiencing absolute freedom from the bondage of incessant pain and her immediate response was one of ecstatic elation accompanied by tears of joy.

When the demon was expelled from the woman on the platform, another woman seated in the back of the auditorium immediately screamed out in pain and leaped to her feet, clutching her head. I cast the demon out of her, also; and she was immediately freed from the migraine headache that had come upon her simultaneously with the first woman's deliverance. After the service, this woman told me that she had disregarded my warning and had refused to cover herself with the blood because she thought it unnecessary to do so. She firmly declared that she would never again neglect to apply the blood at such times!

---

[91] "Now when the unclean spirit goes out of a man, it passes through waterless places seeking rest, and does not find *it*. Then it says, 'I will return to my house from which I came;' and when it comes, it finds *it* unoccupied, swept, and put in order. Then it goes and takes along with it seven other spirits more wicked than itself, and they go in and live there; and the last state of that man becomes worse than the first. That is the way it will also be with this evil generation." *Matt. 12:43-45*

*　　*　　*

Another Case, Same Lesson

Some years later, I witnessed a very similar incident at Parkway Assembly of God, the church my family attended in Revere, Massachusetts. The only exception to the above account was that the demon in this incident hadn't caused migraines, but had been the origin of a choking sensation. This had been the case with one woman, who described the feeling as being similar to having a rubber ball lodged in her throat. In this case, another woman nearby (a close personal friend of ours and a wonderful Christian) was the skeptical doubter. When the demon was forced out of its first hiding place, it quickly gained entry into our friend and she began to gasp and choke as she struggled to breathe. After the second woman was delivered, she admitted to a moment of temporary doubt. She said she had always respected my ministry; but she had found it difficult to accept the possibility that a demon could gain access to a Christian. She then stated that, since it had happened to her, she was now convinced of that very real possibility.

*　　*　　*

A Demonic Assignment Foiled

A large church in a major Midwestern city (which will remain nameless) once invited me to conduct three two-week crusades—one in August, another in October and a third in December. Thousands of people attended each crusade and signs, wonders and miracles became a regular occurrence.

During one sermon, I had made casual reference to the fact that I had once left a counseling practice to return to my true calling of power-evangelism. Following that service, a woman asked me if I would take the time to counsel with her privately about a serious problem in her life. I told her that would be impossible because the temporary nature of evangelistic ministry does not provide sufficient time for effective counseling. She approached me again after another service with the same request and again I refused for the same reason.

Several nights later, the woman again expressed the urgency of her need and said she had arranged for her husband to drive some friends home, and he wouldn't return to get her for at least another hour. Her rationale, therefore, was that there would be ample time for me to advise her regarding the problem. When she approached me the first time, I had sensed that something about her story didn't ring true; but by this time I had become convinced that a hidden motive was behind her request.

Since I firmly suspected insincerity on her part, I led the woman to the center of the platform and sat down on the edge. When I asked her to give me an overview of the problem, she fumbled for words even after repeated requests for an answer. Then she came up with some innocuous "problem" and claimed that the intensely personal nature of the situation would require a more private setting than our present location at the front of the auditorium. I pointed out that we had all the privacy we needed there; and even though there were many people mingling about the sanctuary, none of them were close enough to overhear our conversation. When that answer didn't meet with her approval, I firmly stated that this was all the privacy I would allow. Again I asked the nature of her "serious" problem. When the reply proved to be another innocuous one, I excused myself and left with friends for a bite to eat.

In the service that next night, the same woman came in the prayer line. As soon as she came before me, the Spirit of the Lord spoke forcefully through me and commanded a demon of lust to come out of her. In response to that mandate, the demon threw the woman to the floor where she began to writhe in a singularly sexual manner. I cast several demons of lust and sexual perversion from the woman that night and commanded them never to return. As each demon was evicted, they shrieked their expressions of anguish and despair. When the last one had gone, the woman stopped her sensual contortions and her face literally glowed with radiance! Only someone who has been rescued from that intense darkness and transplanted into the brilliance of God's Presence can truly understand the absolute reality of her relief and joy!

After the service that night, the woman shared her story with me. At some point in the past she had opened herself to demonic spirits. She didn't relate to me the circumstances that had led to her surrender, and I didn't ask; but what followed the revelation was more shocking by far. With tears streaming down her cheeks the woman confessed that she had finally found herself totally under demonic control. In that depraved state, Satan had used her to seduce the previous three evangelists who had ministered in that church and all three had succumbed to her sexual advances! She then revealed Satan's intended plans for me by stating, *"You were supposed to be the next one on my list!"* The woman then expressed genuine gratitude that not only had I seen through the enemy's intentions, but had set her free in the process.

I was also grateful as well—that God had not only rescued that one helpless victim; but He had also spared *me* from becoming entangled in an unspeakable situation! To this day, I remain convinced that I would not have succumbed to a sexual liaison with her or with any other woman. However, had the woman remained undelivered, she could very well have circulated the rumor that I *had* engaged in an illicit relationship; and my reputation and ministry would have been irreparably damaged as a result.

*　　*　　*

A "Burning" Deliverance

Among the many opportunities the Lord has given me was a door He opened in Chicago, where I was invited to minister at Faith Tabernacle, a former wrestling arena that had been transformed into a large, beautiful sanctuary. Thousands of people packed that great auditorium during the crusade and the Presence of God hovered over the congregation in every service. In addition to the many individuals who were healed, we saw many other types of miracles in that church.

In one particular service, the Holy Spirit used me to bring deliverance to people who were involved in the occult realms of spiritism and various aspects of witchcraft. As a result, several practicing occultists were set free.

During the ministry time that night, I singled out one young woman standing on the lower level directly in front of the platform. Using me in a prophetic word, the Holy Spirit revealed that she had become deeply involved with a study of occult practices and the Holy Spirit commanded her to bring all of her occult reference books to the church immediately, after which she would be set free. The friend beside her smugly interjected, "Preacher, you just don't understand! It's impossible for my friend to go get her books now—she lives an hour-and-a-half from here, and the round trip would take over three hours!" In reply to this impertinent comment, I said firmly that the order had not come from *me* but from the Holy Spirit—surely *He* was well aware of how far away the woman lived! I then repeated the Lord's command that the books be brought to the church *immediately*.

The young woman then spoke for herself. "I *do* live that far away, but the books aren't at my house. I stored them at my boyfriend's apartment and that's only three blocks from here; so I'll go and get them." (I have always been grateful that no amount

304

of human logic or reasoning has ever been able to adversely influence me when I know the Holy Spirit has spoken!) I ministered to other people during the interim and the young woman soon returned carrying a large box filled with books on various aspects of occultism.

The ushers brought a metal chair and a large pot from the kitchen because I had told the congregation that we were going to burn the books. When everything was in place, I lit a fire in the pot and we fed the books to the flames. While the books burned, I cast several demons from the woman whose body had harbored them for quite some time. As each foul spirit was commanded to leave, they screamed out in helpless protest, but nevertheless were forced to obey.

A staff member took photos throughout the book burning and deliverance, but until they were developed, we had no idea what unique images were revealed in them. As one demon in particular released his hold (no doubt the controlling entity of the lot), flames in the shape of a devil's head leaped upward and came between the burning books and the area of the young woman's heart! This was a singularly appropriate picture of the process that was taking place at that very moment. Not only was the young woman being cleansed from satanic domination, she was simultaneously surrendering control of her being to the lordship of Jesus Christ and receiving the indwelling Presence of the Holy Spirit!

This was a unique exorcism for me. We have burned satanic paraphernalia during outdoor crusades in foreign lands, but I've never conducted another book burning within a church building since that time.

By way of addendum: the following night, another occultist brought hundreds of his books and various items of satanic worship. We destroyed them by some means or other, but we didn't burn them as we had done in the previous service. That man was also delivered from demons, saved and filled with the Holy Spirit.

*   *   *

The Invisible Shield

Demons will always seek to attack Christians at their weakest point. I have seen this repeatedly all over the world. On numerous occasions I have encountered truly good people who have somehow fallen victim to demonic attack in times of weakness and vulnerability. Satan's mission is to weaken and, if possible, to destroy both the Christians *and* their effectiveness for the Kingdom of God. Conversely, it is the Holy Spirit's mission to heal and deliver the weak, the weary and the wounded—and He is far better able to accomplish His mission than Satan is to overcome with his devices! The following story, which took place at a New Jersey church, illustrates this unassailable truth.

More than a thousand people were in attendance each night during the services and the Holy Spirit moved powerfully, performing miracles of all sorts. During various off-times, I had engaged in brief conversations with a deacon from that church and had enjoyed his fellowship. On one night in particular, the prayer line was stretched from wall to wall across the entire front of the large auditorium and, as I moved down the line, I found myself standing before that same deacon. No sooner had I done so, than the voice of the Holy Spirit revealed a demon of rage that had gained access to the man's mind and was hindering his usefulness for the Kingdom of God. [It's important to note here that, until the Holy Spirit chooses to reveal specific information to me, I have no more knowledge about any individual than anyone else does.]

The man was a high school principal and the Lord showed me that when dealing with students, he sometimes would be overcome by inexplicable rage. So great was his fury that he would become verbally abusive to the point of actually spitting in anger and frustration! As I revealed this information, the demon responded violently, and in a loud, raspy voice it growled its intention to tear me apart and kill me. Simultaneously, the man's expression changed to one of blind rage; and he came toward me with outstretched arms to carry out the demon's threat.

[A word of explanation is needed here, also. Demons don't always respond and come out immediately. Like petulant children they play their malevolent games of hide and seek, sometimes accompanied by outward threats of intimidation, belligerence and defiance. Jesus Himself met up with some evil spirits who didn't come out immediately. On one occasion during His earthly ministry, Jesus encountered a man who had been occupied by a *legion* of demons (6,000) that actually bargained with the Lord Himself![92] Over the years, I've become somewhat accustomed to such egotistical and grandiose proclamations, but I know they are backed by a power far inferior to that of my God!]

As the man lunged toward me, I bound the demonic spirit by the power of God and forbade it to do me any physical or spiritual harm. With that, I backed away a few feet from the enraged man and stood relaxed, arms at my sides. Foaming at the mouth and snarling like a rabid animal, the man rushed to close the gap between us. When he reached a point approximately a foot away from me, he abruptly stopped as though he had crashed into a brick wall. (He *had* literally encountered an invisible "wall"—one that had been erected by the Holy Spirit!) Undeterred, the man began to claw at the wall while he continued to drool, growl and voice his threats.

I asked the people who had gathered for prayer at the front of the church to move aside so that the congregation would be able to see the demonic display as a learning experience in evil supernatural demonstrations. While the man continued to futilely claw at the barrier, I addressed the congregation and asked, "Is *this*

---

[92] See *Luke 8:26-33*

what you're afraid of? You have nothing to fear from the enemy—in fact, the enemy should fear *you*! You can see that this demon is bound and can't even touch me, because the Holy Spirit has erected an invisible shield between us."

[Lest the reader think I was bragging and exhibiting an attitude of pride and arrogance, let me assure you that such was not the case. I felt impressed of the Spirit to allow the congregation to observe the power of God in action as He carried out *His* triumph over the enemy. Throughout my decades in ministry, it has consistently been my goal to encourage believers to face their adversary and know that what *I* can do—*they* can do also! The Holy Spirit can be trusted to always to bring His power to bear for any daring Christian who will challenge the enemy, and I want the church at large to be convinced of that!]

As I was exhorting the people, the demonized man continued to claw frantically at the invisible barrier that separated us while the evil entity within him shrieked out threats against my life. These stated intentions carried no impact whatsoever, since it was abundantly clear that his unfortunate victim was unable even to breach the wall—much less to attack and kill me!

When the Lord indicated that the futile display had gone on long enough, I addressed the demon with an authority born of the Holy Spirit. "In a few moments I'm going to cast you out; and when you obey, you will fall at my feet and declare that the Christ within me is Lord to the glory of God the Father! Following that, you will go wherever Almighty God sends you." (I have a feeling the Lord commands demons to return to their master, report their defeat and cringe before whatever punishment Satan metes out to those who fail in their diabolical missions!)

In order for the congregation to clearly observe the contrast between the demon's frantic cries and the Lord's irresistible command, I drew the microphone closer and spoke very quietly, "Now, *come out* in Jesus' name!" Perspiration poured down the man's face, which was intensely contorted with rage. Meanwhile, the evil entity within him struggled desperately to resist the inevitable outcome. The diabolical spirit continued to snarl his defiance, but the man's legs began to buckle and his body slowly descended until his knees finally gave out and he crumpled to the floor. In a voice dripping with contempt, the evil spirit then cried out, "Jesus Christ is Lord!" (O, how it must hurt a demon's pride to be forced to make that confession![93])

As soon as the raging demon departed, the "wall" came down and the deacon was able to reach out and touch me. Still kneeling, he threw both arms around my torso, laid his head against my chest and wept, "Brother Seavey, that wasn't me, that wasn't me saying those things! I love you and would never hurt you! Please forgive me." The man needed no forgiveness from me—he only needed my love. I helped him rise and we wrapped our arms around each other and wept together as we rejoiced over the Holy Spirit's latest triumph over Satan.

*   *   *

O that the Church of the Lord Jesus Christ would once again contend for the Holy Spirit's gift of discerning of spirits! Whenever I teach on the Gifts of the Holy Spirit,[94] I declare that if the Holy Spirit were ever to tell me I could henceforth be used in only one of the nine spiritual gifts, my immediate choice would have to be the gift of discerning of spirits. The rationale behind my decision would be that this one gift is (as I affectionately refer to

---

[93] "He *(Jesus)* humbled himself by becoming obedient to the point of death, even death on a cross. For this reason also, God highly exalted Him, and bestowed on Him the name which is above every name, so that at the name of Jesus EVERY KNEE WILL BOW, of those who are in heaven and on earth and *under the earth*, and that *every* tongue will confess that Jesus Christ is Lord, to the glory of God the Father." *Phil 2:8b-11 (Author's emphasis added)*

[94] Please read *I Corinthians 12-14* for an introduction to the gifts of the Holy Spirit, which the Lord Himself **gave and** expected to have function in every church then and now.

it) "the watchdog of the church." Many times evil spirits masquerade themselves as being from God,[95] when in reality they are emissaries of Satan sent to deceive and wreak havoc in the church. Those Christians who dare to venture into this giftedness will not be fooled by the enemy, nor will they suffer defeat at the enemy's hands.

*　　*　　*

Always Leave 'em Laughing

A few years ago, my son, Eric and several others accompanied me to a service I was conducting in Indiana. After the teaching time, we were preparing to deliver a man from a demon that had been oppressing him, when I suddenly received a mental picture in which demons were carrying luggage and hurrying from a building that resembled a hotel. I told my companions about the amusing concept and, as we turned our attention to the afflicted man, the demon began to speak through him in a petulant, squeaky tone of voice. Over and over the evil spirit kept repeating, "It's checkout time! It's checkout time! It's checkout time!" Indeed it *was* and we were delighted to oblige and finalize the "checkout" procedure once and for all!

*　　*　　*

The time has also come for me to say, "It's checkout time." My sincere hope is that my readers have been deeply stirred and challenged by this factual retrospective of my own experiences in the supernatural realm. My prayer for each one is that the call of the Holy Spirit will compel my readers to seek Him for whatever supernatural function He has ordained for *them* to fill in his kingdom. To assist in your quest, the back pages of this book contain listings of books I have written, all of which were intended

---

[95] "…Satan disguises himself as an angel of light." *2 Cor 11:14*

to bring members of the Body of Christ to full maturity. I make them available to aid the reader in understanding the various ways in which one can *listen* for and *hear* the voice of the Holy Spirit. May God bless you as you earnestly pursue His Presence!

I will not close this book with the traditional closing phrase, *"The End."* Instead, I challenge my readers to personally explore the endless supernatural possibilities available within the Holy Spirit-led life. Doing so will then lead into many opportunities to exercise each one's unique giftedness and function in God's Kingdom. My sincere prayer is that for those readers this book will have served as merely…

The
Beginning!

*   *   *

PROLOGUE

In each individual reader's pursuit for their personal best in living out the Christian life, may the following words of Scripture provide the ultimate challenge:

"But just as it is written, 'THINGS WHICH EYE HAS NOT SEEN AND EAR HAS NOT HEARD, AND which HAVE NOT ENTERED THE HEART OF MAN, ALL THAT GOD HAS PREPARED FOR THOSE WHO LOVE HIM.' For to us God revealed them through the Spirit..." *I Cor 2:9,10a*

"And He [Jesus] answered and said to them, 'Go and report...what you have seen and heard: the blind receive sight, the lame walk, the lepers are cleansed, and the deaf hear, the dead are raised up, the poor have the gospel preached to them.'" *Luke 7:22*

"For to us God revealed them through the Spirit; for the Spirit searches all things, even the depths of God. For who among men knows the thoughts of a man except the spirit of the man, which is in him? Even so the thoughts of God no one knows except the Spirit of God. Now we have received, not the spirit of the world, but the Spirit who is from God, so that we may know the things freely given to us by God, which things we also speak, not in words taught by human wisdom, but in those taught by the Spirit, combining spiritual thoughts with spiritual words." *1 Cor 2:9-13*

"And as you go, preach, saying, 'The kingdom of heaven is at hand.' Heal the sick, raise the dead, cleanse the lepers, cast out demons. Freely you received, freely give." *Matt 10:7-8*

*   *   *

Please Contact Me

My contact information appears below. It would please me immeasurably to hear from my readers. For those who are seeking a miracle of healing, I encourage you to believe for and receive your personal answer from God. If reading my experiences has been helpful to you in that regard, please send me your testimonies, also. Thank you—I look forward to hearing from you.

Rev. Burton W. Seavey
P.O. Box 37
Osceola, IN 46561
USA

E-mail: BURTseavey@aol.com

*   *   *

OTHER BOOKS BY THIS AUTHOR

"Why Doesn't God Heal *Me*?"

A best-selling book that explores many possible scriptural reasons why some Christians don't seem able to obtain divine healing, despite believing that God's Word promises healing for all Christians.

A revised and expanded edition of this out-of-print classic
will be available soon.
Please contact the author for details.

* * *

"Christian Meditation: Doorway to the Spirit"

A scriptural treatise on the use of meditation throughout the Bible and in the Early Church ages. It points out the distinct differences between dangerous worldly meditation practices and those sanctioned and encouraged in the Word of God.

A companion how-to seminar is available on tape, as well.
Please contact the author for additional information.

* * *

"The SHOCKWAVE"

This book explores the current condition of the church in contrast with the biblical descriptions of the end-time Bride of Christ. It encourages individual Christians and the church at large to return to biblical principles in order to accomplish our ultimate destiny and glorious future before Christ's return.

* * *

The above materials are available from the author.
Please contact us for pricing and ordering details.

Printed in the United States
217378BV00001B/1/P

9 781607 916680